Black Catholic Studies Reader

Black Catholic Studies Reader: History and Theology

David J. Endres, Editor

The Catholic University of America Press
Washington, DC

Copyright © 2021
The Catholic University of America Press
All rights reserved

∞

Cataloging-in-Publication Data available from the Library of Congress
ISBN 978-0-8132-3429-8

Contents

Foreword: Cardinal Wilton Gregory vii

Introduction: David J. Endres ix

Contributor Biographies xiii

Black Catholic Studies

Speaking the Truth: The Black Catholic Intellectual Vocation
Bryan N. Massingale 1

History

Black History and Culture
Thea Bowman, F.S.P.A. 19

Black Catholics in the United States: A Historical Chronology, 1452–2020
Ronald LaMarr Sharps 27

Outsiders Within: The Oblate Sisters of Providence in 1830s Church and Society
Diane Batts Morrow 67

Spirituality

We've Come This Far by Faith: Black Catholics and Their Church
Diana L. Hayes 93

Called to Be Leaven: Reflections on African American Catholic Spirituality
Cyprian Davis, O.S.B. 107

v

"Gonna Move When the Spirit Say Move": A Black
Spirituality of Resistance and Resilience
C. Vanessa White 117

Liturgy

Thank God We Ain't What We Was: The State of the
Liturgy in the Black Catholic Community
Clarence Joseph Rivers 133

The African American Catholic Hymnal and the
African American Spiritual
M. Shawn Copeland 141

Sister Thea Bowman: Liturgical Justice through
Black Sacred Song
Kim R. Harris 163

Lives and Writings

Writing Black Catholic Lives: Black Catholic Biographies
and Autobiographies
Cecilia A. Moore 193

Freeing the Spirit: Very Personal Reflections on
One Man's Search for the Spirit in Worship
Clarence Joseph Rivers 215

Black Catholic Scholarship, 1854–2020
Ronald LaMarr Sharps 239

Index 265

Foreword

EDITING ANY ANTHOLOGY of thematic texts is a risky undertaking because it involves making some tough choices among many possible attractive options. I applaud the editor, Father David Endres, for his selections of the writings of a number of prominent African American Catholics in this *Black Catholic Studies Reader*.

He has made his selections in the midst of an intense period for our Church, our nation, and our world in response to the penetrating and ongoing scrutiny of personal and institutional racism. The selections represent different viewpoints, eras, and backgrounds. Yet, there is a common thread that unites all of the texts. They each demonstrate the depth of faith, dedication, and hope of the authors in our Catholic faith. Each author nudges—some more assertively than others—the Church to live up to our mission of evangelization and welcome.

Anthologies are never exhaustive in their scope, and the best ones should always entice a reader to probe more deeply the issues that are introduced by each author. Father Endres has chosen representatives from the theological and historical sciences. He includes women, men, religious, and lay contributors who represent different perspectives on the challenges that the Church faces in caring for and serving People of Color in an environment where we are not the dominant culture.

Father Endres categorizes his selections in areas that have important significance for African American Catholics: Black Catholic studies, history, spirituality, liturgy, and biography. Each of these topics touches upon the unique religious experiences of Black Catholics, and they are areas where the Black Catholic experience can offer both insight and inspiration for the entire Church.

For those who have little personal experience with or knowledge of the African American religious heritage, these selections will be a helpful introduction to the spiritual legacy that can be found within African American Catholicism. For African American Catholics, these selections will help us to reconnect with a heritage that we share with other Black Christians. Both audiences will find information that can be enlightening and transforming.

I recommend a careful review of the bibliographical references contained in the articles in the anthology. These additional selections expand the possibilities for further studies.

This anthology is a prelude to highlighting the contributions that we Black Catholics have made to the Church in the United States and are eager to continue offering to the entire Church as a valuable gift and contribution to our one family of faith. I recommend it highly as a valuable tool and resource.

Wilton Cardinal Gregory
Archbishop of Washington, D.C.

Introduction

IN 1968, at a time of increased racial tensions and violence, the Black Catholic Clergy Caucus offered a stinging indictment: "The Catholic Church in the United States, primarily a white racist institution, has addressed itself primarily to white society and is definitely a part of that society." It challenged the Church to repudiate all forms of racism and to open itself to Black voices and leadership: "[U]nless it is to remain an enclave speaking to itself, it must begin to consult the black members of the Church, clerical, religious, and lay."[1]

Fifty years later, Church and society continue to grapple with systemic racism. The challenge of the Black Catholic Clergy Caucus, however, is at least partially realized. A significant number of Black Catholic voices have emerged: scholars, activists, teachers, and clergy have taken up the task of reflecting on and communicating the distinctiveness of being Black and Catholic in the United States. The study of Black Catholic history and theology has come of age. Many of the first generation of scholars, including Cyprian Davis, O.S.B., and Thea Bowman, F.S.P.A., have passed on. Inspired by them, a new generation of Black Catholic leaders and thinkers have emerged.

This *Black Catholic Studies Reader* joins the best of the earlier generation of scholars with recent contributions to the history and theology of the Black Catholic experience. Contributions delve into the interlocking fields of history, spirituality, liturgy, biography, and bibliography. Through their contributions, Black Catholic Studies scholars engage theologies of liberation and the reality of racism, the Black struggle for recognition within the Church, and the distinctiveness of African-inspired spirituality, prayer, and worship. By considering their racial and religious identities, these select Black Catholic theologians and historians add their voices to

---

[1] "Statement of the Black Catholic Clergy Caucus (1968)," in Mark Massa and Catherine Osborne, eds., *American Catholic History: A Documentary Reader*, 2nd ed. (New York: New York University Press, 2017), 199–202, quotes at 199 and 201.

the contemporary conversation surrounding culture, race, and religion in America.

Many of the articles contained herein appeared first in the *U.S. Catholic Historian*. Under long-time editor Christopher J. Kauffman (1936–2018), the journal gave voice to American Catholics who are members of ethnic and racial minorities (and those who study them). Over the years, the *U.S. Catholic Historian* has published numerous thematic issues on Black Catholics, racial justice, and slavery.[2]

This volume's introductory essay by Bryan N. Massingale frames the role of the Black Catholic intellectual against the backdrop of racism, reminding readers of the perennial task of "speaking the truth" for and with "communities-of-struggle." The reader's second section outlines the history of Black Catholicism through a historical chronology by Ronald L. Sharps, an essay on history and culture by Sister Thea Bowman, and a survey of the early history of the Oblate Sisters of Providence by Diane Batts Morrow.

The third section, on spirituality, features an influential essay by Diana L. Hayes in which she considers Black Catholics as a "subversive memory," a contribution by Cyprian Davis, O.S.B., reflecting the interplay of Black and Christian values, and an article on contemporary conceptions and markers of Black Catholic spirituality by C. Vanessa White.

The section on liturgy includes an assessment of Black Catholic liturgy by Clarence Joseph Rivers, a study of the formation of *Lead Me, Guide Me: The African American Catholic Hymnal* by M. Shawn Copeland, and a recent survey of Sister Thea Bowman's contribution to the liturgy by Kim R. Harris.

Finally, a section on biography, autobiography, and bibliography includes a survey of Black Catholic lives, including those on the

---

[2] *U.S. Catholic Historian* theme issues devoted to Black Catholics or racial justice include volumes 5, no. 1 (Winter 1986); 7, nos. 2–3 (Spring/Summer 1988); 12, no. 1 (Winter 1994); 19, no. 2 (Spring 2001); 28, no. 1 (Winter 2010); 35, no. 1 (Winter 2017); and 37, no. 2 (Spring 2019).

path to sainthood, by Cecilia A. Moore, an autobiographical excerpt by the pioneer liturgist Clarence Joseph Rivers, and finally, Ronald L. Sharps' bibliographical survey of scholarship written by and about Black Catholics in the United States.

Given the contemporary concerns and activism centered around racial justice, it is hoped that this reader might amplify the voices of Black Catholics and help scholars and students reflect on the gift and challenge of being Black and Catholic in the United States.

David J. Endres
Editor, *U.S. Catholic Historian*

Contributor Biographies

Sister Thea Bowman, F.S.P.A.

Sister Thea Bowman, F.S.P.A. (1937–1990), a convert to Catholicism, was the first African American member of the Franciscan Sisters of Perpetual Adoration. As a member of her religious community, she taught in various grade levels, eventually earning a doctorate in English from The Catholic University of America, Washington, D.C. A founder of the National Black Sisters Conference, she wrote and spoke on the theology, spirituality, and worship of Black Catholics. Her cause for sainthood has been introduced, and she is now known as a "Servant of God."

M. Shawn Copeland

M. Shawn Copeland is a Professor Emerita of Systematic Theology at Boston College. She is the author or editor of six books, including *Knowing Christ Crucified: The Witness of African American Religious Experience* and *Enfleshing Freedom: Body, Race, and Being*, as well as numerous articles and essays on spirituality, theological anthropology, political theology, social suffering, and gender and race.

Rev. Cyprian Davis, O.S.B.

Rev. Cyprian Davis, O.S.B. (1930–2015), a monk of St. Meinrad Archabbey (Indiana), was the leading historian of African American Catholicism. He was a consultant for the U.S. Catholic bishops' pastorals on race, "Brothers and Sisters to Us" (1979) and "What We Have Seen and Heard" (1984). His pathbreaking monograph, *The History of Black Catholics in the United States*, focused attention on the field, leading to numerous studies, conference papers, and symposia.

Kim R. Harris

Kim R. Harris is an Assistant Professor of African American Thought and Practice in the Department of Theological Studies at

Loyola Marymount University, Los Angeles, California. She is a liturgist, composer, and expert in spirituals and freedom songs. Among her compositions is *Welcome Table: A Mass of Spirituals*. Through her research and writing on Servant of God Sister Thea Bowman, Dr. Harris hopes to highlight the traditions of Black Catholic worship and inspire efforts toward racial justice and reconciliation.

Diana L. Hayes

Diana L. Hayes is a Professor Emerita of Systematic Theology at Georgetown University, Washington, D.C. An expert in Black theology and African American and Womanist spirituality, she is the author of numerous books and articles, including *Forged in the Fiery Furnace: African American Spirituality* and *No Crystal Stair: Womanist Spirituality*.

Rev. Bryan N. Massingale

Rev. Bryan N. Massingale holds the James and Nancy Buckman Chair in Applied Christian Ethics at Fordham University (New York). His research interests include the Catholic moral tradition, African American religious ethics, and theologies of liberation. He is a past president of the Catholic Theological Society of America and the author of *Racial Justice and the Catholic Church*.

Cecilia A. Moore

Cecilia A. Moore is an Associate Professor of Religious Studies at the University of Dayton (Ohio). Her research has focused on the conversion of U.S. African Americans to Catholicism. She is co-editor of *Songs of Our Hearts, Meditations of Our Souls: Prayers for Black Catholics*.

Diane Batts Morrow

Diane Batts Morrow is an Associate Professor of History at the University of Georgia. Her research has focused on gender and race in the nineteenth century. She is the author of *Persons of Color and Religious at the Same Time: The Oblate Sisters of Providence, 1828–1860*.

Rev. Clarence Joseph Rivers

Rev. Clarence Joseph Rivers (1931–2004), a convert to Catholicism, was the first African American diocesan priest of the Archdiocese of Cincinnati. Called the father of Black Catholic liturgy or the "soul priest," he became known for liturgical music inspired by African American idioms. Serving as the first director of the Department of Culture and Worship in the National Office for Black Catholics, he wrote and lectured widely on music, worship, and culture.

Ronald LaMarr Sharps

Ronald LaMarr Sharps is an Associate Dean of the College of the Arts at Montclair State University (New Jersey). He earned a doctoral degree in American Studies from George Washington University and has taught courses in American history, art history, and arts management. He previously served as director of the Department of Culture and Worship in the National Office for Black Catholics (1978–1985) and was a member of the editorial committee that produced the first national Black Catholic hymnal, *Lead Me, Guide Me* (1987).

C. Vanessa White

C. Vanessa White is an Associate Professor of Spirituality and Ministry at Catholic Theological Union, Chicago, Illinois. She has a dual appointment as Associate Director of the Th.M. degree program at Xavier University of Louisiana's Institute for Black Catholic Studies. She is active in the Tolton Guild, helping to advance the cause for sainthood of Father Augustus Tolton, the United States' first recognized Black priest.

Speaking the Truth:
The Black Catholic Intellectual Vocation

BRYAN N. MASSINGALE*

THEOLOGICAL REFLECTION is an intellectual activity whose questions and modes of analysis are conditioned by the cultural resources and social interests of those who engage in it. Paraphrasing an insight of the African American theologian James Cone, a people's social and cultural environment in a large measure determines the kinds of religious questions they ask.

The historical circumstance which most decisively affects the theological and ethical intellectual endeavors of African Americans is the reality of racism, that is, the existence of an unequal distribution of power, privilege, and prestige based upon race—and the beliefs used to justify and defend such disparities. Racism has constantly and consistently stymied the quest of black Americans for justice, acceptance, and equal access to social, political, and economic opportunity.

My assertion that black intellectual pursuits are influenced by the reality of racism is not meant to deny either the diversity of the black community or the pluralism present in the black experience. That is, many other factors also influence or condition African American perceptions of reality, not the least of these being gender and class. Such factors notwithstanding, the experience common to all visible African Americans is the rejection, humiliation, and otherwise pejorative treatment which stems from the dominant culture's insidious, pervasive, albeit largely unarticulated, belief that most blacks are intellectually, culturally, and morally inferior to whites.

---

* A version of this essay appeared as "Cyprian Davis and the Black Catholic Intellectual Vocation," *U.S. Catholic Historian* 28, no. 1 (Winter 2010): 65–82.

This essay seeks to articulate—even excavate—the experience of being Black, Catholic, and a scholar of religion.[1] How does the "black experience"—that is, the experience of contending with the crushing ordinariness of daily assaults upon one's talent, beauty, character, and intelligence—qualify theological work so that it makes a distinctive contribution to the Church's understanding of faith and what it requires? What unique insight does this cultural experience provide to the craft of religious scholarship? Why should this experience matter to the rest of the Church? And on a more personal level, but more existentially relevant especially for the Black Catholic faithful: Given the history and continuing reality of the Catholic Church's complicity in white racial privilege, why would a black man choose not only to belong to it, but also to serve it as a scholar and minister? . . .

My goal is to situate the vocation of the Black Catholic religious scholar within the context of both African American intellectual life and Catholic theology. I will structure my remarks by first reflecting upon the vocation or self-understanding of the black scholar; then, of the Catholic theologian; and then of the Black Catholic theologian.

Prolegomenon: The Compounded Marginality of Black Catholic Intellectual Life

Before undertaking this project, it is necessary to consider the marginality of black Americans in accounts of U.S. intellectual life, the omission of religious intellectuals in accounts of black intellectual life, and the absence of Black Catholic scholarship in U.S. and black accounts of intellectual life. Clarence Taylor's conclusion to his pathbreaking study of black religious intellectual life puts the matter directly and without varnish: "Intellectual history in the

---

[1] Throughout this essay, I use the terms "Black Catholic intellectual," "black scholar of religion," and "black theologian" interchangeably. There are nuanced differences among these terms, but they are not significant for the purposes of this project. Also, discussion over the capitalization of "black" still continues. My convention is to use it in the lower case, except in the phrase "Black Catholic" as it refers to a specific group that is the subject of the essay. In quotations, however, the term is cited as it appears in the original source.

United States usually has been described as if it were a Whites Only project."² He laments that only a handful of blacks—"obvious choices such as Frederick Douglass, W. E. B. Du Bois, and the rare minister such as Martin Luther King Jr."—are found in standard works. He charges that this non-recognition of black intellectual thought not only "dismisses the intellectual capital and activities of African Americans," it also "leaves the racist impression that African Americans stress intuition and not analytical thought."³

Taylor's warning that omitting black intellectuals from accounts of U.S. intellectual life feeds racist misunderstandings of African Americans becomes a full-fledged accusation by other black scholars. W. D. Wright's monograph, *Crisis of the Black Intellectual*, attributes the oversight and devaluing of African American intellectual scholarship to the endemic and pervasive racism of American life. His indictment is searing and unsparing:

> The racist belief that Black people were inherently incapable of serious or productive intellectual ability led to two other ... racist beliefs: that Black people could not produce any intellectuals, and owing to this, were incapable of producing knowledge, which is what intellectuals do. This meant that white people had to think for Black people, to speak on their behalf, and to represent them publicly before other white people.
>
> Thus, one can see that the emergence of Black intellectuals in America, which was not only not supposed to happen, but which was believed to be impossible, greatly perplexed and significantly frightened white people.⁴

Wright details how a recognition of black intellectual capacity— much less an acknowledgment of black intellectual life—undermines and challenges one of the core foundations of white supremacy, namely, a visceral belief in white intellectual superiority over other races and in the intellectual inferiority of persons of

---
  ² Clarence Taylor, *Black Religious Intellectuals: The Fight for Equality from Jim Crow to the 21st Century* (New York: Routledge, 2002), 196.
  ³ Taylor, *Black Religious Intellectuals*, 5.
  ⁴ W. D. Wright, *Crisis of the Black Intellectual* (Chicago: Third Word Press, 2007), 12.

African descent. Thus, Wright concludes that the suppression of black intellectual life in American accounts of intellectual activity is not only unsurprising but indeed necessary.[5]

However, we not only have to consider the marginalization of black intellectual life from the dominant discourse, but also the omission of black religious scholars from contemporary accounts of black intellectual life. Taylor contends that "black religious leaders are rarely studied for their intellectual contributions. With the exception of Martin Luther King Jr., Malcolm X, and a few icons of the American civil rights and black power movements, there has been a general tendency among scholars writing on black intellectuals in the twentieth century to ignore the black religious community."[6] Taylor attributes the lack of attention to black religious thought by African American scholars to three factors: 1) the secularization of the black intellectual tradition as more black scholars study nonreligious university disciplines and choose careers other than the ministry; 2) the long history (since the 1920s) of secular black activists and intellectuals critiquing the black church and its ministers as irrelevant or even detrimental to the struggle for freedom; and 3) the trend among those writing on black intellectual life to regard secular black revolutionaries as "much more attractive characters."[7] Thus, black religious scholars suffer from a double marginalization, rendered absent in white and black intellectual histories and accounts.

This double marginalization is further compounded for Black Catholic intellectuals and religious scholars who are rendered absent from and invisible in most accounts of U.S. and black intellectual life. Even works such as Taylor's and Wright's, which attempt to

---

[5] Cf. Wright, *Crisis of the Black Intellectual*, chapter one and passim.
[6] Taylor, *Black Religious Intellectuals*, 1. Taylor notes a handful of exceptions to this general tendency: William Banks, *Black Intellectuals* (New York: W. W. Norton, 1996); Henry J. Young, *Major Black Religious Leaders since 1940* (Nashville: Abingdon Press, 1972); Randall Burkett and Richard Newman, eds., *Black Apostles: Afro-American Clergy Confront the Twentieth Century* (Boston: G. K. Hall, 1978); and Mark Chapman, *Christianity on Trial: African-American Religious Thought before and after Black Power* (Maryknoll, NY: Orbis Books, 1996).
[7] Taylor, *Black Religious Intellectuals*, 2–5.

rectify the grave lacunae in the standard rehearsals of black and religious scholarship, fail to mention Black Catholic scholars and religious thinkers.

We are absent and invisible in the discourse of Black Theology and discussions of black faith in America. Symptomatic of this is that in major works on black liberation theology and African American religious thought, one finds scant reference to Black Catholic scholarship.[8] Indeed, in a "seminal" monograph examining the African American religious experience, there is no mention of Black Catholicism.[9]

We often are rendered invisible in Catholic religious intellectual discourse as well. At times, I and my Black Catholic colleagues have the distinct impression that our white Catholic peers more often dialogue with black Protestant theologians than with us.[10] There have

---

[8] Dwight N. Hopkins, *Introducing Black Theology of Liberation* (Maryknoll, NY: Orbis Books, 1999). One could also point to the edited work of Cornel West and Eddie S. Glaude Jr., *African American Religious Thought: An Anthology* (Louisville: Westminster John Knox Press, 2003). Note that this anthology, despite its omission of Black Catholics, has been hailed as "comprehensive." It should be mentioned that James Cone is a conspicuous exception; he has been in intentional dialogue with Black Catholic theologians and has expressed critical appreciation for our project. See James H. Cone, "Black Liberation Theology and Black Catholics: A Critical Conversation," *Theological Studies* 61, no. 4 (December 2000): 731–747.

[9] Juan Williams, *This Far by Faith: Stories from the African American Religious Experience* (New York: HarperCollins, 2003). The description "seminal" is found on this work's back cover. A welcome exception to this pattern of omission is Anthony B. Pinn's *The African American Religious Experience in America* (Miami: University Press of Florida, 2007).

[10] One of the reasons often given for such omission is that there is a lack of resources for such engagement. Given the existence of four anthologies on Black Catholic thought edited by Black Catholics, this reason is more than a little bewildering (to say the least). Such works include: Jamie T. Phelps, ed., *Black and Catholic: The Challenge and Gift of Black Folk* (Milwaukee: Marquette University Press, 1997); Diana L. Hayes and Cyprian Davis, eds., *Taking Down Our Harps: Black Catholics in the United States* (Maryknoll, NY: Orbis Books, 1998); Cyprian Davis and Jamie Phelps, eds., *"Stamped with the Image of God": African Americans as God's Image in Black* (Maryknoll, NY: Orbis Books, 2003); and M. Shawn Copeland, ed., *Uncommon Faithfulness: The Black Catholic Experience* (Maryknoll, NY: Orbis Books, 2009). One should also note the anthology edited by William J. Kelly, S.J., *Black Catholic Theology: A Sourcebook* (McGraw-Hill, 2000). Moreover, since 2007, there is the annual

been recent noteworthy efforts to redress this matter, specifically the annual Black Catholic Theology consultation at the conventions of the Catholic Theological Society of America (CTSA); the special issue of *Theological Studies* (December 2000) exploring the reception of Black Theology in Catholic theology; several issues of *U.S. Catholic Historian* examining the Black Catholic Experience[11]; two seminal works on white privilege and Catholic theology[12]; and the elections of Shawn Copeland (2003-2004) and myself (2009-2010) to the presidency of the CTSA. These are laudable and significant accomplishments. There remains a long way to go.

The compounded marginality of Black Catholic intellectual endeavors—their absence in American, Catholic, and black intellectual discourse—is an important backdrop for our study of Black Catholic intellectual life.

The Vocation of the Black Scholar[13]

In his magisterial study of African American intellectual life, William Banks defines an intellectual as one who "act[s] self-consciously to transmit, modify, and create ideas and culture."[14] In a seminal article, Vincent Harding further specifies the unique vocation and tasks of black scholars in the U.S. context. His understanding rests

---

Journal of the Black Catholic Theological Symposium, which publishes the significant papers delivered at its annual gatherings. In view of these resources, not to mention the monographs and other publications of Black Catholic scholars, the pattern of omission and nonengagement is all the more "curious."

[11] "The Black Catholic Experience," *U.S. Catholic Historian* 5, no. 1 (Winter 1986); "The Black Catholic Community, 1880-1987," *U.S. Catholic Historian* 7, nos. 2-3 (Spring/Summer 1988); and several essays in "Spirituality, Devotionalism, & Popular Religion," *U.S. Catholic Historian* 8, nos. 1-2 (Winter/Spring 1989).

[12] Jon Nilson, *Hearing Past the Pain: Why Catholic Theologians Need Black Theology* (New York: Paulist Press, 2007); and Laurie M. Cassidy and Alexander Mikulich, eds., *Interrupting White Privilege: Catholic Theologians Break the Silence* (Maryknoll, NY: Orbis Books, 2007).

[13] I discuss the vocations of the black scholar and the Black Catholic scholar in *Racial Justice and the Catholic Church* (Maryknoll, NY: Orbis Books, 2010). The presentation here is an adaptation of what appears in that work.

[14] William M. Banks, *Black Intellectuals: Race and Responsibility in American Life* (New York: W. W. Norton, 1996), xvi.

upon the pivotal assertion that black scholars do not and cannot "exist in splendid isolation from the situation of the larger black community."[15] The black scholar's "essential social, political, and spiritual context," he provocatively argues, "is the colonized situation of the mass of the black community in America."[16] Because of this "colonized situation," he argues that black people in the United States constitute what he calls a "community-in-struggle,"[17] that is, a people engaged in an elusive and ongoing quest for self-definition, self-determination, and the recognition of their authentic humanity. Therefore, the black scholar, as a member of this "community-in-struggle" must "transmit, modify, and create ideas and culture" in a way that furthers the efforts of this community in its quest for justice and well-being.

Echoing the African American poet Mari Evans, Harding believes that a distinctive vocation of the black scholar is that of "speaking the truth" on behalf of a community-in-struggle. A selection from Mari Evans' poem provides the charge which inspires Harding:

> Speak the truth to the people.
> Talk sense to the people.
> Free them with reason.
> Free them with honesty.
> Free them with Love and Courage and Care for their being ...
> Speak the truth to the people
> To identify the enemy is to free the mind
> Free the mind of the people
> Speak to the mind of the people
> Speak Truth.[18]

Harding maintains that fidelity to this vocation requires that the black scholar not only speak the truth, or even live the truth, but

---

[15] Vincent Harding, "The Vocation of the Black Scholar and the Struggles of the Black Community," in *Education and Black Struggle: Notes from the Colonized World* (Cambridge, MA: Harvard Educational Review, 1974), 2–29, at 5.

[16] Harding, "The Vocation of the Black Scholar," 6.

[17] Harding, "The Vocation of the Black Scholar," 7 and passim. Observe how this echoes the dimension of "struggle" highlighted as a core dimension of the black cultural experience.

[18] Mari Evans, *Continuum: New and Selected Poems* (Baltimore: Black Classic Press, 2007), 22–23.

indeed come to be possessed by the truth. He declares, "It is obviously not enough to speak the truth to our people. We must somehow find ways, stumbling ways, to live the truth—to run the risk of being possessed by our struggle for justice and hope."[19]

Harding further specifies the agenda or summons of black scholarship by positing that the following questions guide responsible scholars:

> How can a victimized, oppressed people begin to see its true identity as more than that of victims and sufferers, and begin to grasp the vast potentialities of their humanity? How can we move from talk of "making it" in the system to the work of total transformation of the system? . . . What do liberation, independence, authentic black humanity, self-determination . . . mean in the world of the [twenty-first century]? What is the nature of the society we seek?[20]

I do not believe that Harding intends these questions to be either exhaustive or exclusive. Rather, they illustrate his central thesis: If "struggle" is a constitutive and fundamental dimension of the black experience in the United States, then authentic black scholars must be truly identified with and participants in this "community-in-struggle." In common with other intellectuals, black scholars pursue and speak the truth they have discovered (or believe they have discovered). But black scholarship is pursued in neither cultural isolation nor for mere self-interested curiosity. The black scholar's "speaking the truth" is an activity engaged in, on behalf of, and in solidarity with a community-in-struggle.[21]

---

[19] Harding, "The Vocation of the Black Scholar," 20. Note that this truth is not an abstract, timeless notion, but one which is discovered and verified in the midst of struggle and action for the sake of justice.

[20] Harding, "The Vocation of the Black Scholar," 13.

[21] Black scholars are, in Antonio Gramsci's words, "organic intellectuals." Unlike "traditional intellectuals" who see themselves as functioning somewhat autonomously from society and its influences (the stereotype of the "ivory tower" academic), the Italian social theorist Gramsci describes the "organic intellectual" as one who is intimately involved in a movement for social change and contributes the intellectual justification and analysis necessary for the new ideas upon which a more just society can be founded. He or she also provides the sophisticated critique of the dominant social ideas and values which shore up unjust social situations. In

I find much that is rewarding, demanding, and challenging in Harding's meditation. I lift up three considerations.

First, I present Harding's reflections because I believe that Black Catholic scholars of religion are part of the broader tradition of African American intellectual life. Harding thus reminds us how our self-understanding and the pursuit of our theological vocations are shaped not only by our religious faith and church membership, but also by the African American intellectual tradition and the debates within it concerning the purpose of black scholarship.[22]

Second, it is critical to note how the black scholar's passion—that is, voicing truth on behalf of the "community-in-struggle"—neither demands a blind stance of uncritical apology for black people, nor entails a lack of intellectual rigor and discipline. Harding, in fact, states that the black scholar not only must speak the truth about white America, but also must speak truths about those pathological and self-destructive forces within the black community which impede its struggle for justice and self-determination.[23] Moreover, liberation theologians have maintained that the tasks of disciplined intellectual reflection and passionate advocacy on behalf of the oppressed are not mutually exclusive. As James Cone argues:

> There can be no creative black theology without a disciplined mind, without a solid knowledge of black, third-world, and white theological

---

both of these tasks, the organic intellectual contributes to developing the new consciousness essential to a new social order. For a discussion of Gramsci's notion of the "organic intellectual," see Barry Burke, "Antonio Gramsci, schooling and education," *The Encyclopedia of Informal Education (Infed)*, https://infed.org/mobi/antonio-gramsci-schooling-and-education/.

[22] And there are many debates within this tradition both supporting and disputing Harding's thesis that black scholarship must serve an advocacy role in the quest for black freedom and justice. Banks' work is a masterful recounting of these disputes and debates.

[23] Harding, "The Vocation of the Black Scholar," 14 and 16. He lists as examples: fear, lack of self-discipline, failure to believe in ourselves, and an excessive desire for public recognition. I would offer Malcolm X as an example of one who relentlessly criticized the values of white society, yet also offered searing critiques of self-destructive forces within the black community. Cf. *Malcolm X Speaks*, ed. by George Breitman (New York: Grove Press, 2005).

traditions as they are related to sociology, psychology, philosophy, and history. *But how this knowledge is to be used should be decided by our love for the poor.* Love demands that we participate in their liberation struggles, fighting against the forces of oppression.[24]

Third, while I agree with Harding regarding the organic relationship of black scholars to a specific "community-in-struggle," I also believe that Black Catholic intellectuals do—and ought to—recognize that persons of African descent in America are not the only "community-in-struggle." We have, in the words of Peter Paris, a charge to contribute to the well-being of both "our communities-of-belonging and to the world at large."[25] For example, Black Catholic intellectuals and scholars have been attentive to and in dialogue with our Latino and Asian colleagues. Moreover, many of us are engaged in other justice concerns besides racism; for example, the struggle for environmental justice, the role of women in church and society, and the civil rights of gay and lesbian persons lay claims to our concern. Most of us resonate with Audre Lorde's insight that for the black community there cannot be a single-issue justice struggle because most black folk do not live single-issue lives.[26]

Thus, I argue that the Black Catholic theologian is called to be what Cornel West calls "a race-transcending prophet," by which he means "someone who never forgets about the significance of race but refuses to be confined to race.... [Someone] concerned about the development of each human being regardless of race, creed, gender, [sexual orientation], and nationality.... [One] who moves beyond the confines of race without ever forgetting the impact of

---

[24] James H. Cone, *My Soul Looks Back* (Maryknoll, NY: Orbis Books, 1986), 77-78; emphasis added. Gustavo Gutierrez, a seminal Latin American liberation theologian, likewise declares: "We make no attempt at an aseptic—and elusive!—'objectivity.' We shall not be filling the columns of our ledger with cold analysis. What we enter there will be facts, yes, but facts with which we are passionately involved" (*The Power of the Poor in History* [Maryknoll, NY: Orbis Books, 1983], 77).

[25] Peter Paris, "The Ethics of African American Religious Scholarship," *Journal of the American Academy of Religion* 64, no. 3 (1996): 483-497; at 489.

[26] Audre Lorde, "There is No Hierarchy of Oppressions," in *Dangerous Liaisons: Blacks, Gays, and the Struggle for Equality*, ed. by Eric Brandt (New York: New Press, 1999), 306-307.

racism on Black people in this society."²⁷ In another place, West describes this "race-transcending prophet" as one who "puts forward a vision of fundamental social change for all who suffer from socially induced misery."²⁸ While rooted in a particular "community-of-struggle," Black Catholic scholars are also aware of and concerned about other "communities-of-struggle." Thus, we can conclude that the responsible Black Catholic scholar today has a vocational commitment to "fusing the life of the mind with the struggle for justice and human dignity."²⁹

In summary, in common with other African American intellectuals, Black Catholic scholars are called to be people who take the life of the mind seriously, and link the life of the mind to spiritual, political, and cultural struggle. There is a constitutive ethical dimension to this vocation: "The mission of the African American scholar is a moral mission, because its final aim is the realization of racial justice in the nation's thought and practice. Apart from the realization of that aim, African peoples will surely perish on this continent and elsewhere."³⁰

The Vocation of the Catholic Theologian

It is difficult to give a concise yet comprehensive definition of a Catholic theologian or scholar of religion. I find it helpful to conceive of the theologian as "a thinker for the church."³¹ That is, the

---

²⁷ Bell Hooks and Cornel West, *Breaking Bread: Insurgent Black Intellectual Life* (Boston: South End Press, 1991), 49.
²⁸ Cornel West, *Race Matters* (Boston: Beacon Press, 1993), 46.
²⁹ West, *Race Matters*, 43.
³⁰ Paris, "The Ethics of African American Religious Scholarship," 489.
³¹ One often hears an injunction that the Catholic theologian is to *sentire cum ecclesia*, that is, to "think with the Church" and to harmonize one's theological contribution with the normative faith claims taught by official authorities. I believe this is too narrow an understanding. Rather, the Catholic theologian, in order to serve the faith community well, must also *sentire pro ecclesia*, that is, to think *on behalf of and for the sake of the Church* in its quest for a less and less imperfect understanding of the infinite love and claim that our God has laid upon it. At times this will entail a stance of critical loving critique of some of the Church's concrete practices or current official stances—never out of intellectual arrogance or hubris, but out of deep concern for the adequacy of its internal life and moral witness.

theologian is a fellow believer or disciple in the faith, who offers the faith community the gifts and fruits of his/her education—an in-depth knowledge and familiarity with the Scriptures, the traditions of our faith, and the community's doctrines, customs and practices—to help the community come to deeper and truer insight into the meaning, challenges, and privileges of discipleship in the Lord Jesus. One of the tasks of the theologian, then, is to listen to the stories of the contemporary community and the world in which we live, and then to put them into dialogue with the larger tradition of the faith witnesses who have preceded us. Thus, these scholars are charged with helping the faith community articulate the relevance of its faith to contemporary human experience and help uncover the faith dimension of human experience. In doing so, they help the community to clarify the convictions of faith, the demands of love, and the reasons for its hope in the God of Jesus Christ.

Thus, the theologian is charged with developing a critical reflection upon the faith of the believing community. To this end, the scholar is engaged in the quest to provide serious, disciplined reflection on questions such as: What is the purpose of human existence? Who is God? What does God desire or intend for creation, including humankind? How do we know what God wants? Why should we do what God wants? How do we cooperate with the unfolding of God's intentions for creation? What is the fitting human response to the experience of sacred mystery encountered in human existence? And in light of the importance of tradition for Catholic faith and practice, the theologian must ponder the further questions: How have our forebears in faith answered such questions, and what is the relevance or significance of those responses for contemporary believers?

Catholics are heirs to a complex and complicated religious tradition, one that is marked by both shadow and glory; inspirational witness and horrifying callousness; heroic sanctity and barbarous cruelty; pathetic failure and extraordinary grace; maddening plurality and frightening ambiguity. The factual pluralism and moral ambiguity of the Catholic heritage are evident in matters as mundane as the postures prescribed for our liturgical celebrations, and as weighty as Catholic attitudes and practices concerning slavery, divorce, warfare, indigenous peoples, the Jews, and the papacy. It is difficult to find a single matter on which the Catholic tradition has held a univocal and invariant point of view, that is, a position maintained "always, everywhere, and for everyone." One of the responsibilities of Catholic theologians, then, is to hold the various strands of the Catholic tradition in critical tension, fruitful dialogue, and mutual correction.

Black Catholic theologians, then, are not only formed by our cultural community's struggle for justice and equality. We also belong and contribute to the long and expansive Catholic tradition of "faith seeking understanding." Our particular task, I believe, resonates with Mark Jordan's self-description as a "Talmudic Catholic." He writes: "I choose to inherit Catholic traditions, which means that I have the responsibility to think through them about their contradictions and to wonder with them about who gets to count as part of the tradition."[32] Thinking about the Catholic tradition's pluralism, ambiguity, and contradictions through serious, responsible, careful, and disciplined scholarship—while also being attentive to the dynamics of exclusion, silence, and repression of certain voices in that tradition—strikes me as an essential dimension of the vocation of Catholic theologians today, and especially so for U.S. Catholic scholars of African descent.

The Black Catholic Intellectual Vocation

To be a Black Catholic religious scholar, then, is not to be an "either/or," or a bifurcated reality. Rather, we are "both/and"—in the classic phrasing which has become a rallying cry of the contemporary Black Catholic movement, we are both "authentically Black and truly Catholic." Nor are we simply "hybrids," as in cars which sometimes run on batteries and at other times burn gas. At our best, we do not take off our "black" hat in order to put on the "Catholic" one. Our vocations are shaped by the reality of simultaneous truths and multiple identities, being indivisibly members of the theological academy, the black "community-in-struggle," and the Catholic faith communion.

---

[32] Mark D. Jordan, *Telling Truths in Church: Scandal, Flesh, and Christian Speech* (Boston: Beacon Press, 2003), 110, at note 1.

Therefore if the essence of the black scholar's vocation is that of "speaking the truth" for the sake of a "community-in-struggle," and that of the Catholic theologian to help the faith community come to a less and less imperfect understanding of its response to the Divine, then the vocation of the Black Catholic intellectual can be phrased as "passionate participation in reasoned inquiry on behalf of God's oppressed and despised people."[33] Whatever else can be said of the gospel of Jesus Christ, it is certainly "good news" for the poor, the oppressed, the outcast, the despised, and the disdained. Theology worthy of the name "Christian" must give privileged attention to the tears and moans, the groans and the hopes, the hidden struggles and quiet desperation of those forced to the margins of our society and church. Dealing with what Shawn Copeland has termed "the virulent residue" of slavery and its "protracted and pervasive influence" upon the social order and religious experience of the United States is a cognitive, moral, and existential imperative for Black Catholic scholars.[34]

Black Catholic theological scholarship, then, must originate from a stance of engagement and commitment. It cannot maintain a posture of dispassionate objectivity or academic distance, for theology and intellectual inquiry are matters of life and death for our people. Yet despite its passion on behalf of the victims of systemic injustice—and I would argue precisely because of this bias—this theological scholarship must also be rigorous, disciplined, and painstaking. The complexity and urgency of our situation as black believers in the United States do not permit us the luxury of indulging superficial analyses, simplistic interpretations, irresponsible solutions, or intellectual laziness.

I suggest the following questions as among those which convey the vocation and tasks of Black Catholic theological scholarship:

---

[33] M. Shawn Copeland, "Guest Editorial," *Theological Studies* 61, no. 4 (December 2000): 607.

[34] M. Shawn Copeland, "Theology as Intellectually Vital Inquiry: A Black Theological Interrogation," *CTSA Proceedings* 46 (1991): 51. Copeland elaborates upon the challenges the virulent residue of white racism poses for the entire guild of Catholic theologians regardless of race in her essay, "Racism and the Vocation of the Christian Theologian," *Spiritus* 2 (2002): 15-29.

- What does it mean to exercise the theological vocation—that is, to think through the faith community's complex and complicated faith tradition—in the midst of a church both historically and (still) practically committed to white racial privilege?

- How do Black Catholics "sing the Lord's song in a foreign land" (Psalm 137:4)? That is, what does it mean to affirm the real experience of God found in a church that is sometimes hostile, often indifferent, and seldom fully affirming of one's humanity?

- What does it mean to "speak the truth" to both church and society, on behalf of all who suffer social oppression, out of a Catholic tradition that is tainted with complicity and collusion with the social evil of racism?

- What in the Catholic tradition is "good news" for the oppressed of whatever "community-of-struggle"?

- What in Catholicism resonates with the passions and concerns of persons of African descent, especially those living in North America? What in Catholicism, particularly as it has been lived in the United States, resonates with the heartaches, groans, and cries of black peoples?

- How does the "virulent residue" of slavery and segregation, e.g., the continuing stigmata of black inferiority, challenge the integrity of the Catholic faith, the mission of the Church, and the identity of its theologians?

- What are the distinctive tasks of "speaking the truth" for the sake of and in solidarity with a particular subset of the "community-in-struggle," namely Catholics of African descent in the United States?

These questions are not meant to be all-inclusive or exhaustive. Nor do they have easy or obvious answers. Given the newness of Black Catholic scholarship, it is too soon to attempt comprehensive or definitive answers to such questions. Moreover, I am not implying that my Black Catholic colleagues would totally agree with my questions, the ways that I have phrased them, or the answers I would give to them at this time. However, I do believe that questions such as these get us to the heart of the intellectual vocation of those who are both Black and Catholic. For such questions acknowledge both the task we have in common with all Catholic religious scholars and our solidarity with a community which is still seeking an unambiguous recognition and acceptance of their God-given humanity.[35]

Thus, the vocation of the Black Catholic scholar is to think through the complexities and "ideological deformations"[36] of this faith tradition. Our charge is not only to speak out of Black Catholic experience and culture, but also to speak of the contemporary reality of Black Catholic existence. We undertake this task not merely for self-interest or self-satisfaction, but for the sake of the integrity and credibility of Catholic faith and witness. Our ultimate goal is to help transform the Catholic Christian community into a less and less imperfect witness to the broad, expansive and inclusive "welcome table" which is the Reign of God. Our distinctive vocational challenge is to think through and struggle with the contradictions, paradoxes, and potentials of Catholic faith and then prophetically challenge this faith community's propensity to sinful attitudes and practices of exclusion....

Conclusion: The Significance of the Black Catholic Intellectual Vocation

Why is the vocation of the Black Catholic scholar relevant or of interest to the Catholic faith community and its ongoing quest for a deeper understanding of its faith?

I believe that our vocation should be a concern for at least two reasons. One stems from the meaning of "catholic." Unless we celebrate

---

[35] Shawn Copeland describes the commonality and distinctiveness of Black Catholic religious scholarship with her characteristic lucidity and precision as follows: "Black Catholic Studies involves a three-fold movement: retrieval, critique, and construction.... First, as a division of African American Religious Studies, Black Catholic Studies retrieves, critiques, and evaluates the intellectual, aesthetic, moral, and religious sensibilities and expressions of people of African descent. Second, Black Catholic Studies retrieves, critiques, and evaluates the theological and doctrinal traditions, customs, and expressions of the Catholic Church. Third, Black Catholic Studies synthesizes the decisions and products of the first and second movements: from these materials, Black Catholic scholars construct a distinctive religious, intellectual, and moral horizon or world view." Copeland presented this description in a lecture at the Institute for Black Catholic Studies, Summer 1994.

[36] I borrow this term from my colleague Shawn Copeland, in a personal conversation.

Black Catholic scholarship and nurture more Catholic scholars of African descent, then we will have neither a truly "catholic" nor a genuinely "American" theology. For the black experience is a pivotal and constitutive part of the American experience.

We cannot understand who we are—as Catholics and as U.S. citizens—if the fortunes and misfortunes, the joys and tragedies, the sorrows and exaltations of black peoples are not heard and understood. Despite the overwhelming denials and silences of our curricula, African Americans are central to this country's fortunes and prospects. Nor has there ever been a U.S. Catholicism in which there have not been Black witnesses of Catholic sanctity and faith.[37] But these voices cannot be adequately heard unless there is a critical mass of scholars who are part of this faith community and can speak from within this cultural experience.

The second reason why this particular, and at times peculiar, vocation should be a concern for Catholic life is because the calling of the Black Catholic scholar provides an alternative model and/or needed corrective for understanding the role of the Catholic theologian in the Church and society. Our specific vocation reminds all Catholic religious scholars that the measure of our calling cannot rest in the acclaim of the academy, the achievement of tenure, the holding of a named chair, an increase in salary, or any of the other typical and usual ways of measuring "success" in our guild. Success as a faith-filled intellectual—as a Catholic religious scholar—must include above all else the qualities of constant fidelity to a call in the midst of persistent difficulties; humble service to a people spurned and despised; a willingness to speak unpopular, uncomfortable, yet necessary truths; and a commitment to the life of the mind for the sake of social and ecclesial transformation. Each religious scholar is called to do these things in his or her own fashion. But without some understanding and appropriation of this aspect of the theological vocation, then Catholic intellectual life risks becoming merely a self-serving career and an unworthy witness to the Crucified and Risen One whose message it is our privileged duty to study, share, and speak.

---

[37] As chronicled in Cyprian Davis' seminal work, *The History of Black Catholics in the United States* (New York: Crossroad Publishing, 1990).

Black History and Culture

SISTER THEA BOWMAN, F.S.P.A.*

> We've come this far by faith,
> Leaning on the Lord;
> Trusting in his holy word,
> He's never failed me yet,
> O, can't turn around,
> We've come this far by faith.
>   —Albert S. Goodson, 1965

THAT'S OUR HISTORY, Church. We've come this far by faith. How? Leaning on the Lord. We've come this far. Can't turn around.

Look inside yourself; look into your heart; look into your life; remember the people who brought you in faith and taught you in faith, who led and fed you in faith. Think about your mama, your grandparents, your godparents, the uncles and the aunts, the brothers and sisters, the grands and great-[grands], the ones who led you in the storm, who set a welcoming table for you, who taught you to say "precious Lord take my hand," who convinced you that you were God's child when the world told you you were nobody and would amount to nothing.

When we remember from whence we came, then we can look into our souls, our Black souls, and testify to that we have seen with Black eyes, heard with Black ears, and understood with African hearts. We can embrace the culture that has enabled us to survive. We can't turn around. We've come too far.

---

* This essay was first published in *U.S. Catholic Historian* 7, nos. 2–3 (Spring/Summer 1988): 307–310. It was drawn from an address offered at the Sixth National Black Catholic Congress held in Washington, D.C., May 21-24, 1987.

Let us recall the history, the blood, sweat, and tears, the sacrifices made to bring us this far. Can't turn around. We've come this far by faith.

On this historic occasion of the [Sixth] National Black Catholic Congress, we have come from all over the country, from the Islands, and from Africa saying, "We want to know more about ourselves, we want to look deeply into our past and touch the fabric of our being, for we know that when we know our history and our culture we are fortified as individuals and as a people. When we know ourselves, we bring the gift of our history and our culture to one another, to the Church, and to the world." We sing, "My soul looks back and wonders how I got over." *My Soul looks back*—I learn and claim my history. *My soul wonders how I got over*—I investigate and embrace the spiritual and psychological survival skills embodied in my culture.

Our history includes the services of a Simon of Cyrene, the search of that Ethiopian eunuch; the contributions of Black Egypt in art, mathematics, monasticism, and politics; the art and architecture of Zimbabwe; the scholarship of Timbuktu; the dignity and serenity of textile, gold work, and religion in Ghana; the pervasive spirituality and vitality of Nigeria; the political and social systems of Zaire.

Our history includes enslavement, oppression, and exploitation. As Malcolm X phrased it, "Our people didn't come here on the *Mayflower*." Many of them came in slave ships, in chains. Strong, proud men and women, artists, teachers, healers, warriors and dream makers, inventors and builders, administrators and politicians, they came to these shores in the slave trade.

Those who survived the indignity of the Middle Passage came to the Americas bearing treasures of our African heritage, African spiritual and cultural gifts, wisdom, faith and faithfulness, art and drama. Here in an alien land, African people clung to African ways of thinking, of perceiving and understanding values, of celebrating life, of walking and talking, of healing and learning, of singing, dancing, laughing, of being together and of loving—that's culture. To the Americas our people brought the secret memory of Africa. The celebration of life and values in an African way and style, in song and instrumentation, in story and drums, in verse and anecdote, the memory of African ways of survival; from Africa, the memory of culture, color and texture, of culinary arts that translated even when we ate chitlins and other folks' leftovers.

African people became African-Americans. Relating and communicating, teaching and learning, loving, and expressing faith in the God who loves and saves, they embodied and celebrated themselves and their values, goals, dreams, and relationships.

Our history includes our island experience, the Virgin Islands, Haiti, Cuba; our Hispanic experience, in Central and South America; our Native American experience, African blood commingled with Choctaw, Cherokee; with people of Asian and Asian/Pacific origin; with Europeans from France, Germany, and Spain, and so on and so on. Are you with me, Church? African people of the Diaspora, we are here in this land, and it is truly our land. That's a part of our history too. Our people helped to build this nation, in cotton, grain, beans, and vegetables, in brick and mortar! They cleared land and cooked the food they grew.

They cleaned houses, they built churches, railroad bridges, and national monuments. They defended the country as soldiers and sailors. They taught and molded and raised the children, and I'm not just talking about the Black children. They produced a music that speaks America and that has influenced the music of the world. And during the movement for Civil Rights, they challenged America to live out her freedom creed. The history must be told. In spite of oppression, exploitation, disenfranchisement, and poverty, my people helped to build and form this nation.

Surviving our history, physically, mentally, emotionally, morally, and spiritually, faithfully and joyfully, our people developed a culture that was African and American, that was formed and enriched by all our various experiences.

My folks have been about the business of making Black history. We are making Black history. Black history is in human rights, in economics, in education, in allied health, in the strength that sustains us to do what we need to do so that the Source that has given us life may preserve our life.

Our history is power. We can learn from it. We don't need to make all the mistakes ourselves. If we remember the misery of slavery, the struggles for freedom and Civil Rights, the joys of the past, if we remember how far we have come, our memory is power.

Our culture is power. Within the culture the coping mechanisms of the people survive. Do you remember the folks who could say, "Nobody knows the trouble I have seen, but glory Hallelujah"? Do you remember the people who could say, "God can make a way out of no way and out of nothing"? Do you remember the ones who said, "There is nobody in this neighborhood who is hungry unless we all are hungry"? "We are a people and we are a family and we are walking together toward that new Jerusalem."

Did they tell you that God is, that God is above us, that the spirit world is here and now, and that we are called to build up God's Kingdom? Did they tell you that faith and values must be expressed, must be celebrated, must be lived in song and dance and story? Did they tell you, Church, that feelings and passions and emotions are not to be suppressed, repressed, and denied? They are to be channeled and directed and used to give life to the family and to the community. Did they tell you that the individual finds joy and fulfillment in community, in helping somebody, in building the family, in building the Church? Did they tell you to forget what other folks think and choose the colors that complement your complexion, the music that is expressive of your heart? Did they tell you that the child is the treasure of the community and that the elders are the repository of the wisdom of the community? Do you hear me talking about history, Church? Do you hear me talking about culture?

When we talk about history and culture, we're talking about understanding ourselves, understanding our roots, understanding where we're coming from so we can understand where we are, so we can chart a course toward where we need to go. When we talk about culture, we're just talking about being ourselves, being our best selves, living, claiming, and celebrating and sharing the best of the cultures that have formed, uplifted us, and enabled us to survive. We're talking about naming the goals, values, dreams, and aspirations of our hearts, claiming and celebrating them in family and in community where they can do us some good. If you sit there and keep your faith locked up in your heart, it's not going to help any.

Culture is the expression whereby we as the family of Christian, Black Catholic people learn from our history and accept it all. We have to stop fussing and fighting about who's too yellow, and who's not Creole, who came from what island, and how much money or education or influence it takes to belong to this or that. We are a multicultural people. We must claim our roots and proclaim our peace.

We all have multicultural people in our families. Just look round this room, all kinds of beauty. We need to know the histories and cultures from which we come, to claim all, to use all, all the experience, all the survival and coping mechanisms, all that we need if we're going to get over to that Promised Land, to that new Jerusalem, where there won't be anybody hungry, or lonely or poor, because we're walking together as brothers and sisters in Jesus' Name.

When we know who we are and claim the history, we claim the struggle, the pain, the challenge, the purpose, the journey, and the dream. We are who we are and Whose we are because of all our journeys, and the children that belong to our communities are enriched because of a pluralism that reflects life in a world that is pluralistic. Do we know all we can know, of ourselves, of our history, of our arts, and of our experience, of our goals, and of our values, the full range of what has made us a people? When we know and understand, then we can do what we need to do to help ourselves.

Martin Luther King Jr. was a leader in this nation's struggle, but his learnings were from Africa, the Islands, Europe, India. He could discourse with scholars and presidents; and he could sit down on the back steps with some old woman in Mississippi and eat cornbread and greens with his fingers while he learned the story of her life and struggle. He claimed it all. He claimed the culture of Greece and the glory of Europe. He used all he learned in the universities. He was multicultural. We have to be multicultural in order to survive in this society. We can take that message home to our children. We have to learn. We have to know.

You have to be bicultural to hold a job, don't you? You have to be bicultural in academe, don't you? You have to be bicultural to make it in the political situation. And with all this bicultural experience, we can come into the house of the Lord and say, "We want a liturgical celebration that is of all of us, that satisfies all our Souls."

We must recognize who we are and how we are and celebrate, because in our history and in our culture, we find power. Do you remember the old days when we were out in the fields telling the stories and singing the songs? Some of you never experienced that reality, but that's a part of our history, too. Listening to grown-ups talk on city stoops, or around the family table, or in the message of the Gospel preacher, we heard the stories of our people. The knowledge of their life and culture was power, spirit-power, faith-power, health and healing-power, life-power, love-power. Some of us no longer take time to be together as families and as the families of families which make Church. We no longer have the time or inclination to tell the stories, to pray the prayers or sing the songs, or share the jokes and anecdotes, to shuck and jive and play together, to pass on the old coping mechanisms and survival techniques. We have to get the extra dollar or watch TV. We don't have time to share history and culture.

Where Black culture and spirituality are alive and well in our hearts and homes and neighborhoods, we bring them easily and joyfully into our churches. Where Black culture is alive in our churches, its vitality spills over into our communities. It becomes a source of energy and vitality.

Some of us say we don't need Black Culture. We're comfortable. [Do you hear me? Are you with me? I'm from Mississippi. I don't know how to deal with a quiet audience.] When we talk about culture, we're talking about learning, understanding, and facing ourselves, embracing and educating ourselves, teaching our children, all of them, learning from our elders the stories of history and of survival, and passing them on.

When we as delegates to the National Black Catholic Congress live and celebrate our history and our culture, we will address concerns that many Black Catholics express and that are reflected in the working documents of this National Black Catholic Congress. When we understand our history and culture, then we can develop the ritual, the music, and the devotional expression that satisfy us in church. We can develop the cognitive-based religious education and the catechesis that will speak to the hearts of our people. We can develop the systems of service that respect us, who we are, how we operate as a people, and how our families really are. And we can bring new life.

> We've come this far by faith,
> Leaning on the Lord;
> Trusting in his holy word,
> He's never failed me yet,
> O, can't turn around,
> We've come this far by faith.

Let's remember the ones who brought us this far, in faith, who led us and fed us in faith: St. Simon of Cyrene and the Ethiopian eunuch, Anthony of Egypt, Cyril of Alexandria, Moses the Black, Martin de Porres, Charles Lwanga and the Ugandan martyrs, Frederick Douglass, Harriet Tubman, Sojourner Truth, Henriette Delille, Augustus Tolton, George Washington Carver, Booker T. Washington, W. E. B. Du Bois, Mary Church Terrell, Marian Anderson, Paul Robeson, Langston Hughes, Jackie Robinson, Rosa Parks, Medgar Evers, Malcolm X, Martin Luther King Jr., Andrew Young, James Baldwin, Desmond Tutu, the Black Catholic Bishops, all the priests, sisters, teachers, preachers and leaders, all the fathers and mothers, grandparents and great-grands, adoptive parents, godparents, play parents, brothers, sisters, husbands, wives, friends, neighbors, lovers, and children.

We've come this far by faith. Let us remember our brothers and sisters, in Africa, in South Africa, in Haiti, in Cuba, and the other Islands, our brothers and sisters in this country and everywhere who are in hunger, in poverty, in need. We've come this far by faith. Can't turn around now.

May the Spirit within us and among us inspire us to keep on keeping on, in our homes and families, in our communities and in our Church. May the Spirit inspire us and may we share our spiritual and cultural gifts with the Church and with the world. We've come this far by faith. Can't turn around.

Black Catholics in the United States: A Historical Chronology, 1452-2020

RONALD LAMARR SHARPS*

Fifteenth Century

1452 June 18 Pope Nicholas V promulgates *Dum Diversas*, authorizing Portugal and Spain to press into perpetual slavery the enemies of Christ.

1455 January 8 Pope Nicholas V promulgates *Romanus Pontifex*, sanctioning enslavement, while extending control of discovered lands in sub-Saharan Africa and the New World to Catholic nations.

1492 August 3–October 12 A black Catholic who is not enslaved (identified interchangeably as Juan Prieto or Juan Morano) accompanies Christopher Columbus on his first voyage to the New World.

1493 May 4 Pope Alexander VI promulgates *Inter Caetera*, authorizing Portugal and Spain to colonize the New World and enslave its inhabitants.

Sixteenth Century

1501 Spanish monarchs Ferdinand I and Isabella grant permission to Caribbean colonists to import African enslaved persons.

1502 Juan Garrido (ca. 1487–ca. 1548), an African Catholic conquistador born in the Kongo, joins a Spanish expedition to Santo Domingo.

1537 June 2 Pope Paul III promulgates *Sublimis Deus*, forbidding enslavement of indigenous peoples in the Americas and elsewhere, though colonists and conquistadors ignore the document.

---

* An earlier version of this chronology appeared as "Black Catholics in the United States: A Historical Chronology," *U.S. Catholic Historian* 12, no. 1 (Winter 1994): 119–141. The author has revised, expanded, and updated the chronology.

1565 August 28 As part of Pedro Menéndez de Avilés' colonizing expedition, the first black enslaved persons land in St. Augustine, Florida.

1593–1609 Luis de Molina, S.J., of the University of Salamanca in Spain, writes *De Justitia et Jure* ("On Justice and Law"), including the first theological treatise on the transatlantic slave trade.

Seventeenth Century

1634 March 25 The passengers of the British ships *Ark* and *Dove* arrive at St. Clement's Island to settle the colony of Maryland. Two black indentured servants are aboard, including Matthias de Sousa, a Catholic, who became part of the Maryland General Assembly in 1642, the first black to participate in a colonial British assembly. Disembarking Jesuits celebrate the first Catholic Mass in the British American colonies. By the end of the century, Jesuits introduce enslaved persons of African descent onto their plantations.

1678 Lord Baltimore (Charles Calvert) issues an edict requiring Catholic planters in Maryland to allow the enslaved to receive the sacraments.

1684 March 6 Lourenço da Silva de Mendouça (1620–1698), an Afro-Brazilian layman and procurator-general of the Confraternity of Our Lady Star of the Negroes (Madrid, Spain), petitions Pope Innocent XI to condemn perpetual slavery.

1685 March Louis XIV of France issues the first *Code Noir*, outlining slavery in the French colonies, limiting activities of free blacks, and requiring conversion to Catholicism. As the first formal codification of slave laws in the Americas, the *Code Noir* is applied to the West Indies in 1687 and Guyana in 1704.

1685 Capuchin Franciscan missionaries petition Rome to distinguish between "just" and "unjust" enslavement. In response, Pope Innocent XI condemns unjust enslavement, while recognizing just enslavement as a form of punishment.

1693 Under Charles II, Spain offers freedom in Florida to enslaved runaways owned by British masters provided they convert to Catholicism.

A Historical Chronology, 1452-2020 | 29

Eighteenth Century

1723 April 17 Father Raphael de Luxembourg, Capuchin major superior, arrives in New Orleans and begins work among blacks on Catholic plantations.

1724 September 10 Governor Jean-Baptiste Le Moyne de Bienville publishes the first French *Code Noir* for the Louisiana Colony, requiring Catholic baptism and instruction of the enslaved. Louis XV issues subsequent versions in 1723 and 1724. Slavery is abolished in the French colonies in 1794, reinstated in 1802, and abolished again in 1848.

1724 Francisco Menéndez (ca. 1700–ca. 1770), a runaway African slave from the Carolinas, arrives in St. Augustine, Florida. Converting to Catholicism, he joins the Spanish militia and defends St. Augustine from British attack.

1727 July Led by mother superior Sister Saint Augustine (Marie Tranchepain), Ursuline nuns come to New Orleans and, although owning slaves themselves, establish Ursuline Academy, a school for blacks and Indians (the oldest Catholic school established in colonial America).

1738 March 15 Governor of La Florida, Manuel de Montiano, establishes Fort Gracia Real de Santa Teresa de Mose as a community for freed enslaved persons converted to Catholicism, the first legally sanctioned free black community within the present U.S. boundaries.

1739 September 9 Kongolese (Congolese) Catholic slaves initiate the Stono Rebellion in South Carolina, the largest and deadliest uprising of the enslaved in the British colonies before the Revolutionary War.

1743 May 15 Benedict of Palermo (ca. 1525–1589), known also as Benedict the Moor, is beatified by Pope Benedict XIV. Born to enslaved Africans in Sicily, Benedict joined a religious community of hermits, of which he became superior.

1779 Jean-Baptiste Pointe du Sable (ca. 1745–1818), a hunter/trader of African descent, establishes the first permanent settlement in what would become Chicago, Illinois.

1781 September 4 Governor Don Felipe de Neve recruits eleven Catholic families (Africans, Spanish, and American Indians) to settle on the Porciúncula River—now Los Angeles, California.

1785 Jesuit missionaries estimate that there are 3,000 black Catholics in the United States.

1787 Pierre Toussaint (1766–1853) arrives in New York from Haiti with his owner. He works as a hairdresser and becomes known for his charity, including the care of his master's widow and purchasing freedom for the enslaved.

1789 May 31 Governor Esteban Rodriguez Miró of Louisiana promulgates "Instructions on Slaves for All of the Indies." It acknowledges that the enslaved have souls, requires Catholic baptism and instruction, and allows them to purchase their freedom.

1790 October 15 Carmelite nuns, the first nuns to come to the original thirteen British colonies, dedicate a monastery in Port Tobacco, Maryland, where they maintain enslaved persons whom they instruct in the faith.

1791 Toussaint Louverture/L'Overture (François Dominique Toussaint) (ca. 1743–1803), a devout Catholic and former enslaved person, leads a slave rebellion on the western side of French-controlled Saint-Domingue, and is taken prisoner. His lieutenant, Jean-Jacques Dessalines (1758–1806), completes the fight for independence, establishing the nation of Haiti on January 1, 1804.

1793 July 9 Black refugees from Saint-Domingue (Haiti) land in Baltimore, and Sulpicians associated with St. Mary's Seminary minister to them. Sulpician Father Louis William DuBourg starts a catechism class for black children in 1794. Worship services are later held for blacks in the Sulpician's basement-level "Chapelle Basse."

Nineteenth Century

1803 The first wave of refugees from the Saint-Domingue slave rebellion arrives in New Orleans.

1807 May 24 Benedict the Moor (Benedict of Palermo) is canonized by Pope Pius VII, the first saint of African descent. He is declared patron saint of North American missions to blacks.

1812 April–June Father Charles Nerinckx, a Belgian priest, organizes the Sisters of Loretto in Loretto, Kentucky. They are the first American sisterhood without foreign affiliation. Dedicated to serving the frontier poor, they acquire enslaved persons through novices' dowries.

1828 June 13 Elizabeth Clarissa Lange (1784–1882), a Cuban-born mulatto of Haitian parents, with the assistance of Sulpician priests, establishes the nation's first black Catholic school: the Oblate School for Colored Girls (later St. Frances Academy) in Baltimore, Maryland.

1829 July 2 The Oblate Sisters of Providence, the first community of black sisters in the U.S., is founded in Baltimore by Elizabeth Clarissa Lange and Sulpician Father Jacques (James Marie) Joubert. Pope Gregory XVI officially recognizes the congregation in 1831.

1829 July 19 The Chapel of St. Augustine on Isle Brevelle, Louisiana, is dedicated, the first Catholic edifice in Louisiana designed and built by free non-whites. It is canonically erected as a parish in 1856.

1836 May 21 Bishop John England of South Carolina becomes the first U.S. bishop to ordain a black priest, George Paddington (ca. 1800–1851), in Port-au-Prince, Haiti.

1836 November The Sisters of the Presentation of the Blessed Virgin Mary, a community for women of color, is founded in New Orleans by a freeborn woman of color Henriette Diaz Delille (1813–1862) and Haitian-born Juliette Gaudin (1808–1887). Formed to evangelize blacks, the community receives formal approval as the Sisters of the Holy Family on November 21, 1842.

1836 The Chapel of the Oblate Sisters of Providence in Baltimore moves to a larger facility. It is used by French-speaking Sainte-Domingue and Haitian refugees, becoming the first permanent black Catholic parish church in the U.S.

1837 October 29 Martin de Porres (Juan Martín de Porres Velázquez) (1579–1639), a mulatto from Lima, Peru, is beatified by Pope Gregory XVI. Martin, who had become a Dominican lay brother in 1603, founded an orphanage and hospital, and ministered to enslaved persons brought to Peru.

1838 June 19 The Jesuits sell 272 enslaved persons to cover the debt of Georgetown University.

1839 December 3 Pope Gregory XVI issues *In Supremo Apostolatus Fastigio*, condemning the Atlantic slave trade and future slavery, but not referencing those already enslaved.

1843 December The Society of the Holy Family, the first black Catholic lay prayer group, is established in Baltimore by Haitian Americans and moderated by Sulpician John Hickey.

1844 June 30 Chapel of the Nativity, Pittsburgh, is dedicated for black Catholics.

1845 November 10 Sisters, Servants of the Immaculate Heart of Mary, a predominantly white community, is founded in Monroe, Michigan, by Maria Theresa (Almaide) Maxis Duchemin (1810-1892), formerly of the Oblate Sisters. The first U.S.-born black sister, Duchemin passed for white when founding the Sisters, Servants of the Immaculate Heart.

1848 Catholic families settle Hidalgo Bluff, Texas, bringing ninety enslaved persons with them. They are catechized and baptized, and in 1888, Father Martin Francis Huhn organizes a mission specifically for the African American community.

1850 July 16 Peter Claver is beatified by Pope Pius IX. The Spanish-born Jesuit worked in Cartagena (now in Colombia), ministering among blacks for more than four decades.

1853 William Augustine Williams enters a Roman seminary because of an unwillingness to train blacks in U.S. seminaries, but he leaves before ordination. He later publishes the journal *Truth Communicator* (1855–1863) for freedmen in Baltimore.

1854 June 10 James Augustine Healy (1830–1900) is ordained in Paris for the Archdiocese of Boston. He is the first African American priest to serve in the U.S.

1858 December 15 Alexander Sherwood Healy (1836–1875) is ordained a priest in Paris for the Archdiocese of Boston. He serves as a theologian at the Second Plenary Council of Baltimore (1866) and at the First Vatican Council (1870).

1862 September 1 Cincinnati Archbishop John Baptist Purcell becomes the first U.S. Catholic bishop to advocate for emancipation. On April 8, 1863, Cincinnati's *Catholic Telegraph* joins him, becoming the first diocesan newspaper to offer support.

1862 Louis Charles Roudanez (1823-1890), a physician and son of a free woman of color, founds *L'Union* in Louisiana, the first African American newspaper in the American South. After *L'Union* ceases, Roudanez begins *The New Orleans Tribune,* the first daily paper for blacks, in 1864.

1863 May 27 André Cailloux (1825-1863) is killed during the Siege of Port Hudson, Louisiana, becoming the first black Civil War hero. He was captain of the largely Catholic First Regiment of Louisiana Native Guards, the first black U.S. Army regiment to engage in battle.

1864 February 21 Archbishop Martin J. Spalding dedicates St. Francis Xavier Church in Baltimore to serve blacks.

1864 September 3 Patrick Francis Healy, S.J., (1834-1910) is ordained a priest in Belgium, the first African American Jesuit. Graduating from Saint-Sulpice Seminary in Paris in 1865, he is the first black American known to have earned a doctoral degree.

1865 The U.S. black Catholic population is estimated at 100,000.

1866 February 11 Blessed Martin de Porres Chapel opens as the place of worship for the first black Catholic congregation in Washington, D.C. This congregation becomes part of St. Augustine's Church in 1876.

1866 May 10 St. Ann's Church in Cincinnati, Ohio, opens, the first black Catholic parish in the region.

1866 September 2 The Sisters of St. Joseph of LePuy arrive in St. Augustine, Florida, to educate and catechize formerly enslaved persons.

1866 October 7-21 The Second Plenary Council of Baltimore advocates for evangelization among blacks and debates formation of separate black churches (with the decision left to each bishop).

1868 January 12 St. Peter's Church, Charleston, South Carolina, a parish for blacks, is dedicated by Bishop Patrick N. Lynch.

1869 April The Tenth Provincial Council of Baltimore adopts a proposal that each bishop build schools and churches for African Americans.

1870 February 20 St. Augustine Church, Louisville, Kentucky, opens for blacks, the diocese's first black parish.

1871 December 5 The Mill Hill Fathers of England arrive in Baltimore to work among freed blacks.

1872 Holy Ghost Fathers (Spiritans) begin work among blacks in the U.S. Having ordained their first black (African) priests in Paris in 1842, they begin to serve blacks in Pittsburgh (1888) and Philadelphia (1889).

1873 May 18 St. Elizabeth Church in St. Louis, Missouri, is dedicated for blacks.

1874 May 13 Benedictine priests Gabriel Bergier and Raphael Wissel arrive in Savannah, Georgia, and devote themselves to the spiritual interests of African Americans.

1874 July 31 Patrick F. Healy, S.J., is inaugurated president of Georgetown University—the first African American to head a predominately white university.

1874 The Grand Body of the Sisters of Charity is founded by Celeste Allen in Indianapolis, Indiana, to provide healthcare for blacks migrating from the South.

1875 June 2 James Augustine Healy is ordained Bishop of Portland, Maine, the nation's first African American bishop.

1881 December 26 The Franciscan Sisters of Mill Hill arrive in Baltimore to work among blacks, opening St. Elizabeth's Home for black orphans. The orphanage was built upon the earlier work of a black woman, Mary E. Herbert, who kept deserted infants and children in her home beginning in 1878. The American religious community eventually breaks away from the English order, renaming themselves the Franciscan Sisters of Baltimore.

1882 Eliza Healy (Sister Mary Magdalen) (1846–1919), a mulatto born in Macon, Georgia, takes final vows with the Congregation of Notre Dame, Montreal, Canada. In being named superior of a convent in St. Albans, Vermont, she becomes the first African American superior of a Catholic convent.

1883 February Marie Emilie Gouley (Mother Marie Euphrasia) (ca. 1840–1922), a free Afro-Creole woman, founds a black religious community, the Sisters of Our Lady of Lourdes of New Orleans, Louisiana.

1883 November 18 St. Benedict the Moor Church in New York is dedicated as a black mission parish.

1884 November 9–December 7 Third Plenary Council of Baltimore proposes that lay catechists serve the black apostolate. It institutes the Commission for Catholic Missions Among the Colored People and Indians.

1886 April 24 Augustus Tolton (1854–1897), born to enslaved parents, is ordained a priest in Rome. Tolton is the first recognizable black priest in the U.S. and founder of Chicago's first black parish: St. Monica's.

1886 May 6 The Knights of St. John, a Catholic fraternal organization with African American branches, is incorporated in New York.

1886 Daniel A. Rudd (1854–1933), born into slavery, begins a publication for black Catholics called the *American Catholic Tribune* in Springfield, Ohio. It is later published in Cincinnati and then Detroit.

1887 The first annual collection for the Negro and Indian Missions, authorized by the Third Plenary Council of Baltimore, takes place.

1888 January 15 Peter Claver is canonized by Pope Leo XIII and proclaimed patron of missions among African Americans (and later, all Africans).

1888 May 5 Pope Leo XIII promulgates *In Plurimis*, lending support for the abolition of slavery in Brazil.

1888 September 9 The Mill Hill Fathers dedicate St. Joseph Seminary in Baltimore, Maryland, the first integrated U.S. Catholic seminary. In 1889, they establish Epiphany Apostolic College, Walbrook, Maryland (later moved to Newburg, New York), as a preparatory college for St. Joseph's.

1889 January 1–4 The first Colored Catholic Congress is held in Washington, D.C. Daniel A. Rudd is the principal organizer.

1889 The Sisters of the Third Order of St. Francis is established by Mother Mathilda Taylor Beasley (1832–1903) in Savannah, Georgia. Born into slavery, Beasley organizes the first community of black sisters in Georgia.

1889 Msgr. John E. Burke, the director general of Colored Missions in the U.S., sponsors a movement to encourage devotion to Blessed Martin de Porres, and the first English biography of Blessed Martin is translated from Italian.

1890 July 8–10 The second Colored Catholic Congress convenes in Cincinnati, Ohio. Subsequent congresses are held in Philadelphia (1892), Chicago (1893), and Baltimore (1894).

1890 November 20 Pope Leo XIII issues *Catholicae Ecclesiae*, calling for the abolition of slavery in Africa.

1890 Anna Frances Hartwell (Sister Joseph) founds the Mission Helpers of the Sacred Heart, a religious order to work among blacks, in Baltimore.

1890 The Benedictines of St. John's Abbey, Collegeville, Minnesota, are called to assist the evangelization of blacks in the Bahamas.

1891 February 12 Katharine Drexel takes final vows and soon founds the Sisters of the Blessed Sacrament for Indians and Colored People in Philadelphia.

1891 September The Franciscan Sisters of Glen Riddle (Sisters of St. Francis of Philadelphia) begin work among blacks, taking charge of St. Peter Claver School in Baltimore.

1891 December 19 Charles Randolph Uncles (1859–1933) is ordained a priest for the Mill Hill Fathers in Baltimore, the first African American to receive seminary training and ordination in the U.S.

1891 Mary Rosina Wightman of Charleston, South Carolina, not recognized as black, becomes superior general of Mount St. Vincent Sisters of Charity of New York.

1892 *The Journal*, a weekly Philadelphia newspaper, is founded by black Catholics.

1893 May 30 St. Joseph Society of the Sacred Heart (Josephites) breaks from Mill Hill Fathers to become the first order of Catholic priests dedicated exclusively to work among blacks in America.

1893 June 9 The Sisters Servants of the Holy Ghost (Holy Spirit) and Mary Immaculate are founded by Margaret Mary Healy-Murphy and begin work among blacks in San Antonio, Texas.

1893 November Msgr. John E. Burke, head of St. Benedict's Home for Destitute Colored Children, in Rye, New York, sponsors the U.S. movement to canonize Martin de Porres.

1895 May 19 Archbishop Francis Janssens dedicates New Orleans' first exclusively black Catholic church, St. Katherine. New Orleans' black Catholics, supporting interracial parishes, had co-founded nearly fifty integrated churches in the archdiocese.

1897 September 1 Josephite Father Pierre Lebeau begins to minister in Petite Prairie (now Lebeau), Louisiana. He later goes to New Orleans, where he establishes St. Dominic's Church (renamed St. Joan of Arc) for blacks.

1898 May 1 Josephite Father Thomas Plunkett begins work among blacks in Pine Bluff, Arkansas.

Twentieth Century

1900 St. Joseph College for Negro Catechists (renamed St. Joseph's Catechetical College) is opened by the Josephites in Montgomery, Alabama.

1902 June 21 John Henry "Harry" Dorsey (1873–1926) is ordained a Josephite priest, the second black ordained in the U.S.

1905 June 17 Adrian Esnard (1879–1947) is ordained for the Society of the Immaculate Heart of Mary, becoming a missionary in the Congo.

1905 July 5 The Society of the Divine Word begins work among blacks in the U.S., arriving in Merigold, Mississippi (and later moving to Vicksburg).

1905 Augustine Joseph McNorton, a former seminarian from St. Joseph's Seminary in Baltimore, establishes *The [Colored] Catholic Herald* newspaper in Washington, D.C.

1906 April 26 U.S. bishops establish the Catholic Board for Mission Work Among the Colored People (Catholic Board of Negro Missions) with Msgr. John E. Burke as director.

1907 January Society of Missionaries of Africa (or White Fathers) begins work among blacks in the U.S., starting in Savannah, Georgia.

1907 September 14 Joseph C. Burgess (1880–1923), the first African American ordained by the Holy Ghost Fathers, is assigned to Haiti.

1908 August 25 Lincoln Charles Valle (1864–1932), a black Catholic layman and newspaper editor, arrives in Milwaukee, Wisconsin, and helps establish a black mission.

1908 The Missionary Sisters, Servants of the Holy Spirit (or Blue Sisters) begin work among African Americans, staffing an elementary school in Vicksburg, Mississippi. In 1946, they begin to accept African Americans as members.

1909 November 7 Through the collaboration of black laymen and Josephite priests, the Knights of Peter Claver, a black fraternal organization, is founded in Mobile, Alabama.

1909 Charles Marcellus Dorsey (1876–?) founds the *Colored Catholic* newspaper in Baltimore.

1910 June 8 Stephen Louis Theobald (1874–1932) is ordained in St. Paul, Minnesota, the first black diocesan priest ordained within the U.S.

1910 November *The Shield* (later called *The Claverite*) is published as the official organ of the Knights of Peter Claver.

1912 As a gesture for healing, the Sisters of Charity of Nazareth in Nazareth, Kentucky, invite those formerly enslaved by them and their descendants to celebrate the congregation's centennial.

1913 The Knights of the Holy Name of Jesus, a Catholic society for black men, is founded in Memphis, Tennessee.

1915 Katharine Drexel and the Sisters of the Blessed Sacrament lay the foundation for Xavier University of Louisiana, opening the coeducational Xavier High School for blacks in New Orleans. In 1925, it becomes Xavier University, the nation's first and only black Catholic university.

1916 October 15 The Handmaids of Mary, a community of black sisters in Savannah, Georgia, is founded by Mother M. Theodore (Elizabeth Barbara) Williams (1868–1931) and Father Ignatius Lissner of the Society of African Missions. In 1924, they move to Harlem and become known as the Franciscan Handmaids of the Most Pure Heart of Mary.

1916 James Wendell, S.V.D., publishes *The Colored Messenger* magazine.

1917 January 14 The Junior Knights of Peter Claver are authorized.

1917 January The Federation of Catholic Societies for the Colored People of the Gulf States is founded in New Orleans.

1917 February 8 Emma Lewis (1869–1921) organizes the first community of black Catholics in the Diocese of Camden, New Jersey, founding the mission of the Church of St. Nicholas of Tolentine (later, St. Monica) in Atlantic City.

1917 The Committee Against the Extension of Race Prejudice in the Church (later, the Committee for the Advancement of Colored Catholics) is founded by Catholic layman Thomas Wyatt Turner (1877–1978).

1919 November 30 Pope Benedict XV issues *Maximum Illud*, lamenting the absence of native priests and bishops in missionary lands.

1920 September Sacred Heart College is opened in Greenville, Mississippi, for the formation of black members of the Society of the Divine Word. This first seminary for blacks in the U.S. is moved to Bay St. Louis, Mississippi, and renamed St. Augustine Seminary in June 1923.

1921 November 16 The Society of the African Missions' St. Anthony Mission House in Highland, New Jersey, becomes an early integrated house of formation.

1922 August The Ladies Auxiliary of the Knights of Peter Claver is established in Opelousas, Louisiana.

1923 May 15 Willis Richardson's (1889–1977) drama *The Chip Woman's Fortune* becomes the first nonmusical play by an African American produced on Broadway.

1923 Anita Rose Williams (1891–1983) joins the staff of Catholic Charities, becoming the first known black social worker to be employed by a Catholic charitable institution.

1924 December 29 The Federated Colored Catholics of the U.S. are founded in Washington, D.C., as a federation of colored parishes and societies. Thomas Wyatt Turner is elected president and its first annual meeting is held in December 1925.

1925 Delilah Leontium Beasley (1867–1934), historian and newspaper columnist, becomes the first black woman to regularly publish in a major metropolitan newspaper—the *Oakland Tribune*.

1926 February 7 Norman Andrew Dukette (1890–1980) is ordained, the first black priest for the Diocese of Detroit.

1928 The Catholic Layman's Union of New York City, an organization of black professionals and businessmen, is founded in Harlem by John LaFarge, S.J.

1928 The U.S. black Catholic population is estimated at 200,000.

1931 Pope Pius XI extends the feasts of St. Peter Claver and the Ugandan Martyrs to the United States.

1932 Internal conflicts among its leadership, especially regarding the organization's new interracial character, lead to a schism in the Federated Colored Catholics. Supporters of Father William Markoe reorganize as the National Catholic Federation for the Promotion of Better Race Relations (later, National Catholic Interracial Federation). Supporters of Thomas Wyatt Turner continue as the Federated Colored Catholics.

1933 March The Sisters of St. Mary of the Third Order of St. Francis open St. Mary's Infirmary in St. Louis to black patients, attended by an integrated nursing staff. They later open St. Mary's Infirmary School of Nursing, the first Catholic nursing school to train black nurses.

1933 November 12 The Northeast Clergy Conference on Negro Welfare, composed primarily of Catholic priests serving black congregations, is formed during a meeting in Newark, New Jersey.

1934 May 20 The Catholic Interracial Council is founded in New York by John LaFarge, S.J. Its *Interracial Review* begins publication and the council's interracial forums begin in 1939.

1934 May 23 The first black priests trained at St. Augustine Seminary in Bay St. Louis, Mississippi, are ordained: Anthony Bourges (1904-1991), Maurice Rousseve (1906-1985), Vincent Smith (1894-1952), and Francis G. Wade (1894-1976).

1934 *The Voice: A Journal of Catholic Negro Opinion* is established by black laymen in Philadelphia.

1935 The Blessed Martin Guild is founded by Dominican Edward Hughes to coordinate Martin de Porres' cause for canonization in the U.S.

1935 Llewellyn J. Scott (1892-1978), a member of the Third Order of St. Francis, founds the Blessed Martin de Porres Home in Washington, D.C., a hospice for indigent men of all races.

1935 The first U.S.-born black Benedictine, Dom Basil Matthews (1911-1999), is ordained in Belgium.

1937 July 6 The Society of St. Edmund establishes a Southern Mission, forming St. Elizabeth's Church for blacks and Good Samaritan Hospital, both in Selma, Alabama.

1937 Edward Hughes, O.P., founds the Blessed Martin chapter of Dominican tertiaries.

1937 Brother Vincent (Louis) Webb (1908-2005) professes vows, becoming the first African American brother in the Society of Divine Word.

1938 February 23 To promote racial equality, Catherine de Hueck Doherty begins Friendship House, a Catholic lay apostolate.

1938 The Midwest Clergy Conference on Negro Welfare, composed of priests active in African American apostolates, is established in Cincinnati.

1939 October 20 Pope Pius XII issues *Summi Pontificatus*, decrying racial ideologies.

1939 The Catholic Committee of the South is formed as a network of clergy and laity promoting social change in the South through religious principles.

1940 Ellen Tarry (1906–2008) publishes the first African American picture book, *Janie Belle*.

1940 The U.S. black Catholic population is estimated at 297,000.

1941 At its second annual Liturgical Week, the Liturgical Conference addresses race issues in light of the liturgy and calls for social action.

1942 Martin de Porres Friendship House is founded in Chicago. Additional houses are opened in Washington, D.C. (1948), Portland, Oregon (1951), and Shreveport, Louisiana (1953).

1944 December Justine B. Ward forms the Catholic Interracial Council of Washington, D.C., seeking to change archdiocesan practices contributing to racial discrimination and segregation.

1944 Saint Louis University in St. Louis, Missouri, becomes the first historically white university in a former slave state to admit black students.

1945 Mary Elaine Gentemann of the Sisters of Divine Providence composes a *Mass in Honor of Blessed Martin de Porres*, the first Mass composition to incorporate Negro spirituals.

1945 (James) Richmond Barthé (1901–1989) is elected a member of the American Academy of Arts and Letters.

1946 March 17 The Friendship House movement opens St. Joseph's Farm in Marathon, Wisconsin.

1947 June 9 Five black women, including Sister M. Antona Ebo (1924–2017), profess vows in the Sisters of St. Mary of the Third Order of St. Francis in St. Louis, Missouri.

1947 June 15 Prosper Edward Meyer (1912–1961) is ordained, the first black Benedictine in the U.S.

1947 The St. Benedict the Moor Interracial Charity Apostolate begins under the direction of the Franciscans of Holy Name College, Washington, D.C.

1947 The U.S. black Catholic population is estimated at 344,000.

1948 Peter Hogan, S.S.J., forms the Josephite Archives in Baltimore to assist in historical research of the Josephites and black Catholicism.

1949 November 21 The community of Sisters, Home Visitors of Mary, is established in Detroit to evangelize African Americans.

1949 The Benedictines form St. Maur Interracial Priory in South Union, Kentucky. The order accepted blacks at St. Vincent Archabbey Seminary in Latrobe, Pennsylvania, beginning in 1929, and at St. John's Abbey Seminary in Collegeville, Minnesota, since 1939.

1949 Rollins E. Lambert (1922-2009) is the first black diocesan priest ordained in the Archdiocese of Chicago. He was the first black student to attend the University of St. Mary of the Lake/Mundelein Seminary.

1951 Helen Caldwell Day (1926-2013) founds the Blessed Martin House in Memphis, Tennessee, providing aid for the indigent.

1951 Brother Cyprian Lamar Rowe (Donald Rowe) (1935-2008) becomes the first African American member of the Marist Brothers (U.S. Province).

1952 Sister Thea (Bertha) Bowman, F.S.P.A., (1937-1990) becomes the first African American to join the Franciscan Sisters of Perpetual Adoration.

1953 April 22 Joseph Oliver Bowers, S.V.D., (1910-2012) becomes the first alumnus of St. Augustine Seminary appointed as bishop. He is consecrated bishop of Accra, Ghana, the first (recognized) African American to be consecrated bishop in the U.S. Before leaving for Accra, he ordains two black priests, both students at St. Augustine Seminary.

1956 May 3 Cyprian (Clarence John) Davis, O.S.B., (1930-2015) is ordained a priest, the first African American to join the Benedictine community at St. Meinrad, Indiana.

1956 Clarence Rufus Joseph Rivers (1931-2004) is ordained, the first black priest of the Archdiocese of Cincinnati.

1956 William Henry Adams, S.V.D., (1913-2002) is the first black priest to be appointed rector of St. Augustine Seminary, Bay St. Louis, Mississippi.

1957 The U.S. black Catholic population is estimated at 576,000.

1958 November 14 Condemning Jim Crow laws, the U.S. bishops issue "Discrimination and the Christian Conscience."

1959 October 1 St. Benedict the Moor Interracial Charity Apostolate is adopted as a national movement by the Third Order of St. Francis.

1959 To coordinate local interracial councils, John LaFarge, S.J., founds the National Catholic Conference for Interracial Justice.

1960 St. Thomas More Society, a group of Catholic professionals in New York devoted to spiritual life, culture, and social action, sponsors the first in a series of annual Civil Rights Masses.

1962 May 6 Martin de Porres is canonized by Pope John XXIII.

1962 June 9 Ugandan Francis X. E. Kabuleta is ordained in Washington, D.C., the first African-born priest ordained in the U.S. He is assigned to the Diocese of Fort-Portal, Uganda.

1962 November 3 Mary Lou Williams (1910–1981) performs a "Hymn in Honor of St. Martin de Porres: Black Christ of the Andes" at St. Francis Xavier Church in New York. Williams is the first jazz composer to write music intended for the liturgy and composes her first jazz Mass in 1966.

1962 November Edward Joseph "Ed" Dwight (1933–) is the first African American trained as an astronaut. Facing discrimination, he resigns from the Air Force in 1966, never having gone into space. Becoming a sculptor, Dwight creates major monuments, including the Mother of Africa Chapel at the Basilica of the National Shrine of the Immaculate Conception in Washington, D.C. (1997).

1962 One hundred eighteen African bishops attending the Second Vatican Council advocate for reforms, especially for indigenized ministry and cultural adaptation of the liturgy.

1962 Sister Julian Griffin (ca. 1944–1986) becomes the first African American to enter the Vincentian Sisters of Charity in Phenix City, Alabama.

1963 January 14–17 The National Conference on Religion and Race is held in Chicago. The National Catholic Conference for Interracial Justice serves as lead organizer.

1963 August 23 The U.S. bishops issue "On Racial Harmony," a document on the moral and religious dimensions of racial justice and charity.

1963 September Patricia Ann Haley (1945-2018) of Columbus, Georgia, becomes the first African American postulant of the Sisters of Charity of Nazareth.

1963 December 13 Bernardine Joseph Patterson, O.S.B., (1923-2001) is the first black elected major superior of men in the U.S.

1963 Uganda Martyrs Center, Washington, D.C., is opened by the Society of African Missions to assist efforts to canonize the Ugandan Martyrs.

1963 Father Clarence Rivers records "An American Mass Program," blending Gregorian chant and Negro spirituals. It is released by the World Library of Sacred Music. In 1966, Rivers receives a gold medal from the Catholic Art Association, stating that it is the start of a revolution in liturgical music.

1963 The North American Federation of the Third Order of St. Francis is reportedly the first Catholic group to honor the Rev. Martin Luther King Jr. for his efforts at racial justice.

1963 At the invitation of President John F. Kennedy, Harold Robert Perry, S.V.D., (1916-1991) participates in the White House Conference on Civil Rights. He becomes the first black clergyman to deliver an opening prayer to the U.S. Congress.

1964 April 9 The Midwest Clergy Conference on Negro Welfare is renamed the Catholic Clergy Conference on the Negro Apostolate. By 1965, they reorganize as the Catholic Clergy Conference on the Interracial Apostolate, a racially mixed but predominately white group of priests, sisters, and laity working among African American communities.

1964 August 24-27 Father Clarence Rivers presents "God is Love"—the first liturgical composition by an African American using a black musical idiom—during the first approved English-language liturgy in the U.S., coinciding with the National Liturgical Conference's Annual Liturgical Week, held in St. Louis, Missouri.

1964 September 18 Martin Luther King Jr. meets Pope Paul VI at the Vatican. The pope declares his commitment to the cause of civil rights in America.

1964 October 18 The Ugandan Martyrs (St. Charles Lwanga, St. Matthias Kelemba Mulumba, and companions) are canonized by Pope Paul VI.

1964 Harold R. Perry, S.V.D., is elected the first black provincial of the Southern Province of the Divine Word Missionaries.

1965 March 7 Catholics participate in the civil rights March on Selma. Sister Mary Antona Ebo, F.S.M., joins with several other women religious. In the aftermath of "Bloody Sunday," sister nurses care for injured marchers. Among the nurses is Sister Anne Benedict, the first black member of the Sisters of St. Joseph of Carondelet.

1965 October 3 Carlos Ambrosio Lewis Tullock, S.V.D., (1918–2004), an alumnus of St. Augustine Seminary, is ordained a bishop, becoming auxiliary bishop of Panama City, Panama. He becomes coadjutor bishop of David, Panama, in 1986.

1965 December 7 Pope Paul VI issues the *Pastoral Constitution on the Church in the Modern World* (*Gaudium et Spes*), observing that "whatever is opposed to life" and insults human dignity—including forms of slavery—are a "supreme dishonor to the Creator."

1966 January 6 Harold R. Perry, S.V.D., (1916–1991) is ordained a bishop, becoming auxiliary bishop of New Orleans, the first black bishop in the U.S. since Bishop James Healy (d. 1900).

1966 May 8 Edward (Eddie) Valentine Bonnemere (1921–1996) performs *Missa Hodierna* (Mass for Today), at St. Charles Borromeo Church in New York. It is the first jazz Mass celebrated in a Catholic rite in the U.S.

1966 November 19 The U.S. bishops issue a "Pastoral Letter on Race Relations and Poverty."

1966 Robert M. Kearns, S.S.J., establishes the Josephite Pastoral Center in Washington, D.C., as an educational and pastoral extension of the Josephite mission.

1967 July 2 With the Billy Taylor Trio, Father Clarence Rivers performs the music for his "Mass Dedicated to the Brotherhood of Man" at the Newport Jazz Festival in Rhode Island.

1967 July Mary Lou Williams' jazz Mass (simply called "Mass") is performed in concert at St. Paul's Cathedral in Pittsburgh. Her second Mass setting, "Mass for Lenten Season," is performed at St. Thomas the Apostle Church in New York in 1968. Her third Mass, "A Mass for Peace" (commissioned by the Vatican in 1969), is used for Mass at St. Patrick's Cathedral in New York on February 18, 1975. Alvin Alley choreographs dance to accompany the musical settings.

1967 George F. O'Dea, S.S.J., the Josephite superior general, advocates for the restoration of the permanent diaconate as a means of developing black Catholic leadership. On June 18, 1967, Pope Paul VI issues *Sacrum Diaconatus Ordinem*, restoring the permanent diaconate.

1967 Joseph Abel Francis, S.V.D., (1923-1997) is appointed provincial of the Western Province of the Society of the Divine Word.

1967 The Council of Catholic Negro Laymen (later, the Council of Black Catholic Laymen) is founded in Cleveland by Anthony J. Delgado to integrate black middle-class and poor.

1967 Sister M. Antona Ebo, F.S.M., becomes executive director of St. Clare Hospital, Baraboo, Wisconsin, the first African American female hospital administrator.

1967 The U.S. black Catholic population is estimated at 808,000.

1968 April 16-18 The National Black Catholic Clergy Caucus (NBCCC) is founded during the annual meeting of the Catholic Clergy Conference on the Interracial Apostolate in Detroit. The caucus drafts a statement calling the U.S. Catholic Church "a predominantly white racist institution."

1968 April 25 U.S. bishops issue a "Statement on National Race Crisis."

1968 August 18-24 The National Black Sisters Conference (NBSC) is established in Pittsburgh. Martin de Porres Grey, R.S.M., (Patricia Grey Tyree) (1942-), the only sister to take part in the inaugural meeting of the National Black Catholic Clergy Caucus, is elected president of the NBSC.

1968 August 19–22 Edward Bonnemere performs his "Mass for Every Season (Trinity to Advent)" at the Liturgical Conference's Annual Liturgical Week dedicated to Rev. Martin Luther King Jr. in Washington. The Mass incorporates a variety of musical genres: calypso, jazz, gospel, folk, and rock.

1968 Stimuli Inc. is founded by Father Clarence Rivers to demonstrate how to synthesize Afro-American and Euro-American culture in worship. Through liturgical music workshops called "Freeing the Spirit," he presents his vision to parishes and dioceses across the country.

1968 The Office of Black Catholic Affairs, the first diocesan office of black Catholic ministries, is established in Detroit with Garland Jaggers (1933–) as director.

1969 January 12 A dispute over the selection of parish leadership leads to accusations of racism against Cardinal John Cody of Chicago. As a form of protest, concerned parishioners—black and white—organize a Black Unity Mass at Chicago's St. Dorothy Parish. The liturgy includes an altar draped in tiger skin, African-inspired vestments, and liturgical dancers. The controversy resolves when Cody promotes three black priests, including Father George Harold Clements (1932–2019).

1969 June Father George Clements, the first black pastor of Holy Angels Parish in Chicago, becomes an advisor to the Black Panthers. He is the first black graduate of Quigley Academy Seminary (1945).

1969 July 31 Paul VI becomes the first pope to visit Africa. During his visit to the Shrine of the Ugandan Martyrs, Pope Paul VI addresses the African bishops, urging them to share their "blackness with the Church."

1969 National Black Catholic Seminarians Association (NBCSA) organizes under the NBCCC through the leadership of Clarence Williams, C.PP.S (1950–).

1969 Calling for increased black vocations and black awareness in religious life, a caucus of black religious brothers presents a position paper to the Brothers Institute held in North Easton, Massachusetts.

1970 July 1 The National Office for Black Catholics (NOBC) is established with Brother Joseph Davis, S.M., (1938–1992) serving as its first executive director (1970–1977).

1970 August 21-24 The National Black Lay Catholic Caucus (NBLCC) is formed in Washington.

1970 The Archdiocese of Pittsburgh establishes the Black Catholic Ministries and Laymen's Council.

1971 January 16 Bishop Joseph Oliver Bowers, S.V.D., is appointed bishop of St. John's-Basserterre in the British Virgin Islands.

1971 June 12 Americus Melvin Roy (1929–2004) of Baltimore is the first black ordained to the permanent diaconate in the U.S.

1971 August 13-22 During the NBLCC meeting in Detroit, the NOBC holds its first liturgical music workshop under the direction of Father Clarence Rivers, the NOBC's first director of the Department of Culture and Worship.

1971 The NBCCC initiates investigation of a possible African American Catholic rite, but is opposed by Auxiliary Bishop Harold Perry as divisive.

1971 Eugene Antonio Marino, S.S.J., (1934–2000) is the first black priest elected vicar general of the Josephites.

1971 The NBSC initiates its Institute on Black Sister Formation, using an all-black staff to instruct major superiors, formation and vocation directors, and personnel—most from predominately white religious congregations.

1972 Barbara Jean LaRochester, O.C.D., (ca. 1939–) becomes the first black American to join the Carmelite Sisters of Baltimore.

1972 Joseph Abel Francis, S.V.D., is elected president of the Conference of Major Superiors of Men in the U.S.

1972 *Freeing the Spirit* magazine is launched by NOBC with Father Clarence Rivers as editor.

1973 January 28 Joseph Lawson Howze (1923–2019) is ordained a bishop, becoming auxiliary bishop of Natchez-Jackson, in Mississippi.

1973 November 17 Prince Joseph Moultry, a black seminarian, records the first Gospel Soul Mass: "Freeing the Spirit Gospel Soul Mass." In 1974, Moultry releases "Get On The Good Foot," sacred music in a Funk style.

1974 September 12 Eugene Marino, S.S.J., is ordained a bishop, becoming auxiliary bishop of Washington, D.C.

1974 September The Archdiocese of Washington Secretariat for Black Catholics (later, Office of Black Catholics) is established.

1974 November NBCCC/NOBC outlines a plan to the U.S. bishops for the recruitment and education of indigenous priests, deacons, and religious for Catholic parishes serving black Americans.

1974 James E. Goode, O.F.M., preaches the first black Catholic revival in America, held at Our Lady of Perpetual Help Church, Archdiocese of Chicago.

1974 The U.S. black Catholic population is estimated at 855,000. Parishes in which black Catholics predominate number 636. The number of black clergy and religious include 180 priests, 30 permanent deacons, 130 religious brothers, 715 sisters, and 442 seminarians.

1975 April 19 Martin J. Carter, S.A., (ca. 1930–) becomes the first black priest of the Franciscan Friars of the Atonement.

1976 January The Rochester, New York, Diocesan Office of Black Catholics is established. Jerome R. Robinson, O.P., (ca. 1948–) serves as its first director.

1976 June 25 Joseph Abel Francis, S.V.D., (1923–1997) is ordained auxiliary bishop of Newark, New Jersey.

1976 October 7–8 Garland Jaggers and Jerome Robinson, O.P., help develop an organization to support diocesan black ministry offices. The National Association of Black Catholic Administrators (NABCA) holds its inaugural meeting in Rochester, New York.

1976 The National Association of Pastoral Musicians (NPM) is founded in collaboration with Father Clarence Rivers and other black musicians to help ensure African American programming.

1976 The Pierre Toussaint House of Studies in New York is founded to encourage black vocations. Similar houses are formed in Baltimore (Benedict the Moor House of Studies) in 1977 and New Orleans (The Society of Divine Word's Augustus Tolton House of Studies) in 1983.

1976 The U.S. black Catholic population is estimated at 917,000.

1977 June 6 Joseph Lawson Howze is named the founding bishop of Biloxi, Mississippi.

1977 The Academy of the Afro-World Community is founded by Clarence Williams, C.PP.S. In 1985, he establishes the National Black Catholic Televangelization Network, producing radio broadcasts and videos.

1977 Grayson Warren Brown (1948–) releases *Hymns of A Soulful People*, a collection of liturgical music with gospel influences, through North American Liturgy Resources.

1977 The first Kujenga Leadership Conference is organized in the Archdiocese of Chicago. The conference for black Catholic youth extends to other locations in the country through the efforts of Franciscan Friar of the Atonement Father Martin Carter.

1978 October 25 Raymond Rodly Caeser, S.V.D., (1932–1987), a black American, is appointed coadjutor bishop of Goroka, Eastern Highlands-Papua New Guinea. He becomes bishop of Goroka in 1980.

1978 December 1 Sister Josephine Margaret Bakhita (1869–1947) is declared venerable by Pope John Paul II. Kidnapped into slavery as a child in the Sudan and forced to become Muslim, she converted to Catholicism and joined the Congregation of the Daughters of Charity. The cause for her canonization was begun in 1959.

1978 December 10 Emerson John Moore (1938–1995) is elevated to monsignor by Cardinal Terrence J. Cooke, Archbishop of New York, becoming the first U.S. black monsignor.

1978 Sponsored by the NBCCC, the Black Catholic Theological Symposium is established under the leadership of Thaddeus Posey, O.F.M., (1944–2013). Holding its first and second meetings in 1978 and 1979, the symposium begins meeting annually in 1991.

1979 May 19 Cordell J. Long is the first black ordained a priest in the Diocese of Mobile, Alabama.

1979 July Cardinal William A. Baum, Archbishop of Washington, issues a pastoral letter attacking racism as sinful.

1979 August 1 James Patterson Lyke, O.F.M., (1939–1992) is ordained a bishop, becoming auxiliary bishop of Cleveland.

1979 November 14 The U.S. bishops issue "Brothers and Sisters to Us," declaring racism a sin.

1979 NBCCC establishes the Institute for Black Catholic Studies (IBCS) at Xavier University of Louisiana. It offers its first classes in the summer of 1980.

1980 August 6–9 The National Office for Black Catholics (NOBC) holds its first national conference in Chicago and issues a Black Catholic Action Agenda for the 1980s.

1980 October 4 Allan John Roberts (1944–2006) is the first African American priest ordained for the Archdiocese of Los Angeles.

1980 To assist black women in discerning religious vocations, the Sojourner House is founded in Detroit by NBSC.

1980 The Catholic Negro-American Mission Board joins the Bureau of Catholic Indian Missions and the Commission for Catholic Missions among Colored People and Indians. The three agencies continue their respective missions with a shared staff and consolidated board of directors.

1981 February 25 The Catholic Committee of the South (CCS) is reactivated during a gathering of church workers at Tupelo, Mississippi.

1981 August NBCCC, NBSC, and NBCSA hold their first joint conference in Washington, at which they formally withdraw from NOBC.

1981 Leonard G. Scott Jr. (1939–) of Camden, New Jersey, is elevated to monsignor—the second black American monsignor. In 1984, he becomes the first black to serve on the Board of Governors of the Canon Law Society of America (CLSA), and in 1987, he is the first black elected CLSA president.

1981 Ethnic Communications Outlet is founded by the Society of the Divine Word Northern Province.

1981 Father George Clements adopts a thirteen-year-old African American boy. He subsequently adopts three other children. His "One Church, One Child" program, advocating for the adoption of racial minorities, extends to thirty-two states.

1981 Dolores Harrall, S.N.D., (ca. 1937–1988), a founding member of the NBSC, receives the National Association for the Advancement of Colored People (NAACP) Unsung Hero Award for her work as an educator and activist. She was the first African American to enter the New England Province of the Sisters of Notre Dame.

1982 February 5 Rev. Jesse Jackson, Baptist minister and activist, meets with Pope John Paul II, asking the pontiff to use his influence with President Ronald Reagan to allow Haitian refugees to enter the U.S.

1982 Sept 8 Emerson John Moore (1938–1995) is ordained a bishop, becoming auxiliary bishop of New York.

1982 The Media Production Center is founded by the Society of Divine Word Southern Province.

1983 January 27 Moses Bosco Anderson, S.S.E., (1928–2013) becomes auxiliary bishop of Detroit.

1983 September 17 Vanessa Williams (1963–) is the first African American crowned Miss America. Due to a scandal over the unauthorized publication of nude photographs, she relinquishes her crown less than a year later.

1983 December 13 Wilton Daniel Gregory (1947–) is ordained a bishop, becoming auxiliary bishop of Chicago.

1983 The Black Catholic Hymnal Project Committee is organized by NBCCC and coordinated by James P. Lyke, leading to the publication of *Lead Me, Guide Me* in 1987, the first U.S. black Catholic hymnal.

1983 The Africa Faith and Justice Network is founded by three Catholic missionary congregations (Missionaries of Africa, the Congregation of the Holy Spirit, and the Society of African Missions) to shape U.S. policy towards Africa and Africans.

1983 Through the efforts of Nigerian Aniedi Okure, O.P., the National Conference of Catholic Bishops establishes an Office for the Pastoral Care of Migrants and Refugees.

1984 February 10 James Terry Steib, S.V.D., (1940–) is ordained a bishop, becoming auxiliary bishop of St. Louis.

1984 June 30 Sarah Vaughn (1924–1990), black American jazz singer, performs a concert based on the poems of Pope John Paul II in Dusseldorf, West Germany. It is televised across Europe.

1984 July 2 John Huston Ricard, S.S.J., (1940–) is ordained a bishop, becoming auxiliary bishop of Baltimore.

1984 September 9 "What We Have Seen and Heard," the first joint pastoral letter of the U.S. black bishops, is issued.

1984 Subcommittee on Black Worship (Black Liturgy Subcommittee) is established under the National Conference of Catholic Bishops' Committee on the Liturgy. Bishop Wilton Gregory serves as chair.

1985 January 3 Bishop Emerson Moore and the Rev. Jesse Jackson meet with Pope John Paul II at the Vatican to discuss the Church's role in opposing South African apartheid. In late 1984, Bishop Moore had been arrested for participating in an anti-apartheid protest at the South African consulate in New York.

1985 August 11–18 The 43rd International Eucharistic Congress is held in Nairobi, Kenya. Edward K. Braxton (1944–), a priest of the Archdiocese of Chicago, is the only black American to speak.

1985 November 9 Bishop Eugene Marino, S.S.J., is elected secretary of the National Conference of Catholic Bishops, the first African American to hold the position.

1985 Compiled by Sister Thea Bowman, "Families: Black and Catholic, Catholic and Black" is issued by the U.S. Catholic Conference. It urges black Catholics to maintain and strengthen black rootedness, traditions, and rituals, and transmit faith and values.

1985 Inspired by the black Catholic congresses of the nineteenth century, Bishop John Ricard reestablishes the National Black Catholic Congress (NBCC) as a coalition of black Catholic organizations. It is incorporated on March 21, 1986.

1985 The U.S. black Catholic population is estimated at 1,294,000.

1986 November 12 The National Conference of Catholic Bishops establishes a standing Committee for Black Catholics and a Secretariat for Black Catholics. Auxiliary Bishop John Ricard is elected ccchairman of the Committee for Black Catholics during the November 1987 U.S. bishops' meeting.

1986 The *U.S. Catholic Historian* dedicates an issue to black Catholics, marking the centennial of the ordination of Father Augustus Tolton.

1986 The National African American Catholic Youth Ministry Network is founded in Louisville, Kentucky, as an affiliate of the National Federation for Catholic Youth Ministry.

1987 January 26 Katharine Drexel is declared venerable by Pope John Paul II. Her cause for canonization was launched by Cardinal John Krol in 1959.

1987 February 22 Carl Anthony Fisher, S.S.J., (1945-1993) is ordained auxiliary bishop of Los Angeles.

1987 May 21-24 In the tradition of the first five Black Catholic Congresses (1889-1894), the Sixth National Black Catholic Congress convenes in Washington, D.C. Future congresses are held every five years: New Orleans (1992), Baltimore (1997), Chicago (2002), Buffalo, New York (2007), Indianapolis, Indiana (2012), and Orlando, Florida (2017).

1987 September 12 Pope John Paul II, while in New Orleans, addresses black Catholics and is presented with resolutions of the National Black Catholic Congress. It is the first time that a pope has met with black Catholics in the U.S. as a body.

1988 January 3 The Secretariat for Black Catholics of the National Conference of Catholic Bishops is established, with Beverly A. Carroll (1946-) as director, to help implement the National Black Catholic Pastoral Plan. In 1991, it is renamed the Secretariat for African American Catholics.

1988 February 19 Curtis J. Guillory, S.V.D., (1945-) is ordained a bishop, becoming auxiliary bishop of Galveston-Houston. In 2000, he becomes bishop of Beaumont, Texas.

1988 April Henriette Delille's cause for canonization is introduced by the Archdiocese of New Orleans. She is the first U.S.-born black to have a cause for canonization opened. The Sisters of the Holy Family establish a guild to promote the cause in March 1991.

1988 May 5 Eugene Marino, S.S.J., is installed as archbishop of Atlanta, becoming the first black archbishop in the U.S.

1988 August 8 The Order of the Brothers of St. Martin de Porres is founded in the Diocese of Richmond, Virginia, by Bruce Edward Greening, S.D.S., (1951–2018) to train black men to minister to the black community.

1988 November 20 Katharine Drexel, S.B.S., is beatified by Pope John Paul II.

1988 December 20 Leonard James Olivier, S.V.D., (1923–2014) becomes auxiliary bishop of Washington.

1988 The U.S. bishops issue "In Spirit and Truth: Black Catholic Reflections on the Order of Mass."

1988 Toni Morrison (Chloe Anthony Wofford Morrison) (1931–2019) receives the Pulitzer Prize in Fiction for *Beloved* (1987).

1989 February The National Day of Prayer for the African American and African Family is created by James Goode, O.F.M., calling families to pray on the first Sunday of Black History Month.

1989 June 17 Sister Thea Bowman, F.S.P.A., gives a major address on evangelization, "To Be Black and Catholic," before the National Conference of Catholic Bishops. She is the first African American woman to address the U.S. bishops.

1989 July 2 George Augustus Stallings Jr. (1948–), a priest of the Archdiocese of Washington, breaks with the Church and organizes the Imani Temple African-American Catholic Congregation. After incurring excommunication, he seeks ordination as a bishop. In 1990, he is ordained a bishop by a representative of the Old Catholic Church, a church not in communion with Rome. A year later, Stallings ordains Rose M. Vernell, a former Oblate Sister of Providence, as the first female priest of the Imani Temple.

1989 July 23-28 The NBCCC, meeting in Milwaukee, announces the plan to study the creation of an African American rite within the Church and "a personal prelature or vicariate" for black Catholics.

1989 August Bruce Greening joins the Imani Temple African-American Catholic Congregation, assuming the pastorate of the Umoja Temple in Washington. He is dismissed by his religious order, the Salvatorians, and excommunicated.

1989 November 6-9 "Here I Am, Send Me" is approved by the U.S. bishops as a response to the evangelization of African Americans and the National Black Catholic Pastoral Plan.

1989 December Pierre Toussaint's cause for sainthood is reintroduced by Cardinal John O'Connor of New York. The canonization movement had begun in the early 1940s and the cause was introduced in 1968, but no records could be found.

1989 NBCCC initiates the Pan African Roman Catholic Clergy Conference to assist in communication with clergy in Africa and develop support systems on their behalf in the U.S.

1990 February 5 Bruce Greening breaks away from Imani Temple African-American Catholic Congregation, renaming his parish in Washington, St. Martin de Porres. Initially intending to reconcile with the Catholic Church, he declares independence and is ordained a bishop of the Independent African American Catholic Rite—a religious body created and so-named by Greening.

1990 February 28 Emerson Moore is the only bishop to sign the "Call for Reform in the Catholic Church: A Pastoral Letter," which calls for open dialogue on women's ordination, married priests, and racial, ethnic, and gender marginalization in the Church.

1990 July 10 Archbishop Eugene Marino resigns and Bishop James P. Lyke is appointed apostolic administrator of the Archdiocese of Atlanta. Lyke is installed as archbishop a year later.

1990 July 24 The NBCCC designates November as Black Catholic History Month. Coinciding with St. Martin de Porres' feast day (November 3), the first celebrations occur.

1990 July Cyprian Davis, O.S.B., is the keynote speaker of the Association of Catholic Diocesan Archivists' conference, addressing "Documenting Black Catholic History at the Diocesan Level."

1990 November 13–19 To ensure awareness of the black contributions to the Church, Grayson Warren Brown conducts the North American Conference on Cultural Awareness in Liturgy in Rome. Similar efforts included a gospel choir performance for Pope John Paul II on August 23, 1989, and a conference held in Rome on "Evangelization and Culture: An African-American Perspective," November 9–16, 1989.

1990 Cardinal John O'Connor exhumes and examines Pierre Toussaint's body as part of the canonization process before moving it to a crypt under the main altar at St. Patrick's Cathedral in New York, the first lay person so interred.

1990 The Catholic African World Network (CAWN) begins to provide worldwide communication services for Catholics of African descent. It is the result of collaboration between Bishop James Odongo, Chairman of the Social Communication Committee for East Africa, and Clarence Williams, C.PP.S, of the U.S.-based Black Catholic Televangelization Network.

1990 Cora Marie Billings, R.S.M., (1939–) is appointed pastoral coordinator at St. Elizabeth's Church in North Richmond, Virginia, the first black woman to lead a Catholic congregation in the U.S.

1991 April 28 The Mother Mary Elizabeth Lange Guild is established by the Oblate Sisters of Providence to promote their founder's cause for sainthood.

1991 July 1 Clarence Thomas (1948–) is nominated by President George H. W. Bush to serve on the U.S. Supreme Court. Once confirmed, he becomes the second African American justice to serve.

1992 May 17 Sister Josephine Margaret Bakhita is beatified by Pope John Paul II.

1992 July 9–12 The seventh National Black Catholic Congress convenes in New Orleans. One resolution calls for a committee to study the feasibility of an African American Roman Catholic Rite.

1993 February 11 Dominic Carmon, S.V.D., is ordained a bishop, becoming auxiliary bishop of New Orleans.

1993 May 5 James Terry Steib, S.V.D., is named bishop of Memphis. In 2016, he is elected Provincial Superior, Society of Divine Word Southern Province.

1993 June 20 An African American Catholic Ministries Program is initiated by the National Black Catholic Congress and the DeSales School of Theology in Washington to prepare lay and pastoral ministers for service in African American communities.

1993 July 25 The National Association of African American Catholic Deacons is founded in Louisville, Kentucky, with Frederick A. Mason of the Archdiocese of Chicago as president. In 2010, the association is renamed National Association of Black Catholic Deacons (NABCD).

1993 October Toni Morrison receives the international Nobel Prize in Literature for *Beloved* (1987), the first African American woman to receive the prize.

1993 December 12 Elliot Griffin Thomas (1926–2019) is ordained a bishop, becoming bishop of St. Thomas, American Virgin Islands.

1994 February 10 Wilton Daniel Gregory is installed as bishop of Belleville, Illinois.

1994 Father George Clements initiates the One-Church-One-Addict program to help recovering drug abusers.

1995 March 20 George V. Murry, S.J., (1948–2020) becomes auxiliary bishop of Chicago and in 1998 is appointed bishop of St. Thomas, American Virgin Islands.

1995 May 17 Edward K. Braxton is ordained a bishop, becoming auxiliary bishop of St. Louis.

1995 Sister Mary Wilhelmina (Mary Elizabeth Lancaster) (1924–2019), formerly of the Oblate Sisters of Providence, founds the Benedictines of Mary, Queen of Apostles of the Priory of Our Lady of Ephesus, under the auspices of the Priestly Fraternity of St. Peter in Scranton, Pennsylvania. The integrated monastic community later moves to Gower, Missouri.

1997 March 13 John Ricard, S.S.J., is installed as bishop of Pensacola-Tallahassee.

1997 August 30 During the National Black Catholic Congress, the Shrine of Our Mother of Africa is dedicated in the Basilica of the National Shrine of the Immaculate Conception in Washington, a gift from black Catholics.

1997 December 17 Pierre Toussaint is declared venerable by Pope John Paul II.

1997 National Black Catholic Apostolate for Life (NBCAL), a prolife ministry of prayer and education, is initiated by Father James Goode as president of the NBCCC.

1997 Brother Cyprian Rowe, F.M.S., former executive director of NOBC (1978–1981) and NBCCC (1981–1983), leaves the Catholic Church to join the Imani Temple African-American Catholic Congregation. He returns to Roman Catholicism in 2000, but is not readmitted to the Marist order.

1997 Due to an increase in the number of African-born priests and religious serving in the U.S., the African Women Religious Conference is founded. A year later, the African Catholic Clergy Association is established. Through annual joint conferences beginning in 2000, the African Conference of Catholic Clergy and Religious in the U.S. is formed in 2005.

1998 March 3 Gordon Dunlap Bennett, S.J., (1946–) is ordained a bishop, becoming auxiliary bishop of Baltimore, and on September 24, 2004, assumes duties as bishop of Mandeville, Jamaica.

1998 June 29 Joseph Nathaniel Perry (1948–) is ordained a bishop, becoming auxiliary bishop of Chicago.

1999 Father George Clements initiates the One-Church-One Inmate program, providing aftercare for incarcerated individuals.

1999 William L. Norvel, S.S.J., (1944–) serves as first rector of the St. Joseph House of Formation in Iperu-Remo, Nigeria, opening a pipeline for future vocations to serve the U.S. Church.

Twenty-First Century

2000 February 22 Edward K. Braxton is appointed bishop of Lake Charles, Louisiana. In 2005, he is named bishop of Belleville, Illinois.

2000 May 7 Pope John Paul II celebrates Martin Luther King Jr. as a twentieth-century martyr and example of Christian faith during ceremonies at the Roman Colosseum recognizing the third millennium of Christianity. Although not calling for canonization, King is included on the Church's official martyrology.

2000 September 9 Coinciding with the United Nations' Millennium Summit, the National Black Catholic Apostolate and the NBCCC host a memorial for victims of the civil war in Sudan, calling on the intercession of soon-to-be saint Josephine Bakhita.

2000 October 1 Katharine Drexel and Josephine Margaret Bakhita are canonized by Pope John Paul II. Drexel is the second U.S. citizen saint, after Elizabeth Ann Seton in 1975.

2000 The Sisters of Loretto commission a monument to acknowledge mistakes of the past and honor blacks that the congregation had held in slavery before the Civil War.

2000 The U.S. bishops issue "Love Thy Neighbor as Thyself."

2001 November Wilton Daniel Gregory becomes the first black president of the U.S. Conference of Catholic Bishops (USCCB), having served as vice president (1998–2001).

2001 Patricia Chappell, S.N.D.deN., (1952–) becomes the first African American elected to the Sisters of Notre Dame de Namur Provincial Leadership Team (Connecticut Province).

2003 July 24–27 The NBCCC and the Pan African Roman Catholic Clergy Caucus convenes its first joint meeting in Techny, Illinois.

2003 September 12 Archbishop emeritus Harry J. Flynn of St. Paul and Minneapolis issues "In God's Image: Pastoral Letter on Racism," recounting his personal perspective as a white bishop confronting racism.

2003 M. Shawn Copeland (1947–) is the first African American to serve as president of the Catholic Theological Society of America.

2004 March 29 Edward P. Jones (1950–) receives the Pulitzer Prize in Fiction for his novel, *The Known World* (2003).

2004 July 2 Martin David Holley (1954–) is ordained a bishop, becoming auxiliary bishop of Washington. He becomes bishop of Memphis in 2016.

2005 January 17 Wilton Daniel Gregory is installed as archbishop of Atlanta.

2006 August 22 Guy A. Sansaricq (1934–), born in Haiti, is ordained a bishop, becoming auxiliary bishop of Brooklyn.

2007 February 28 Shelton Joseph Fabre (1963–) is ordained a bishop, becoming auxiliary bishop of New Orleans. He becomes bishop of Houma-Thibodaux, Louisiana in 2013.

2007 March 28 George V. Murry, S.J., is installed as bishop of Youngstown, Ohio. Later that year he becomes secretary of the USCCB.

2007 The Black Catholic Theological Symposium begins publication of the *Journal of the Black Catholic Theological Symposium*.

2008 July Teresita Weind, S.N.D.deN., (1942–) is the first African American to become Congregational Leader (superior) of the Sisters of Notre Dame de Namur.

2009 July 10 President Barack Obama, the first African American U.S. president, visits Pope Benedict XVI at the Vatican. The president gives the pope a liturgical stole of St. John Neumann. Pope Benedict gives the president a mosaic of St. Peter's Basilica and an autographed copy of his encyclical *Caritas in Veritate*.

2009–2010 The Black and Indian Mission Office establishes the National Advisory Council on Catholic Missions among Black and Native American Peoples. Its board is comprised of lay Catholics.

2010 March 2 The canonization cause of Augustus Tolton is announced by the Archdiocese of Chicago. Bishop Joseph Nathaniel Perry is named postulator for the cause. Tolton is proclaimed Servant of God on February 13, 2012.

2010 March 27 Henriette Delille, S.S.F., is declared venerable by Pope Benedict XVI.

2011 June 13-17 William L. Norvel, S.S.J., is elected the first Black superior general of the Josephites in Washington. He had served as consultor general, 1983-1987.

2011 July 7-August 1 The National Black Catholic Survey is conducted by Knowledge Networks. It is the first national survey to assess African American Catholics' religious engagement.

2011 Patricia Chappell, S.N.D.deN., is the first black executive director of Pax Christi USA, an international Catholic peace movement.

2012 May 29 Toni Morrison receives the Presidential Medal of Freedom, the highest award given to a civilian, from President Barack Obama.

2012 July 19-21 At the National Black Catholic Congress meeting in Indianapolis, Beverly A. Carroll of the U.S. bishops' Secretariat for Cultural Diversity receives the first "Servant of Christ" lifetime achievement award.

2012 July Three Kentucky-based religious communities (Sisters of Loretto, Sisters of Charity of Nazareth, and Dominicans of St. Catherine) hold a joint reconciliation service to ask forgiveness for the congregations' role in slavery, pledging to continue to work to eliminate racism.

2012 The Sisters of Charity of Nazareth, Kentucky, commission a monument to acknowledge mistakes of the past and honor blacks that the congregation had held in bondage.

2013 March 22 General Lloyd James Austin III (1953-) becomes the first African American to command the U.S. Central Command (CENTCOM).

2014 February 8 The feast day of St. Josephine Bakhita becomes the International Day of Prayer and Awareness against Human Trafficking.

2014 March 27 President Barack Obama visits Pope Francis at the Vatican. The president gives the pope a custom-made box of seeds used in the White House garden. The pope gives two medallions and a copy of *Evangelii Gaudium*.

2014 July 4 Kirk P. Gaddy (1965–2020), an educator, creates a black Catholic history rosary. The mysteries recount black Catholic history and the struggle for civil rights.

2014 September 9 The U.S. bishops issue a statement in recognition of the fiftieth anniversary of the Civil Rights Act.

2015 March 23 Fernand Cheri III, O.F.M., (1952–) is ordained a bishop, becoming auxiliary bishop of New Orleans.

2015 July 28 Members of the NBCCC, NBSC, NBCSA, and NABCD visit Emanuel African Methodist Episcopal Church in Charleston, South Carolina, where a white supremacist killed nine black congregation members.

2015 September 23 Pope Francis meets with President Barack Obama at the White House. The president gifts the pope a one-of-a-kind sculpture of an ascending dove. Pope Francis gifts the president with a bronze bas-relief plaque commemorating the 2015 World Meeting of Families in Philadelphia.

2015 December 10 Nadja Yudith West (1961–) is confirmed by the U.S. Senate as the 44th Army Surgeon General, becoming the first black female surgeon general and the first black woman to hold the rank of (three-star) lieutenant general in the Army.

2016 July The USCCB forms the Peace in Our Communities Task Force in response to race-related shootings in Baton Rouge, Minneapolis, and Dallas. Archbishop Wilton Gregory serves as chairman.

2016 September 1 The Georgetown University Working Group on Slavery, Memory, and Reconciliation recommends renaming two campus buildings memorializing Jesuits connected to slavery. One of the rededicated buildings honors Isaac Hawkins, an enslaved person sold by the Jesuits in 1838, and Anne Marie Becroft (Sister Mary Aloysius) (1805–1833), a free woman of color who established a school for Catholic girls in Georgetown.

2016 December The cause for canonization of Julia Greeley (ca. 1840–1918) is opened by the Archdiocese of Denver. Born into slavery in Missouri, Greeley joined the Catholic Church and became a member of the Third Order of St. Francis.

2017 April Amanda Gorman (1998–) becomes the first National Youth Poet Laureate. The author of poetry addressing civil rights, oppression, and marginalization, Gorman recites her poem "The Hill We Climb" at U.S. President Joseph Biden's inauguration (2021).

2017 August 23 In the wake of the white supremacist "Unite the Right" rally in Charlottesville, Virginia, the USCCB creates an Ad Hoc Committee Against Racism chaired by Bishop George V. Murry, S.J.

2018 June 9 M. Shawn Copeland is the first African American theologian to receive the John Courtney Murray Award, the highest honor bestowed by the Catholic Theological Society of America.

2018 June 9 Descendants of enslaved persons the Jesuits sold in 1838 to cover Georgetown University debts hold a reunion in Iberville Parish, Louisiana, hosted by the GU272 Descendants Association.

2018 November 14 The U.S. bishops issue "Open Wide Our Hearts: The Enduring Call to Love—a Pastoral Letter Against Racism."

2018 November 18 Sister Thea Bowman's cause for canonization is opened by the Diocese of Jackson, Mississippi. U.S. bishops give unanimous approval to the cause and she is declared a Servant of God.

2019 March 21 Roy Edward Campbell Jr. (1947–) is ordained a bishop, becoming auxiliary bishop of Washington, D.C.

2019 May 21 Wilton Daniel Gregory is installed as Archbishop of Washington.

2019 June 11 Pope Francis declares Augustus Tolton venerable.

2019 June Retired Bishop John Ricard, S.S.J., is elected as superior general of the Josephites.

2020 May 31 The U.S. bishops issue a statement on the death of George Floyd, an unarmed black man who died at the hands of police, declaring his death "a sin that cries out to heaven for justice." On June 3, Pope Francis calls Floyd's death "tragic" and prays for all who have lost their lives due to racism.

2020 **July 13** Bishop David Zubik of Pittsburgh designates St. Benedict the Moor Church as a non-territorial parish for the city's black Catholics. His decision to separate the parish's administration from two nearby churches is in response to a task force recommendation.

2020 **August 12–14** The Leadership Conference of Women Religious bestows Patricia Chappell, S.N.D.deN., with its 2020 Outstanding Leadership Award.

2020 **November 28** Washington Archbishop Wilton Daniel Gregory is elevated to cardinal in Rome, the first black U.S. cardinal.

2020 The U.S. black Catholic population is estimated at 3,000,000. Approximately 800 U.S. parishes are predominately African American, but more than 75% of black Catholics attend parishes in which African Americans are not the majority. U.S. black Catholic religious vocations include 250 priests, 437 deacons, 400 sisters, 50 brothers, and 75 seminarians. In addition, there are more than 700 African-born priests serving in the U.S.

Outsiders Within: The Oblate Sisters of Providence in 1830s Church and Society

DIANE BATTS MORROW*

THE OBLATE SISTERS OF PROVIDENCE formed the first permanent community of Roman Catholic sisters of African descent in the world.[1] Elizabeth Clarisse Lange[2] and the Sulpician priest James Hector Joubert co-founded the Oblate community in Baltimore in 1828. These two individuals also shared a French cultural heritage, Caribbean refugee status, a fervent devotion to the Catholic faith, and an abiding commitment to the education of black children. Theirs proved to be a collaboration of extraordinary individuals. As a Catholic priest and white male in the antebellum South, James Joubert transcended prevailing institutional and social attitudes towards both black people and women in conceptualizing the Oblate Sisters of Providence. In aspiring to establish a community of black women religious, Elizabeth Lange defied the subordinate status ascribed her as a free woman of color in a slave society.

Unlike founders of white religious communities serving white society, Lange and Joubert proposed to provide for a despised population both a corps of teachers from its own ranks and an education, which the general public considered neither serving a public need

---

* This essay was first published in *U.S. Catholic Historian* 15, no. 2 (Spring 1997): 35–54.
[1] Grace Sherwood, *The Oblates' Hundred and One Years* (New York: Macmillan, 1932), 118; John T. Gillard, *Colored Catholics in the United States* (Baltimore: Josephite Press, 1941), 118.
[2] Most accounts list her as Elizabeth Clovis Lange, but documentation discovered by the author lists her name as Elizabeth Clarisse Lange. John W. Bowen, Sulpician priest and archivist, suggested that "Clovis" may reflect a misreading of "Clarisse."

nor consonant with prevailing social values. Indeed, some Americans proscribed education for free Negroes as much as for slaves.[3] The Oblate Sisters' very existence as free women of color organized into a community of Catholic religious to educate black girls challenged prevailing social and episcopal attitudes about race and gender. If not revolutionary, the foundation of the Oblate Sisters constituted a heroic feat.[4]

As the term "culture" denotes the total way of life of a society at a given time, so the term "charism" signifies the culture of a religious community. Just as unique cultural practices differentiate societies, the specific charisms informing religious communities serve as spiritual fingerprints distinguishing one from the other. In defining themselves in their original Rule as "a religious society of Coloured women ... [who] renounce the world to consecrate themselves to God and to the Christian education of young girls of color,"[5] the Oblate Sisters stated their awareness that the issue of race informed their particular charism. Although they shared many traits with other sisterhoods, this articulated racial consciousness proved unique to the Oblate experience. While issues of gender woven into the nineteenth-century social context affected the Oblate Sisters and white sisterhoods comparably, the pervasive strands of racism woven warp and woof into the American social fabric ensnared the Oblate community alone.

---

[3] James A. Wright, *The Free Negro in Maryland, 1634–1815*, Studies in History, Economics, and Public Law, no. 222 (New York: Columbia University, 1921), 200–202; Michael F. Rouse, *A Study of the Development of Negro Education under Catholic Auspices in Maryland and Washington, D.C.* (Baltimore: Johns Hopkins University Press, 1935), 10–11, 16–17, 102.

[4] Several sources assert the extraordinarily pioneering nature of the Oblate foundation. See Maria M. Lannon, *Response to Love: The Story of Mary Elizabeth Lange, OSP* (Washington, DC: Josephite Pastoral Center, 1992), 6; Sr. Reginald Gerdes, "Service on the Cutting Edge" (Unpublished Paper, 1994), OSPA; Sr. Reginald Gerdes, "To Educate and Evangelize: Black Catholic Schools of the Oblate Sisters of Providence (1828–1880)," *U.S. Catholic Historian* 7, nos. 2–3 (Spring/Summer 1988): 188; Thaddeus J. Posey, "An Unwanted Commitment: The Spirituality of the Early Oblate Sisters of Providence, 1829–1890" (Ph.D. dissertation, Saint Louis University, 1993), 157–158.

[5] The "Original Rule of the Oblate Sisters of Providence," cited in Posey, "An Unwanted Commitment," 314.

During the 1830s the Oblate Sisters forged the patterns of their communal life and executed their teaching ministry.[6] Both Church and society ascribed to the Oblate membership outsider-within status, predicated on Oblate identity as both women of color and as institutionalized religious. The Oblate Sisters nevertheless sought acceptance as a legitimate constituency within both the Roman Catholic Church and Southern society. The Oblate community functioned in a climate of heightened racial tension in Church and society. Yet, even in their first decade, the Oblate Sisters demonstrated "the utility of Black women's relationships with one another in providing a community for Black women's activism and self-determination."[7] This essay examines how the extraordinary faith of the Oblate Sisters of Providence empowered them as black women and committed religious, in spite of their social ascription as "other" or outsiders within both the American Church and society of the 1830s.

Oblate provenance in Baltimore, the capital of the Catholic United States in 1830, proved to be a defining feature of their nineteenth-century experience. The Oblate Sisters joined three other communities of women religious previously established in the archdiocese: the Carmelite nuns (1790), the Visitation Sisters of Georgetown (1800), and the Sisters of Charity of St. Joseph, Emmitsburg (1809).[8] By 1837, all four sisterhoods maintained missions in the city of Baltimore.[9] The Oblate community enjoyed exceptional exposure to and recognition from the national and international Church dignitaries and officials who visited Baltimore, the premier See, or unofficial seat, of the American Catholic Church. Yet, in addition to other issues, considerations of race informed the Oblate Sisters' position within the antebellum Church.

---

   [6]   For a treatment of these issues see Diane Batts Morrow, "The Oblate Sisters of Providence: Issues of Black and Female Agency in their Antebellum Experience, 1828–1860" (Ph.D. dissertation, University of Georgia, 1996), 91–135.
   [7]   Patricia Hill Collins, *Black Feminist Thought: Knowledge, Consciousness, and the Politics of Empowerment*, Perspectives on Gender, vol. 2 (Boston: Unwin Hyman, 1990), 4.
   [8]   Barbara Misner, *"Highly Respectable and Accomplished Ladies": Catholic Women Religious in America 1790–1850* (New York: Garland Publishing, 1988), 257, 260, 262.
   [9]   Misner, *"Highly Respectable and Accomplished Ladies,"* 259, 262, 263, 268.

From 1789 through the 1830s, the Church in the South remained the foundation of American Catholicism. In 1789, over half of the 35,000 Catholics in the United States lived in the South, the largest number by far in Maryland.[10] Waves of European Catholic immigration shifted the concentration of the American Catholic population from Maryland to the cities of the Northeast from the 1840s,[11] but the Catholic Church in the United States retained the imprint of its Southern provenance through the nineteenth century. In fully embracing the tenets of Southern nationalism,[12] the Catholic Church in the South accommodated racism and the institution of slavery.

Although allowing that slavery as practiced in the United States constituted a social evil, Church teachings maintained that in principle slavery did not constitute a sin. Insisting on the equality of all people before God, the Church nevertheless interpreted such equality in its moral and spiritual dimensions only, not in a social sense. The universal Church historically had not perceived its role as that of social reformer and had challenged neither serfdom nor slavery, considering them exclusively social institutions. However, because the Church held that enslaved status did not deprive an individual of her or his humanity, it insisted that the owner-slave relationship entailed reciprocal obligations. Neither more nor less than did Protestant denominations, the Roman Catholic Church condemned abuses and atrocities perpetrated by slaveholders against their slave property.[13]

---

[10] Randall M. Miller and Jon Wakelyn, eds., *Catholics in the Old South: Essays on Church and Culture* (Macon, GA: Mercer University Press, 1983), 6; Raymond H. Schmandt, "An Overview of Institutional Establishments in the Antebellum Southern Church," in Miller and Wakelyn, *Catholics in the Old South*, 55; Richard Duncan, "Catholics and the Church in the Antebellum Upper South," in Miller and Wakelyn, *Catholics in the Old South*, 87-90.

[11] Stephen Ochs, *Desegregating the Altar: The Josephites and the Struggle for Black Priests, 1871-1960* (Baton Rouge: Louisiana State University Press, 1986), 15; Thomas Spalding, *The Premier See: A History of the Archdiocese of Baltimore 1789-1989* (Baltimore: Johns Hopkins University Press, 1989), 160.

[12] Randall Miller, "A Church in Cultural Captivity: Some Speculations on Catholic Identity in the Old South," in Miller and Wakelyn, *Catholics in the Old South*, 14-17.

[13] For a thorough discussion of the antebellum Church's position on slavery see James Hennesey, *American Catholics: A History of the Roman Catholic Community*

American clergy and religious not only tolerated the institution of slavery, they also actively participated in and profited from the ownership and sale of human chattel. Several distinguished prelates, including John Carroll, the first Roman Catholic bishop in the United States, and his colleagues and successors Louis DuBourg of Louisiana, Benedict Flaget of Kentucky, and Samuel Eccleston of Baltimore, owned or had owned slaves.[14] Communities of priests including the Jesuits, the Vincentians, the Sulpicians, and the Capuchins owned slaves.[15] Congregations of women religious such as the Carmelites, the Sisters of the Visitation, and the Sisters of Charity also owned slaves.[16]

The Oblate Sisters of Providence were free women of color; nevertheless, racism and consequences of the system of racial slavery entrenched in the United States intruded on their antebellum experience. In sanctioning the foundation of the Oblate Sisters of Providence as a community of black women religious in 1829, the Church affirmed free black people as a legitimate spiritual constituency. Yet the pervasive debasement of all black people ensuing from the racial basis of slavery in the United States convinced most white people in America—including the Catholic hierarchy—of universal black inferiority. The existing evidence fails to corroborate a recent assertion that the Catholic clergy and religious of Baltimore "found no difference between the Oblates and other religious."[17] Throughout the antebellum period, ambivalence toward the Oblate Sisters as black women religious plagued the institutional Church.

---

in the United States (New York: Oxford University Press, 1981), 143–149; Duncan, "Catholics and the Church in the Antebellum Upper South," 77–98; Randall M. Miller, "A Church in Cultural Captivity," 11–52, and "The Failed Mission: The Catholic Church and Black Catholics in the Old South," in Miller and Wakelyn, *Catholics in the Old South*, 149–70; John C. Murphy, *An Analysis of the Attitudes of American Catholics toward the Immigrant and the Negro, 1825–1925* (Washington, DC: Catholic University Press of America, 1940), 33–51, 76–79, 136–44; Cyprian Davis, *The History of Black Catholics in the United States* (New York: Crossroad, 1990), 35–57.

[14] Duncan, "Catholics and the Church in the Antebellum Upper South," 90; Davis, *History of Black Catholics in the United States*, 43.
[15] Davis, *History of Black Catholics in the United States*, 38–39.
[16] Misner, "*Highly Respectable and Accomplished Ladies,*" 75–88.
[17] Posey, "An Unwanted Commitment," 125, 136.

In June 1829 the disapproval of the Oblate foundation expressed within the Baltimore Catholic community—evidently by clergy as well as laity[18]—dismayed the four charter Oblate members. Oblate spiritual director James Joubert noted, "these good girls ... admitted to me that after all they had heard said, only through obedience would they be determined to take the religious habit."[19] Joubert further revealed, "I had myself heard much talk. I knew already that many persons who had approved the idea of a school for pupils disapproved very strongly that of forming a religious house, and could not think of the idea of seeing these poor girls (colored girls) wearing the religious habit and constituting a religious community."[20] That same month Sulpician priest John Chanche had refused a favor requested by Joubert on the Oblate community's behalf. Chanche's refusal had "amazed and mortified" Joubert.[21]

The outcry against the idea of black sisters had come to the attention of even Archbishop James Whitfield who, according to Joubert, "knew very much himself, even more than I did, and he advised me not to be in the least discouraged."[22] The "persons" who confronted the sisters, challenged Joubert, and complained to the archbishop about the concept of a community of black women religious undoubtedly included clergy—Sulpicians among them—who were more likely to have access to the sisters, Joubert, and Whitfield than the general laity.

Joubert had told the four dismayed Oblate novices to "rest on the purity of their intentions, and since their actions were misinterpreted by certain persons, they should put their confidence in God; that until now their work seemed good, so they must not stop

---

[18] Posey, "An Unwanted Commitment," 29, 184.
[19] Translation of "The Original Diary of the Oblate Sisters of Providence" typescript copy, 5, Oblate Sisters of Providence Archives, Baltimore, Maryland (hereafter OSPA), hereafter cited as "Original Diary."
[20] "Original Diary," 5.
[21] "Excerpts from Louis Deluol's Diary Concerning the Oblate Sisters of Providence," June 20, 1829, Archives of the Associated Sulpicians of the United States, Associated Archives at St. Mary's Seminary & University, Baltimore, Maryland.
[22] "Original Diary," 5.

because of the judgment of men who often judge things through their passions and prejudices."[23] The Oblate Sisters incorporated Joubert's sage words into their communal response to all encounters with racial discrimination.

From their beginning the Oblate Sisters of Providence enjoyed the support of several extraordinary individuals among the clergy who both affirmed and promoted the spiritual mission of the Oblates.[24] Yet clerical support of the Oblate Sisters never included significant financial donations commensurate with those that the communities of white women religious established in the Archdiocese of Baltimore received at their foundations.

Carmelite nuns formed their first foundation in the United States at Port Tobacco, Maryland in 1790. The Jesuit priest Charles Neale, a scion of the long-established, immensely wealthy, and devotedly Catholic Neale family of Maryland, served as both spiritual director and generous benefactor to this first Carmelite mission in America. Within three months of their arrival in Maryland in 1790 from the Antwerp, Belgium, Carmelite community, the four charter American Carmelites took possession of an 800-acre plantation provided them by Charles Neale in exchange for his own property and a cash payment of approximately $6,535. By 1830 the Carmelite order owned slaves valued at $9,000.[25]

When in 1830 economic reversals forced the Carmelites to move to Baltimore, Archbishop James Whitfield involved himself personally in the task of locating suitable accommodations for the cloistered nuns. On June 6, 1830, after "looking all over Baltimore," Whitfield wrote triumphantly to the Carmelite mother superior, "I have discovered a most beautiful garden, with a brick house, in a

---

[23] "Original Diary," 5.
[24] For a fuller discussion of this issue, see Morrow, "The Oblate Sisters of Providence," 189–192.
[25] "Dollar-Sterling Mint Parity," *Journal of Economic History* 43, no. 3 (1983): 579–616; Charles Warren Currier, *Carmel in America: A Centennial History of the Discalced Carmelites in the United States* (Baltimore: John Murphy, 1890), 69, 187; Misner, *"Highly Respectable and Accomplished Ladies,"* 17–18, 257–258.

very respectable part of the city...." The property was within a half-mile of the archbishop's own residence and included

> a fine green house, a bath room for warm and cold baths, a pump of good water within the lot and, close to the house, a variety of the choicest flowers, large beds of cauliflowers, and plenty of room and good soil for planting sufficient vegetables for your community.[26]

The Carmelite order purchased the house in 1830 for $6,250. Whitfield personally contributed $100 towards their expenses.[27]

The Sisters of the Visitation established their first foundation in the United States in Georgetown in 1800. Leonard Neale—Jesuit priest, brother to Charles, and future archbishop of Baltimore—made the Visitation Sisters "the principal focus of his interest and energies until the assumption of his archiepiscopal role."[28] Between 1800, when the Georgetown Visitation began with three charter members, and 1805, Neale served as the sisters' spiritual director and also purchased an entire block of Georgetown real estate for $5,670. He then deeded all of the property to the Visitation Sisters in 1808 for one dollar.[29] The French priest Joseph Clorivière, the third spiritual director of the Visitation Sisters from 1819 until his death in 1826, contributed $9,354,605 of his own money to their community.[30]

Elizabeth Ann Seton founded the Sisters of Charity of St. Joseph in Baltimore in 1809. Seton professed her vows before Archbishop John Carroll in March 1809. Samuel Cooper, a student preparing for the priesthood at St. Mary's Seminary, generously donated $10,000 to Seton for the purchase of property suitable for a convent and school. Three months after professing her vows, Seton and the four

---

[26] Currier, *Carmel in America*, 184, 189.
[27] Currier, *Carmel in America*, 185, 187.
[28] Spalding, *Premier See*, 66.
[29] Eleanore C. Sullivan, *Georgetown Visitation Since 1799* (privately printed, 1975), 42, 49–51, 98; Misner, "Highly Respectable and Accomplished Ladies," 19–20, 260.
[30] Misner, "Highly Respectable and Accomplished Ladies," 145, 260–261; Sullivan, *Georgetown Visitation Since 1799*, 72.

other charter Sisters of Charity occupied their new estate at Emmitsburg, Maryland.[31]

The only detail in which the experience of the Oblate Sisters of Providence in their early years resembled that of the three sisterhoods preceding them in the Archdiocese of Baltimore was in the number of their respective charter members: the Carmelite nuns, four; the Visitation Sisters, three; the Sisters of Charity, five; and the Oblate Sisters, four. In 1829, the year of their formal profession, the Oblates included their original 4 members compared to 25 Carmelite nuns, 60 Visitation Sisters of Georgetown, and 120 Sisters of Charity.[32] By 1850 the Oblates had received 29 candidates; the Carmelites, 53; the Visitation Sisters, 178; and the Emmitsburg Sisters of Charity, 680.[33] The inchoate state of the Oblate community in the 1830s, the minuscule size of the national black Catholic population relative to its white counterpart—100,000 black Catholics in 1865 compared to 3,103,000 white Catholics in 1860—and the single Oblate mission in Baltimore compared to the numerous missions the Visitation Sisters and the Sisters of Charity established in other regions of the nation account for the difference in the complements of the Oblate community and the white sisterhoods.[34]

Significantly, Oblate student enrollments compared favorably with those of the archdiocesan white girls' academies. In 1830 Archbishop Whitfield advised the Carmelite nuns that an enrollment of 50 to 60 pupils would constitute a viable student body capable of supporting their institution.[35] The Oblate School for Coloured Girls enrolled 56

---

[31] Christopher J. Kauffman, *Tradition and Transformation in Catholic Culture: The Priests of Saint Sulpice in the United States from 1790 to the Present* (New York: Macmillan, 1988), 77; Misner, "Highly Respectable and Accomplished Ladies," 28-29; Charles Herbermann, *The Sulpicians in the United States* (New York: Encyclopedia Press, 1916), 222-223.

[32] "Statement Concerning the Diocese of Baltimore Prepared and Forwarded to the Editor of the *Annals of the Propagation of the Faith* by His Grace Archbishop Whitfield," June 27, 1829, *Historical Records and Studies* 2 (1900): 136-137.

[33] Misner, "Highly Respectable and Accomplished Ladies," 92.

[34] Gillard, *Colored Catholics*, 88, 99; Ochs, *Desegregating the Altar*, 15; Misner, "Highly Respectable and Accomplished Ladies," 118-119, 126-127.

[35] Currier, *Carmel in America*, 184.

pupils in 1839; the Georgetown Visitation Academy, 50 in 1830; the Carmelite school, approximately 50 pupils in the early 1840s.[36]

No priest or bishop appeared as a *deus ex machina* disbursing thousands of dollars in cash or property to the fledgling Oblate community. The priest Adolphus Williamson repeatedly recognized the Oblate Sisters with non-pecuniary favors.[37] Although in 1830 Williamson donated $3000 of his personal fortune to provide cut granite for the facade of the Sulpician institution St. Charles College,[38] some fifteen miles outside Baltimore, evidently he did not consider financial support of the Oblate Sisters a suitable investment.

When circumstances required the Oblate Sisters to relocate three times between June 1828 and December 1829,[39] no priest or bishop personally interceded on their behalf or helped defray their moving expenses. Unlike the other archdiocesan sisterhoods, the Oblate Sisters of Providence had to rely exclusively on their own resources and the generosity of the lay community for financial support.

In 1836 both the Oblate Sisters and the Carmelite nuns constructed new chapels. The Oblate Sisters borrowed money to finance construction and organized a fair in 1837 to meet the expense of outfitting their new chapel.[40] Acting on behalf of the Carmelites, their resident chaplain, Matthew Herard, not only donated $3,000 from his personal funds for the project, but also engaged some "ladies of the city" to organize a fair which raised an additional $3,500 for the Carmelite chapel.[41] The discrepancy between the unencumbered $7,500 for the Carmelite chapel and the begged, borrowed, and earned total of $3,301.02[42] for the Oblate chapel in 1836 accurately reflected the relative positions of these two communities of women religious in Baltimore.

---

[36] *Laity's Directory* (1839), 96; Sullivan, *Georgetown Visitation Since 1799*, 73; *Laity's Directory* (1843), 64; (1847), 80.
[37] Morrow, "The Oblate Sisters of Providence," 191.
[38] Herbermann, *Sulpicians in the United States*, 201.
[39] "Original Diary," 2–4, 7.
[40] "Original Diary," 43, 52.
[41] Currier, *Carmel in America*, 203–204.
[42] "Original Diary," 43, 52.

In describing the ceremonies consecrating the altar stone on July 31, 1836, and the one blessing the chapel cornerstone on August 27, the Oblate annalist declared, "We followed exactly all the ceremonies prescribed in the ritual."[43] This statement revealed the Oblate Sisters' awareness of their anomalous position as outsiders within Catholic Baltimore society. As if in response to an anticipated, if unarticulated, challenge from the white Catholic community, the Oblate Sisters explicitly noted their knowledge of and conformity to established religious ritual. They thus asserted their status as a legitimate constituency within the Baltimore religious community.

In December 1837 forty-nine black women and girls conceived, planned, and executed the Oblate Fair which realized almost $1,000. In the aftermath of this fair, the Oblate Sisters and the black community confronted further evidence of their status as outsiders within the nineteenth-century Catholic Church and Baltimore society. The Oblate annalist recalled:

> The Fair for which we had been working for more than three months began today in the Catholic School on Saratoga Street which the gentlemen wardens of the Cathedral very willingly loaned. It lasted four days. We took all precautions that everything might pass orderly. Angela Noel and her mother had the first idea of this fair. It was they who first spoke to the Sisters. They were seconded by a certain number of colored persons, who took very much interest in it.[44]

The annalist gratefully acknowledged the generosity of the white wardens of Baltimore's Cathedral of the Assumption who "very willingly loaned" the use of the cathedral school on Saratoga Street as the site for the Oblate function. But the statement, "We took all precautions that everything might pass orderly," again documented the Oblate Sisters' awareness of their precarious position within Baltimore society. Trebly scrutinized as black, Roman Catholic, and women religious, the Oblate community enjoyed no margin for error in any of their endeavors. Their fishbowl existence in 1830s Baltimore demanded that the Oblate membership remain ever vigilant "that everything might pass orderly."

---

[43] "Original Diary," 43, 44–45.
[44] "Original Diary," 52.

At the same time the Oblate Sisters explicitly acknowledged the initiative and effort on their behalf exerted by black women in the Baltimore community. On December 10, 1837, the Oblate Sisters hosted a celebratory luncheon "for all those good persons who were employed at the different tables at the fair . . . to show by this how grateful they were for the services which they had rendered."[45] During the festivities Joubert made a significant announcement to the assembled women.

In an awkward and slightly cryptic entry which constitutes one of the most poignant passages in the Oblate *Annals*, Joubert revealed "the order arranged in the chapel, and the reservation that was made of the six benches in the back of the chapel for the white people who came to the services." He cited "gratitude" and a "measure of safety" as the reasons for the seating segregation. Although, Joubert admitted, the sisters "were fully persuaded that this separation, as just and as reasonable as possible, would inconvenience certain persons," he maintained, "but they did not hesitate." Joubert concluded that "all the people present seemed pleased with the reasons."[46]

The stilted style of this passage reflects more than the inevitable loss of semantic nuance in translating from the original French to an English text. The challenge to articulate "as just and as reasonable as possible" a policy of racial segregation exceeded Joubert's—or anyone's—verbal facility in any language.

Joubert, sensitive to the racial indignities which assailed the Oblate Sisters and the black community in general, could not have anticipated this announcement with equanimity. His reference to the seating restriction as "this measure of safety" implied real or potential danger to black Catholics in the absence of such restrictions. Concerns for safety raised to justify segregated seating in a black Catholic church attested to the racially charged atmosphere of 1830s Baltimore. The long arm of racial discrimination reached even to the last six pews in the Oblate Sisters' chapel.

---

[45] "Original Diary," 52.
[46] "Original Diary," 52.

On December 10, 1837, the Oblate Sisters and their guests confronted a bitter dimension of the reality of their anomalous position as outsiders within 1830s Church and society. At the very occasion celebrating black initiative and agency in raising $1,000 to furnish the Oblate chapel, the black community faced the institutionalization of their inferior status even within the premises of that chapel. Joubert's admission that the sisters realized the demeaning impact of seating segregation on the black congregation suggested the turmoil the debate on this issue generated within the Oblate community. It seems improbable that either the Oblate Sisters or their guests would have been genuinely "pleased with the reasons" for racial discrimination in the Oblate chapel. But, as they had in the past and would again in the future, these black women endured.

Few clerics matched the unstinting zeal and total commitment to the Oblate cause evinced by their co-founder, James Joubert. Archbishop James Whitfield approved the Oblate foundation in 1829. Several Sulpician and other priests and prelates demonstrated varying degrees of support for the Oblate Sisters throughout the 1830s. Yet clerical support of these black women religious never equaled the clerical patronage bestowed on the white sisterhoods in the Archdiocese of Baltimore. Issues of race and the grip of the institution of slavery on social attitudes inhibited the response of the institutional Church to the Oblate community.

Issues of race, ethnicity, and religion informed the position of the Oblate Sisters of Providence within Southern society. Their Catholic identity potentially estranged these black sisters from the sympathies of a substantially Protestant nation, which viewed the Church alternately as the perpetrator of a popish plot to conquer the United States and as the evil genius holding in thrall the teeming masses of immigrants invading America. Indeed, the Oblate Sisters themselves claimed immigrant roots. As author Grace Sherwood asserted, a French priest formed a community of women of color "French in language, in sympathy, and in habit of life."[47]

---

[47] Sherwood, *The Oblates' Hundred and One Years*, 5.

Ethnic categorization often resulted in discrimination in the European immigrant experience in America. Yet being identified ethnically as French by white Baltimoreans actually mitigated the Oblate Sisters' negatively perceived racial identity.[48] Certainly the Oblate Sisters' Francophone ethnicity in concert with their Catholic faith recommended these black women religious to their supporters among both the French Sulpician priests and the white San Domingan exile community.

As black women religious, members of the Oblate community observed vows of chastity in a society which denigrated the virtue of all black women—slave or free—and consequently considered the concept of chaste black women an oxymoron. Indeed, the commitment to chastity embraced by all sisterhoods would have found favor with few nineteenth-century Americans, who subscribed to the cult of domesticity and its promulgation of the virtues of matrimony and maternity. As women religious living in community, the Oblate Sisters of Providence endured with other sisterhoods nativist hostility in 1830s Baltimore. Whatever concerns for their safety the white sisterhoods entertained in the wake of nativist agitation, the black Oblate Sisters also experienced concerns for their safety derived from their racial identity.

During their first decade the Oblate Sisters encountered incidents of racism, both subtle and overt, in their interactions with the citizenry of Baltimore. The racial identity of the sisters and their students complicated their securing a suitable, permanent residence. Unexpectedly evicted from their first rented property in April 1829, the Oblate Sisters experienced a discriminatory housing market familiar to minority populations in both the nineteenth and twentieth centuries. Joubert reported that the Oblate community "found several [houses] but the price asked was exorbitant; several refused absolutely to let us have them, when they were informed that it was for a school, and still more a school for colored children."[49] Fortunately for the community, within a month of their eviction notice Dr. Peter Chatard, a wealthy white San Domingan

---

[48] Spalding, *Premier See*, 109.
[49] "Original Diary," 2.

émigré, offered them his Richmond Street property on generous terms.⁵⁰

In 1832 a cholera epidemic ravaged several eastern cities, including Baltimore. The Trustees of the Bureau of the Poor requested eight Sisters of Charity to nurse indigent cholera victims at the city almshouse. Supplied with only four Sisters of Charity, the trustees then approached Joubert on August 26, 1832, to request four Oblate Sisters to nurse the sick. Evidently the Trustees of the Poor had not known of the Oblate Sisters of Providence until the Sisters of Charity informed them of the existence of that "society of religious colored women." Joubert informed "these gentlemen that the Sisters of Charity were by the spirit of their institute obliged to look after the sick; but that the Sisters of Providence were not, as they are obliged to the education of young girls of their color." Cautioning the officials that "my authority over them [the Oblates] did not allow that I should force them to obey in a thing other than the spirit of their institute," Joubert nevertheless hoped to "find four among them who were willing, and who felt courage enough to expose themselves to possible contagion; these were to give me their names." In response, the entire Oblate membership of eleven sisters volunteered "and filled with joy and happiness, they all cried that they were ready to undertake it, that they should find much happiness in being able to serve our Lord in the person of the sick; all I had to do was to make a choice."⁵¹

Joubert chose Sisters Mary Lange, Anthony Duchemin, Magdalene Barclay, and Scholastica Bourgoin to nurse at the almshouse for a month. Oblate nursing at the almshouse earned a formal letter of thanks from Archibald Stirling, Secretary of the Trustees of the Poor.⁵²

The Oblate Sisters' willing service as nurses during the cholera epidemic of 1832 demonstrated their strong sense of mission and empowerment. However, significant racial dimensions inhered in this Oblate service to the city of Baltimore. Except for the letter from

---

⁵⁰ "Original Diary," 3.
⁵¹ "Original Diary," 16.
⁵² "Original Diary," 17–18.

Archibald Stirling, the Oblate Sisters enjoyed no public recognition for their civic service in nursing the sick. Yet the white Sisters of Charity received significant public acknowledgement of their efforts.[53] The existing evidence does not specify whether the Oblate Sisters nursed black or white cholera patients at the almshouse; it does suggest, however, that the cholera incident provided another opportunity for the Oblate Sisters to serve the Baltimore black community.

The outbreak of cholera in Baltimore in 1832 ravaged the free black community disproportionately to its presence in the total population. In the first week in September, 254 Baltimoreans died from cholera; 104 victims were black and of these, 92 were free. Although composing only 14% of the city's population, in that one week, free black victims accounted for more than one-third of the cholera dead.[54] Crowded and inadequate housing conditions for Baltimore's black residents and municipal negligence in maintaining minimum standards of public sanitation partially explain this severe black mortality from cholera.[55]

Most nineteenth-century public and private institutions, asylums, hospitals, and orphanages did not accept black inmates. Those that did—like the Baltimore City and County Almshouse—enforced a policy of strict racial segregation. A city medical report published in 1851 detailed the inferior, segregated facilities provided Baltimore's black population at the city almshouse.[56] The report's account of "cholera as it appeared at this institution in 1832" established that these racially segregated facilities had also existed in

---

[53] Sherwood, *The Oblates' Hundred and One Years*, 59; Misner, "Highly Respectable and Accomplished Ladies," 47, 229–230; Posey, "An Unwanted Commitment," 137–139.

[54] Ira Berlin, *Slaves Without Masters: The Free Negro in the Antebellum South* (New York: Pantheon Books, 1974), 258–259.

[55] Thomas H. Buckler, *A History of Epidemic Cholera as it Appeared at the Baltimore City and County Alms-house in the Summer of 1849* (Baltimore: J. Lucas, 1851), 13–14, 30–32; Bettye J. Gardner, "Free Blacks in Baltimore, 1800–60" (Ph.D. dissertation, George Washington University, 1974), 188–197; Christopher Phillips, "'Negroes and Other Slaves': The African-American Community of Baltimore 1790–1860" (Ph.D. dissertation, University of Georgia, 1992), 280–283.

[56] Buckler, *A History of Epidemic Cholera*, 7–9.

1832.[57] The Trustees of the Bureau of the Poor had requested eight Sisters of Charity, evidently to minister to both black and white almshouse cholera victims. Had the Sisters of Charity provided half the number of requested nurses, expecting the "society of religious colored women" to nurse black almshouse inmates?

Even as they valiantly agreed to serve the city of Baltimore as nurses, the Oblate Sisters experienced the intrusion of racial discrimination. In informing the city officials of the sisters' consent, Joubert "also told these gentlemen that I should wish these colored Sisters in a department of the hospital entirely separate from those of the Sisters of Charity, so that they would not come in contact with them. The gentlemen understood perfectly, and promised that this should be done."[58]

However much at the time "the gentlemen understood perfectly," Joubert's unexplained yet explicit request to segregate the Oblate Sisters from the Sisters of Charity at the almshouse remains puzzling. Did Joubert anticipate some racial friction should "the colored Sisters . . . come in contact with" the white Sisters of Charity? Was Joubert attempting to minimize the humiliation of legally enforced racial segregation by insisting on such racial segregation as a condition of Oblate service? Was Joubert ensuring that the colored Oblate Sisters would nurse only where the white Sisters of Charity would not—in the segregated black wards of the municipal almshouse? Perhaps the lack of acknowledgement by the Baltimore public of the Oblate service in the almshouse reflected, in part, not only the racial identity of the Oblate Sisters themselves, but also the racial identity of the beneficiaries of their care.

Yet circumstances beyond race may have dictated the respective public acknowledgements accorded the nursing efforts of the white Sisters of Charity and the colored Oblate Sisters of Providence. The Sisters of Charity, Emmitsburg, who taught, nursed, and cared for orphans as their mission, constituted the largest congregation of

---

[57] Buckler, *A History of Epidemic Cholera*, 27.
[58] Buckler, *A History of Epidemic Cholera*, 27.

women religious within the Archdiocese of Baltimore.[59] The outbreak of cholera precipitated requests for their nursing services from civic authorities in Philadelphia and Washington, D.C., as well as Baltimore.[60] Before the Trustees of the Poor solicited assistance from the Sisters of Charity for the almshouse, the Baltimore City Board of Health had requested their services on August 19, 1832, at two provisional hospitals set up in the city. Two Sisters of Charity died nursing at these hospitals.[61] In their annual reports in 1832 both the Commissioner of Health and the Consulting Physician called to "the attention of the City Council" the deaths of these sisters in service to the city.[62]

The Sisters of Charity nursed at more locations and in greater numbers than did the Oblate Sisters. While two Sisters of Charity died, all four Oblate Sisters survived exposure to cholera to return to their convent. Two separate bureaucratic agencies, the Board of Health and the Bureau of the Poor, requested the services of the Sisters of Charity; only the latter approached the Oblate Sisters. The City Council formally acknowledged the services of the Sisters of Charity at the specific request of two city officials. Visibility, mortality, and bureaucracy as much as issues of race may explain the different public acknowledgements of the nursing services rendered by the Sisters of Charity and the Oblate Sisters of Providence during the cholera epidemic of 1832.

In 1834 the Oblate community decided to buy the lot adjoining their Richmond Street location. Evidently the Oblate neighborhood, unlike that of the Carmelites, was not located in a very respectable part of the city. Joubert wrote that in part "the fear of seeing the small wooden house which is on the lot converted into a

---

[59] Misner, *"Highly Respectable and Accomplished Ladies,"* 28–29; Spalding, *Premier See*, 107.
[60] Misner, *"Highly Respectable and Accomplished Ladies,"* 227–230.
[61] *Baltimore City Health Department: The First Thirty-Five Annual Reports 1815–1849* (Baltimore, 1953); "Report of the Commissioner of Health," December 31, 1832, n.p.
[62] *Baltimore City Health Department: The First Thirty-Five Annual Reports*; "Report of the Commissioner of Health"; "Consulting Physician's Report," December 31, 1832, n.p.

grocery store, or what would be still worse, a house of ill-repute" prompted the sisters to forestall such an eventuality by buying the property. Joubert noted that "the persons to whom this house belonged felt the need we had of this lot and sold it more dearly, perhaps, than they would have to anyone else but the Sisters."[63] Whether the racial identity or the religious state of the Oblate Sisters evoked such illiberality from the owners of the property remains unclear. Having to pay premium prices for inferior goods and services proved another experience familiar to minority populations in both the nineteenth and twentieth centuries.

The Oblate Sisters of Providence endured without complaint discrimination in the guise of minimal public acknowledgement of their public service and exploitation by unscrupulous businessmen. Yet the racially charged atmosphere of 1830s Baltimore required Joubert and the Oblate Sisters to remain ever alert to potential threats to their physical safety as well.

On October 8, 1834, Joubert noted, "Some alarming rumors had been current for some days of the ill will born to all religious houses of the city and the desire they had to renew in Baltimore the horrible scenes enacted in the Convent of the Ursulines in Charleston near Boston."[64] The "they" referred to nativist agitators. Nativists—descendants of earlier waves of immigrants who considered themselves "native" Americans—feared and resented the newer wave of mostly Catholic immigrants as competition for scarce jobs in the port cities and as purveyors of foreign papism. The "horrible scenes enacted in the Convent of the Ursulines" referred to the violence perpetrated by a nativist mob in Massachusetts that burned the exclusive Ursuline convent school to the ground on August 11, 1834.[65] Convents proved particularly vulnerable targets of nativist wrath during the Jacksonian period. As institutions which allegedly denied freedom of choice to the individual, convents appeared antithetical to the family values of marriage and motherhood. Furthermore, convents "offered a disturbingly different

---

[63] "Original Diary," 5.
[64] "Original Diary," 34.
[65] Misner, "*Highly Respectable and Accomplished Ladies,*" 6–9.

lifestyle that served as a role model for impressionable girls in convent schools."[66]

"A good Catholic of the city" had informed Joubert "of the threats that were made in particular against the Carmelite Sisters and the Colored Sisters"; Joubert consequently applied to the mayor of Baltimore for protection.[67] Anxious about the safety of the Oblate Sisters, Joubert obtained permission from the archbishop to spend the night in the Oblate parlor with two other priests. The night passed without incident, to the relief of all concerned.[68]

Although Joubert attributed this threat against the "colored Sisters" to nativist sentiment, racial animosity provides an equally plausible explanation. In 1833 the abolitionist movement had launched a frontal assault on the institution of slavery, demanding the immediate, uncompensated manumission of slaves. This movement evoked significant anti-Negro reaction in several urban areas. Anti-black sentiment had sparked mob violence against Negroes in New York, Philadelphia, and Columbia, Pennsylvania, in July and August 1834.[69] Reports of these three incidents of racial violence could have instigated the threat against the Oblate Sisters as readily as news of the convent arson in Massachusetts.

Historian Barbara Misner disputed the year reported in the Oblate *Annals* for this threat, primarily because Carmelite sources recorded no similar threat to their order in 1834.[70] Ascribing greater accuracy to the Carmelite than to the Oblate source, Misner concluded that the Oblate incident occurred in 1839 to correspond to mob demonstrations at the Carmelite convent that year.[71] In

---

[66] Joseph G. Mannard, "The 1839 Baltimore Nunnery Riot: An Episode in Jacksonian Nativism and Social Violence," in *Urban American Catholicism: The Culture and Identity of the American Catholic People*, edited by Timothy J. Meagher (New York: Garland Publishing, 1988), 194–195.
[67] "Original Diary," 34.
[68] "Original Diary," 34.
[69] Leon Litwack, *North of Slavery: The Negro in the Free States, 1790–1860* (Chicago: University of Chicago Press, 1961), 100–102.
[70] Misner, "*Highly Respectable and Accomplished Ladies*," 47–48.
[71] Misner, "*Highly Respectable and Accomplished Ladies*," 269; Spalding, *Premier See*, 134.

presuming a monolithically nativist, anti-Catholic motivation which would have targeted both the Carmelites and the Oblates as communities of women religious, Misner has ignored the defining characteristic of race distinguishing the Oblate Sisters from the Carmelites as motivation for mob action.

Historian Joseph Mannard maintained that the nativist mob in 1839 focused exclusively on the Carmelite convent, "threatened neither individual Catholics nor their churches, nor any other religious buildings ... [and] refrained from a wholesale condemnation of the Catholic Church and its convent system."[72] Mannard's argument challenges Misner's insistence on conflating the threat to the Oblate Sisters in 1834 with the Carmelite riot in 1839. If the Oblate Sisters alone among the Baltimore sisterhoods suffered a threat of violence in 1834, racial antipathy as much as nativist anti-Catholic sentiment probably served as animus.

The Oblate Sisters did not directly protest their marginal social status. They functioned within the parameters of racial discrimination sanctioned by Church and society. When Oblate Sister Stanislaus Kostka (Cassandra Butler) died in 1832, Joubert sought from the trustee of the cathedral "a lot in that part of the cemetery where they buried colored people,"[73] without hesitation or comment. In 1837 the sisters evidently agonized over imposing the policy of pew segregation in their new chapel; nevertheless, they implemented this racially discriminatory policy,[74] so prevalent in Catholic churches.

The Oblate Sisters acceded to socially and religiously sanctioned racial discrimination. Yet they resisted real and potential threats to their status as women religious. In 1835 the superior of St. Mary's Seminary, Louis Deluol, requested two Oblate Sisters to manage the domestic affairs of the seminary household. Oblate Superior Mother Mary Lange responded to this request with a letter which reflected her astute grasp of both the promise and the perils of the Oblate community's anomalous position as outsiders within Southern Church

---

[72] Mannard, "The 1839 Baltimore Nunnery Riot," 196–197.
[73] "Original Diary," 18.
[74] "Original Diary," 52.

and society. In a forthright manner, Lange articulated the Oblate perception of their unique racial and religious status:

> We do not conceal the difficulty of our situation [a]s persons of color and religious at the same time, and we wish to conciliate these two qualities in such a manner as not to appear too arrogant on the one hand and on the other, not to miss the respect which is due to the state we have embraced and the holy habit which we have the honor to wear. Our intention in consenting to your request is not to neglect the religious profession which we have embraced.[75]

Lange insisted on the guaranteed integrity of the Oblate religious state as a precondition to Oblate employment at the seminary. Oblate experience with clerical disapproval of the concept of a black sisterhood in 1829 had prompted Lange's apprehensions about full recognition and respect for the Oblate Sisters' religious state at the seminary.

The 1830 and 1840 United States censuses indicated the presence of slaves at St. Mary's Seminary.[76] Citizens of Maryland conflated slaves and free Negroes so thoroughly that they institutionalized this practice and perspective in the distinctive legal phrase "Negroes and other slaves" which recurred in state legislation.[77] The Oblate Sisters might well have questioned their prospective position within the seminary household among certain individuals who conflated slaves and free Negroes or denigrated the idea of black sisters.

Lange stipulated in her letter that Oblate Sisters assigned to the seminary not "have any other relation with the other servants and outside people than our obligations require." She requested "an express prohibition" against visitors in the seminary kitchen to

---

[75] "Original Diary," 38–39.
[76] National Archives: Record Group No. 29, Records of the Bureau of the Census; Fifth Census (1830), population schedules, Maryland, vol. 2, sheet 500; Sixth Census (1840), Maryland, vol. 3, sheet 162.
[77] Jeffrey R. Brackett, *The Negro in Maryland: A Study of the Institution of Slavery*, Johns Hopkins University Studies in History and Political Science, ed. Herbert Adams, Extra Volume VI (Baltimore: Johns Hopkins University, 1889), 32–34; Wright, *The Free Negro in Maryland*, 24–26; Phillips, "'Negroes and Other Slaves,'" 37.

comply with the Oblate Rule enforcing partial cloister.[78] In requesting seclusion of the sisters from the other seminary servants—slave and free—Lange attempted to indemnify for the Oblate Sisters a distinctive social position, based on their status as women religious, among other black people within the seminary household.

In response to Deluol's proposal, Joubert stated that "this unexpected request worried and troubled him and that he wished to remain neutral in the affair, which concerned all at one time."[79] Such sentiments indicated Joubert's own uncertainty about the racial and religious reception the seminary would afford black sisters, perhaps fueled by his personal knowledge of Sulpician opposition to their existence. He enjoined the sisters to seek God's help in their decision-making and to be respectful and humble towards Deluol as "becomes good religious." Otherwise, he left them at full liberty to set their conditions and requested only that he see the letter before the sisters sent it to Deluol.[80]

In his reply Sulpician Superior Deluol addressed Oblate Superior Lange on terms of unaccustomed equality. He denied any intention "to enter in any manner into the borders of your Community." He requested reciprocal rights of consultation on the sisters assigned to the seminary and prior notification of any changes, "as I need not tell you that a Superior can sometimes make remarks which deserve consideration."[81] In answer to Lange's numerous stipulations, Deluol responded, "You write the paper which shall contain the conditions under which you will come and I shall sign it."[82]

Deluol may have neither intended nor attached any racial significance to his request that Oblate Sisters serve in a domestic capacity at the seminary. Evidently the custom of procuring the services of women religious to perform domestic duties in seminaries and

---

[78] "Original Diary," 39.
[79] "Original Diary," 38.
[80] "Original Diary," 38
[81] "Original Diary," 40.
[82] "Original Diary," 40.

colleges originated in France.[83] Sisters of Charity served in this capacity at Mount St. Mary's College at Emmitsburg, Maryland, from 1815 to 1852.[84] Yet the racial component inherent in the Lange-Deluol correspondence certainly heightened the exceptional nature of the assertiveness of the black sister and the acquiescence of the white priest within the contexts of the antebellum South and Roman Catholic Church.

The pursuit of spiritual perfection—the common, primary goal of all religious life—provided a unique perspective which viewed suffering and hardship meekly endured as purifying experiences in imitation of Jesus Christ.[85] From their inception the Oblate Sisters had demonstrated such religious devotion and committed spirituality that in 1834 Father John Odin reported to the Society for the Propagation of the Faith that "piety and fervor reign among them, and they are rendering a great service to religion."[86]

The Oblate Sisters of Providence experienced in common with their peer sisterhoods purifying trials of poverty, cold, hunger, and other hardships. But these black women religious utilized their spiritual agency to transmogrify the racial slights, indignities, and humiliations that the institutional Church as well as American society imposed on them into purifying trials unique to their experience.

In forming a community of black women religious within the Roman Catholic Church, the Oblate Sisters of Providence had exercised their spiritual agency to indemnify the virtue of black women in defiance of prevailing social attitudes. In responding to incidents of racial discrimination—even within the Catholic Church—as opportunities for spiritual transcendence, they exercised their

---

[83] Mary Ewens, *The Role of the Nun in Nineteenth Century America* (Ph.D. dissertation, University of Minnesota, 1971; reprint, Salem, NH: Ayer Company Publishers, 1984), 104.

[84] Misner, *"Highly Respectable and Accomplished Ladies,"* 262; correspondence with John W. Bowen, S.S., Sulpician Archivist Emeritus, October 20, 1996.

[85] Eileen Mary Brewer, *Nuns and the Education of American Catholic Women, 1860–1920* (Chicago: Loyola University Press, 1987), 22.

[86] *Annales De La Propagation De La Foi*, vol. 7, English translation typescript copy, OSPA.

spiritual agency to transform intended racial denigration and humiliation into spiritual benefit, in defiance of prevailing social intent.

The blossoming of the Oblate community in 1830s Baltimore proved a remarkable achievement. These black women religious both challenged and responded to the prevailing attitudes of the Catholic Church and the South about race, gender, religion, and ethnicity. As Oblate Sisters of Providence, women of color in the antebellum South utilized their piety and spiritual fervor to defy their socially ascribed inferior status and to exercise agency in service to others. As black people, as women, as Roman Catholics, as religious living in community, the Oblate Sisters formed the antithesis of the white, male, Protestant family patriarch who typified the empowered citizen in nineteenth-century American society. Oblate membership never exceeded twenty sisters before 1860. Nevertheless, this small band of determined women forged an institution suffused with religious fervor and inculcated into their communal consciousness positive senses of themselves as black women and as committed religious, in defiance of their racially derived status as "other" or outsiders within Church and society. Their spiritually empowered self-image prevailed for the Oblate membership over both the ambivalence toward them as black women religious plaguing the institutional Church and the disdain toward them as both black people and women religious demonstrated by white Southern society.

We've Come This Far by Faith: Black Catholics and Their Church

DIANA L. HAYES*

THE BLACK CATHOLIC BISHOPS of the United States issued their first pastoral letter, "What We Have Seen and Heard," in 1984.[1] They did so in recognition of their belief that "the Black Catholic community in the American Church has now come of age." This coming of age, they noted, "brings with it the duty, the privilege and the joy to share with others the rich experience of the 'Word of Life.'"[2]

Today, we are witnesses to further signs of that coming of age. We African American Catholics[3] are claiming our rightful place in the Roman Catholic Church, nationally and globally. Basing our claim for recognition and inclusion on our history in the American church that predates the Mayflower, our persistent faith gives living expression to the "Word of Life" that we have received and that we fully embrace:

> You are no longer strangers and sojourners, but you are fellow citizens with the saints and members of the household of God, built upon the foundation of the apostles and prophets, Christ Jesus himself being the cornerstone, in whom the whole structure is joined together and grows into a holy temple in the Lord; in whom you also are built into it for a dwelling place of God in the Spirit (Eph 2:19–22).

---

* This essay was first published in *U.S. Catholic Historian* 19, no. 2 (Spring 2001): 15–25.
[1] *"What We Have Seen and Heard": A Pastoral Letter on Evangelization from the Black Bishops of the United States* (Cincinnati: St. Anthony Messenger Press, 1984).
[2] *"What We Have Seen and Heard,"* 2.
[3] In this work, "African American Catholic" and "Black Catholic" will be used interchangeably to depict Catholics of African descent now living in the United States, whether their arrival in this country lies in the distant past or in the present.

Strangers and sojourners no longer, African American Catholics will no longer be required, in the words of the Psalmist, to "sing the Lord's song in a foreign land" (Ps 137). Instead, we are taking down our harps and converting that "foreign land" into a homeland, one rich with the woven tapestries of our voices, lifted in praise and song; of our spirituality expressed in deep and heartfelt prayer and preaching; and of our cultural heritage—a colorful mixture of peoples of Africa, the Caribbean, the West Indies, South America, and North America.

Evidence of this newfound land can be seen throughout the United States today in dioceses large and small, rural, urban, and suburban; all blessed and invigorated by the presence and spirit of Black Catholics who are busy about the work of Jesus Christ. We are seeking, in Jesus' name, to "preach good news to the poor,... to proclaim release to the captives, and recovering of sight to the blind, to set at liberty those who are oppressed, to proclaim the acceptable year of the Lord" (Lk 4:18-19). For in their holistic worldview all of life is necessarily interconnected; the sacred and the secular, the workplace and the Church, are all imbued with the spirit of God and thus are the responsibility of people of faith.

A New Birth

In many ways the voices of these new and yet-so-old Catholics can be understood as calling forth a new witness. We see ourselves as "a chosen race, a royal priesthood, a holy nation, God's own people" who work to "declare the wonderful deeds of him who called [us] out of darkness into his marvelous light." Throughout our existence in the United States, we were seen as "no people," but today African American Catholics affirm that we "are God's people"; once little mercy was given us "but now [we] have received mercy" from God on high (1 Pt 2:9-10).

As part of that witness, we recognize the necessity of exposing the inaccurate education received by all, of whatever race, who dwell in this land regarding the contributions of our Black and Catholic foremothers and forefathers to the present status of the United States. The truth of our history, both in this and other adopted lands and in our motherland as well, must be recovered, for that history reveals the proud and distinctive heritage that is ours, one which predates the Greek and Roman empires as well as Christopher Columbus. We Black Catholics must also tell our story within our Church, a story which has as part of its richness a cherished role in the life of the Church dating back to Africa. For it was our African foremothers and forefathers who received the teachings of Christ from the Church's earliest beginnings; they who nurtured and sheltered those teachings, preserving them from the depredations of those still pagan; they who received, revitalized, and rechristianized those teachings, too often distorted at the hands of their would-be masters, in the new lands of the Americas. As Father Cyprian Davis has written of those early years of African history:

> Long before Christianity arrived in the Scandinavian countries, at least a century before St. Patrick evangelized Ireland, and over two centuries before St. Augustine would arrive in Canterbury, and almost seven centuries before the conversion of the Poles and the establishment of the kingdom of Poland, this mountainous Black kingdom [Ethiopia] was a Catholic nation with its own liturgy, its own spectacular religious art, its own monastic tradition, its saints, and its own spirituality.[4]

This cherished heritage must, once again, be brought forth, exposed to the light of a new day, and shared with all of the Catholic Church.

Arguably, one can say that the continued presence of Black Catholics in the Catholic Church in the United States serves as a subversive memory, one which turns all of reality upside-down, for it is a memory of hope brought forth from pain, of perseverance maintained in the face of bloody opposition, and of faith born of tortured struggle. It is the memory of a people forced to bring forth life from conditions conducive only to death, much as Christ himself was restored to life after a scandalous death. Ours is a memory of

---

[4] Cyprian Davis, O.S.B., "Black Spirituality: A Catholic Perspective," in *One Faith, One Lord, One Baptism: The Hopes and Experiences of the Black Community in the Archdiocese of New York*, vol. 2 (New York: Archdiocese of New York, Office of Pastoral Research, 1988), 45.

survival against all odds. It is the memory of a people, born in a strange and often hostile land, paradoxically celebrating Christ's victory over death as a sign of God's promise of their eventual liberation from a harsh servitude imposed by their fellow Christians. Today, we Black Catholics are affirming that we are no longer sojourners, we are no longer just passing through; we are here to stay and intend to celebrate our presence as only we can.

The Persistent Presence of Racism

This memory becomes even more challenging when we recognize the demographic shifts taking place both in the United States and in the Roman Catholic Church as we enter upon the third millennium. The most recent U.S. Census statistics present a picture of a very different American society and American Catholic Church, one in which persons of color, as a whole, are the majority rather than the minority. African American Catholics will be a part of this majority, which can be seen, depending on one's perspective, as threatening to the very stability and identity of both church and state or simply as a sign of the changing times that must be dealt with.

These changes do provide a critical challenge for us as Church today as we seek to affirm the new understandings of theology, ministry, and liturgy that are already emerging from persons heretofore marginalized on the Church's periphery. Black Catholic theology is only one example of these shifts in understanding that must be acknowledged and placed in dialogue within the academy and the Church. This theology was born out of the struggle to maintain both our Catholic faith and our Black culture in the face of the racism that still besets our Church, institutionally and individually. The Pontifical Peace and Justice Commission noted in 1989:

> Today racism has not disappeared. There are even troubling new manifestations of it here and there in various forms, be they spontaneous, officially tolerated or institutionalized.... The victims are certain groups of persons whose physical appearance or ethnic, cultural or religious characteristics are different from those of the dominant group and are interpreted by the latter as being signs of

innate and definite inferiority, thereby justifying all discriminatory practices in their regard.[5]

Racism is a fact of life that continues to torment Black Americans regardless of their particular faith. It has its roots in the very foundations of our society, where, in drafting the Constitution, the enslavement of Blacks was recognized and accepted. The revolutionary phrases of the Founding Fathers, proclaiming liberty and justice for all and declaring the equality of all "men," ignored the condition of Black humanity. As the late Supreme Court Justice Thurgood Marshall noted, "The famous first three words of that document, 'We the People,' did not include women who were denied the vote, or blacks, who were enslaved."[6] The intent was clearly expressed in the notification that Blacks counted as only three-fifths of a White person and then only for the purpose of White male representation in the new Congress. The Constitution was developed not as a color-blind document but as one assuring the hegemony of White, propertied males over all others living in the newly formed union.

Racism has changed its face, however. Rather than the blatant, overt racism of prior years, today we are confronted with a more sinister, because less visible, form of covert racism. Institutional racism "originates in the operation of established and respected forces in the society and thus receives far less public consideration."[7]

As such, institutional racism is more than a form "sanctioned by the Constitution and laws of a country,"[8] as the Vatican commission suggests. For even after that Constitution has been expunged of its color bias, and the laws mandating segregation and second-class citizenship have been removed, the aura of institutionalized racism still persists. It persists in the very warp and woof of that society which

---

[5] "The Church and Racism: Toward a More Fraternal Society," *Origins* 18, no. 37 (February 23, 1989): 617.

[6] In Janet Dewart, ed., *The State of Black America, 1988* (New York: National Urban League, 1988), 6.

[7] S. Carmichael and C. V. Hamilton, *Black Power: The Politics of Liberation in America* (New York: Vintage Books, 1967), 4.

[8] "The Church and Racism," 617.

has, for so long, been imbued with an ideology supported all too often by an erroneous interpretation of the teachings of Sacred Scripture.

The 1960s and 1970s saw significant changes in the laws governing American society with regard to African Americans. Yet, today, many of those changes are being nullified and labeled as preferential treatment, thereby ignoring the centuries of slavery and second-class citizenship that have hindered the descendants of African slaves from attaining equal opportunity before the law. All too often persons of faith have been silent in the face of these assaults against the human dignity of persons of color.

Racism still persists. It is a mindset that flies in the face of Sacred Scripture and the teachings of the Christian church. It is a distortion of the teaching that "all are endowed with a rational soul and are created in God's image."[9] Racism is incompatible with God's design. It is a sin that goes beyond the individual acts of individual human beings. Racism, to be blunt, is sin that becomes a constituent part of the framework of society, sin that is the concentration to the infinite of the personal sins of those who condone evil.

The U.S. Catholic bishops have affirmed this understanding:

> The structures of our society are subtly racist, for these structures reflect the values which society upholds. They are geared to the success of the majority and the failure of the minority. Members of both groups give unwitting approval by accepting things as they are. Perhaps no single individual is to blame. The sinfulness is often anonymous but nonetheless real. The sin is social in nature in that each of us in some measure are accomplices. . . . The absence of personal fault for an evil does not absolve one of all responsibility. We must seek to resist and undo injustices we have not caused, lest we become bystanders who tacitly endorse evil and so share in guilt for it.[10]

---

[9] Vatican II, *Gaudium et Spes*, https://www.vatican.va/archive/hist_councils/ii_vatican_council/documents/vat-ii_const_19651207_gaudium-et-spes_en.html, no. 29.

[10] National Conference of Catholic Bishops, *Brothers and Sisters to Us: The U.S. Bishops' Pastoral Letter on Racism in Our Day* (Washington, DC: United States Catholic Conference, 1979), 3.

Reflecting on the Journey

Theology, in its simplest understanding, can be seen as "God-talk." We, as African American Catholics, often become intimidated when asked to reflect theologically on a matter of importance to us, such as our relationship with God or how we see our role in the Church, because we see ourselves as academically unqualified. There are too few of us with academic degrees in systematic theology. Yet, when asked to simply talk about God's action in our lives or the working of the Holy Spirit in our midst, our reaction is quite different.

Although the world of academe may not recognize our reflections as such, we are indeed speaking theologically when we do this. And as African Americans, we have been doing so for all of our existence. What we have done, as a holistic people in whom the sacred and secular are intertwined rather than alienated, is simply to talk about God, about Jesus Christ, about the Holy Spirit, and about their importance in our lives, a God that you can lean on, a brother you can depend on in your darkest hours, a Spirit who walks with you and brings peace to a troubled soul. We have not put our theology down in dry, dusty tomes that no one can or really wants to read; we have lived it in the midst of our daily lives. That theology has been expressed most clearly in our songs, in our stories, in our prayers. We talk of a God who saves, a God who preserves, a God who frees and continues to free us from the "troubles of this world."

Theology also can be seen as "interested conversation." In other words, theology is talk, dialogue, discussion, conversation about God and God's salvific action in the world, not from an objective, unbiased stance—because no such stance truly exists—but from the perspective of one who is "involved," one who is caught up in that discussion, one whose involvement is "colored," as it were, by his or her own history, heritage, and culture. We cannot speak about the Church, Jesus Christ, or anything else except from within the context of who we are, a people caught in a daily struggle to survive despite the constant assaults of racism, prejudice, and discrimination from the institutional structures of both our society and our Church.

This is to say, on one hand, that there are as many different theologies within the Church as there are persons talking about God, but, on the other hand, that all of these theologies have, as their foundation, the context of Roman Catholicism with its particular teachings, traditions, and faith beliefs. Our theology as African American Catholics is "interested conversation" about that "ultimate reality" which is central to the core of our being, our faith in Jesus Christ. As such, it cannot be understood or conceived of apart from our being and the place in which we find ourselves. All theologies are particular, rooted in and arising from a particular context, the context of the people engaged in their development. Theology arises out of their loves and their angers, their joys and their sorrows, their sufferings and their hopes for a better tomorrow as they express these in the light of their faith.

Today, we, as an African American Catholic people, are engaged in the development of a theology that speaks truly to us and expresses who we are and whose we are for the enlightenment of the entire Church.

We are African Americans: a people with roots deeply sunk in the history and culture of our African homeland yet also a people with a long and proud history in these United States. Both strands of our heritage are important in defining who we are. Neither can be denied without denying an important part of our very selves. That understanding of "who we are and whose we are" affects our theologizing. It "colors," quite simply, our concept of God, our faith in Jesus Christ, our existence in the Holy Spirit, our total understanding of what it means to be truly Black and authentically Catholic. Our reflections are not abstract or objective; they are particular because they are grounded in the particular context of African American history, which is a history of slavery, of second-class citizenship, of discrimination, both in U.S. society and our mother Church as well. More importantly, it is also a history of struggle, of perseverance, of hope, of faith, and of survival against all odds and all obstacles placed in our path.

As a holistic people, however, the pain does not outweigh the hope, the struggle does not diminish the faith. We rejoice in the intertwining, rather than the separation, of the many strands of our life, for we are a people for whom religious faith has been and remains an integral part of who and what we are. Thus, the context of our theologizing is a grounding in our faith, examined in the light of Christ's teachings and a religious tradition dating back to the early Church. Accordingly, our lives must be a witness to the ongoing and pervasive presence of the gospel within us and must reflect that presence back into the world in which we live.

We therefore cherish our memories, painful though they may often be, for they serve as subversive memories, memories that turn all of reality upside-down, as Jesus Christ did in his life, death, and resurrection. These memories transform that which is seen as worthless to that which is of the highest value. We remember, not with an eye toward revenge but in order to prevent faintheartedness in the struggle. We remember that we, as a people, survived and continue to survive despite it all. The apostle Paul's words have a particular significance for us: "God chose what is foolish in the world to shame the wise, God chose what is weak in the world to shame the strong, God chose what is low and despised in the world, even things that are not, to bring to nothing things that are" (1 Cor 1:27–28).

We have been, and too often continue to be, seen as the "low and despised" in the world in which we find ourselves, but paradoxically we see ourselves also as that chosen race and priestly people commissioned to overturn the inaccurate education of ourselves and all Americans regarding African Americans. Knowledge and understanding of our chosenness comes to us from our God, who nurtured and sustained us like a bridge over the troubled waters of our sojourn here. It is from God that we received our faith, and it is to God that we turn in the bosom of our Church, the Roman Catholic Church. For it is the Church that our foremothers and forefathers nurtured and sustained long before many who now claim total ownership of it even knew of its existence.

Black Catholics have remained in the Church, feeling both love and hate, forgiveness and frustration, concern and impatience. We, too, the darker brothers and sisters of this country, are a vital and vibrant part of the Roman Catholic Church. We, too, have gifts of song, story, and praise to offer the Church universal. And we know that those gifts are not only needed but welcomed by the number of our Catholic brothers and sisters who attend our services of worship and even join our gospel choirs, recognizing, perhaps, the absence in their lives of a joy-filled praise of God that brings a comforting peace.

Yet, still, we wonder at the coldness with which we are so often received and at the anger that is directed toward us. How do we prove that we are who we say we are? Why must we even do so? As W. E. B. Du Bois recognized almost a century ago, African Americans, and especially African American Catholics, are often caught in a quandary. He states:

> It is a peculiar sensation, this double consciousness, this sense of always looking at one's self through the eyes of others, of measuring one's soul by the tape of a world that looks on in amused contempt and pity. One ever feels his twoness—an American, a Negro; two souls, two thoughts, two unreconciled strivings; two warring ideals in one dark body, whose dogged strength alone keeps it from being torn asunder.[11]

This has been our quandary in the four hundred years of our sojourn in this land. But the confusion is now at end; the turmoil is over; the strivings are reconciled. There is evidence throughout this nation that our Catholic African American sisters and brothers are taking down their harps from the walls, they are taking them out of the dark trunks and closets where they have been gathering the dust of the ages and are proclaiming, as our poetic brother did years ago, that we, too, sing America.

We are proclaiming to the Church and the world at large that to be Black and Catholic is not a paradox; it is not a conflict; it is not a contradiction. To be Black and Catholic is correct, it is authentic, it is who we are and have always been. For, ironically, it must also be recognized that questions about our faithfulness have come not just from our Catholic family but from the greater Black community. This is further evidence of the critical need for the full history of the

---

[11] W. E. B. Du Bois, "Of Our Spiritual Strivings," in *The Souls of Black Folk* (New York: New American Library [Signet Classics], 1969), 45.

African presence in early Christianity as well as in the United States predating the English-speaking Protestant colonies to be told. For in so telling, naysayers will have to acknowledge that there have been African peoples in the Catholic Church as long as that Church has existed. Black faith is not and cannot be limited to one church or one expression. But it does share in a richness of heritage that predates Christianity and continues to shape and form it into a new creation.

The time finally has come for African American Catholics to articulate fully our self-understanding and to present that articulation not only to our brothers and sisters in the Roman Catholic Church but to all with whom we come into contact. If theology is "God-talk," if it is "interested conversation," then we must become full and active participants in that conversation, one which has been going on for too long a time without our input.

In our gatherings, discussions, dialogues, days of reflection, revivals, and congresses, we are developing a theology, a way of speaking about God, Jesus, the Holy Spirit, the Church and all that pertains to them in a way that is indigenous to us, that is Afri-centric, that is truly Black and authentically Catholic. Our way of doing theology stems from our understanding of and faith in a God who is an active, interested, and loving participant in our history.

We say this not to be divisive, not to deny the truths and teachings of our Catholic faith, but simply to acknowledge for ourselves and to demand from others the recognition of our distinctive Catholicity, a Catholicity with African roots and myriad branches.

Speaking the Truth

It is time to "speak the truth to the people."[12] It is time for the history of the darker peoples of the Catholic Church to be set forth so that all can learn not only of the dark days of colonization and enslavement but also of the days of civilizations ancient and

---

[12] Mari Evans, "Speak the Truth to the People," in *Trouble the Water: 250 Years of African-American Poetry*, ed. by Jerry W. Ward Jr. (New York: Mentor, Penguin Group, 1997), 217–219.

renowned throughout the world. Instead of others' stories, we must learn of and share our stories so that we see ourselves as a new people empowered by our knowledge to take our rightful place in the ranks of peoples of the world. Pope Paul VI noted when in Africa that we, as Africans and people of African descent, are now missionaries to ourselves. He stated further: "You must now give your gifts of Blackness to the whole church,"[13] a sentiment reaffirmed by Pope John Paul II in his meeting with Black Catholics in 1987.

We must learn of ourselves and then share that knowledge with others. "We have come this far by faith," in the words of our gospel heritage, and we will and must continue to explore and uncover the truth of our past so that we may move forward into the future.

African American Catholics have retained, despite the strains of slavery, segregation, discrimination, and second-class citizenship, a steadfast faith in God. Remaining unseduced by the distortions of Christianity force-fed them during slavery, they have always believed in a God who saves, one who was on the side of the poor and oppressed, like them. This steadfast faith in a God who promised eventual deliverance grounds all that is said and done, providing thereby a freedom, both spiritual and physical, for there is no dichotomy between the life lived on earth and the life to be lived with the coming of the Kingdom.

In order to learn of ourselves, in order to understand and accept "who and whose" we are, we must reflect on both faith and its praxis, seeking to understand for ourselves, in language of our own choosing, the constant presence of God within our lives while recognizing with St. Anselm that theology in its truest sense is "faith seeking understanding." We must then share that understanding with all of the Church. For it is in learning the "truth" of ourselves that we are empowered to continue the struggle, "leaning on the everlasting arms" of our God.

---

[13] "To the Heart of Africa," Address to the bishops of the African Continent at the closing session of a symposium held in Kampala, Uganda, in *The Pope Speaks* 14 (1969), 219.

Plenty Good Room

We are all called to defend the faith that is ours (1 Pt 3:15). This is especially true on the local level, for it is in the parish setting that we are called upon to spread the gospel of Jesus Christ, both in and outside of the Church itself. We are all called as Christian faithful who have been anointed in baptism to share in the mission and ministry of Christ (canon 204). It is our responsibility and our joy to evangelize, to spread the good news of the life, death, and resurrection of our Lord and Savior Jesus Christ to all around us. This must be done for those outside the Church but even more so for those within. We must rekindle the spirit of love within the hearts of our brothers and sisters in Christ. But we must do so in a way that is uniquely ours. As a people of God, we are called to witness to the working of the Holy Spirit within us, while recognizing the different gifts which the Spirit has bestowed.

It is the Spirit of God which has empowered us as African American Catholics to speak of our faith and to present that faith without shame, recognizing that as African American Catholics, we are "no longer simply recipients of the ministry of others, [but] are called to be full participants in the life and mission of the Church, on both the local and national levels."[14]

It is now time for African American Catholics to take ownership of this Church in which they have for so long lived marginalized and often alienated lives. We are called to express that ownership in all that we say and do, in our workshops, programs, liturgies, parishes, and every part of our lives.

Today we recognize and affirm that to be both Black and Catholic is not a contradiction but a proclamation of historical pride, for to be truly Black and authentically Catholic means that we, as an African and American and Catholic people, have, indeed, come of age and are beginning to act in accordance with our adulthood. It means that we

---

[14] "Here I Am, Send Me: The U.S. Bishops' Response to the Evangelization of African Americans and the National Black Catholic Pastoral Plan," *Origins* 19, no. 30 (December 28, 1989), 487.

are challenging the all-too-prevalent understanding of Roman Catholicism as a Western, Euro-centric religion. We are proclaiming by our presence in the Church that there is, indeed, "plenty good room" in our Father's Kingdom for a diversity of expressions of the Catholic faith. We are challenging the Church Catholic to acknowledge that recognition and acceptance of the cultures and heritages of the many peoples who make up the Church, as they are lived out in the faith and worship of these people, are no longer luxuries but necessities. Otherwise, there is the risk of preaching not the transcendent Christ, but a cultural Christ, one who is embodied in a particular time, a particular context, a particular culture.

As the Church finally opens itself to the contributions of peoples of every race and ethnicity, it must also expand its understanding and expression of God and Jesus Christ. This correlates with our understanding of the incarnation of Jesus Christ. If God became incarnate in a human being, a male, a Jew, taking on all of the characteristics and appearances of that humanity, so must the Church, expressive of Christ's body, incarnate itself today in the peoples and cultures with whom it has come in contact. This is not optional; it is mandated.

There is "plenty good room" in God's Kingdom. We must only choose our seats and sit down. As African American Catholics, however, we must ensure not only that we are doing the choosing but that the seats actually "fit" us, that we have participated fully in their construction and placement at the center, not the periphery, of our Church.

As Black Catholics we are full members of the Catholic communion. We have struggled for a long time, but the journey is nearing its end. As we continue towards that end, we take as our mandate the words of the prophet Isaiah: "They who wait upon the Lord shall renew their strength, they shall mount up with wings like eagles, they shall run and not be weary, they shall walk and not faint" (40:31). Our faith has not faltered, and our Spirit has been renewed. We are truly Black and authentically Catholic. As we continue to deepen our own understanding of ourselves, we offer the gift of ourselves to the Roman Catholic Church, acknowledging that there is still much work to be done. Yet, we have come this far by faith, and that faith will in time lead us home.

Called to Be Leaven: Reflections on African American Catholic Spirituality

CYPRIAN DAVIS, O.S.B.*

DANIEL RUDD, JOURNALIST, lecturer, polemicist, convinced Catholic, and newspaper editor, was directly responsible for the convening of the first Black Catholic Lay Congress in 1889. In the columns of his newspaper, the *American Catholic Tribune*, Rudd talked about the importance of Black Catholics coming together to know each other and to exchange ideas. He saw them as uniting among themselves and, as he put it, "taking up the cause of the race." Expressing it in another way, he wrote: "Colored Catholics should step forward and convince their people, that none love them better; none [are] more anxious for their welfare; none more ready to advance their cause than their brethren of the Catholic Church."[1] Rudd was responding to the notion that "[the] Colored Catholic must at times, feel that his Colored brethren look upon him as an alien"; in other words, one who did not fit into the African American world.

In response to this notion, Rudd suggested that the African American Catholic community had what one might call "a mission." He defined this mission in this way: "The Catholics of the Colored race should be the leaven, which would raise up their people not only in the eye of God but before men." Later in the article, he referred to Black Catholics in this country as deliberating together and "uniting on a course of action, behind which would stand the majestic Church of Christ, they must inevitably become . . . the bearer of their race." Typically, Rudd unconsciously had lapsed into the language of Scripture. This leaven or yeast is from the parable of the woman preparing

---

* This essay was first published as "Some Reflections on African American Catholic Spirituality," *U.S. Catholic Historian* 19, no. 2 (Spring 2001): 7–14.
[1] *American Catholic Tribune*, May 4, 1888.

to bake bread: "To what shall I compare the kingdom of God? It is like yeast that a woman took and mixed in with three measures of wheat flour until the whole batch of dough was leavened."[2] The number of Black Catholics might be small, but, like the Kingdom, they can transform the entire Black American community.

The notion of being "bearers of the race" suggests Paul's Letter to the Galatians: "Even if a person is caught in some transgression, you who are spiritual should correct that one in a gentle spirit, looking to yourself, so that you also may not be tempted. Bear one another's burdens, and so you will fulfill the law of Christ."[3] Rudd seems to say that the African American Catholic community is called to bear the burdens of race. It is called to bear some responsibility for solving some of the problems besetting the African American community. Such words as "leaven" and "bearing burdens" suggest a people not only called upon to make a certain self-sacrifice and self-giving but also possessing a certain vocation. To put it in other words, the Black Catholic community has its own spiritual ethos.

Is There a Black Spirituality?

Spirituality is one of those words that everyone seems to use without precisely defining it. For many Protestants the word means devotion and devotional practices. Catholics, on the other hand, speak of the Inner or Interior Life, the life of the spirit, the life of prayer, or the prayer experience as spirituality. It includes asceticism or discipline, because one cannot pray well without practices that curb the appetites and create good habits or virtues. As we are physical beings, our prayer experience is affected by our language and bodily expression. Whatever may be our ascetical practices, they are always within the context of a given culture. Moreover, whatever may be our cultural environment, the discipline that governs our behavior varies from culture to culture and from people to people. Thus, we speak of classical French spirituality, meaning the writings of

---

[2] Lk 13:21; also Mt 13:33.
[3] Gal 6:1-2. See also Col 3:13: "Put on then, as God's chosen ones, holy and beloved, heartfelt compassion, kindness, humility, gentleness, and patience, bearing with one another and forgiving one another."

Cardinal de Bérulle, St. Francis de Sales, and others of seventeenth-century France. We speak of the school of English spirituality in the fourteenth century, and we think of the *Cloud of Unknowing*, works by Richard Rolle, and the *Revelations* of Julian of Norwich. The ways of searching for God and experiencing his presence in our lives is not done within a vacuum but in a cultural context.

For African Americans this context is the African experience lived out in America. Jamie Phelps, O.P., wrote in an article on African American spirituality: "Black spirituality is a vital and distinctive spirituality forged in the crucible of the lives of various African peoples.... No matter where or when they live, black people are fundamentally *African* people, whose perspective and way of life have been conditioned by their roots in Mother Africa."[4]

African Spirituality

Chris Egbulem, a Nigerian Dominican theologian, summarized African spirituality under several basic themes: God is the creator of all and all creation is one and good; life on all levels is God's gift; each person must find one's meaning within the extended family and the community; and within the context of the community the influence of the ancestors and the handing down of the oral tradition also give meaning. To put it another way, African spirituality embraces all creation as good. There is no dualism, no rejection of the physical and the real. God is our father and mother. All things have their origin in God and his presence permeates all things. The individual is incomplete without the extended family and the community. There is a power in the oral tradition; there is a power in the environment in which we live.[5]

This vision of African spirituality with its sense of the holy and the emphasis on God, who is both transcendent and immanent, is a

---

[4] Jamie Phelps, O.P., "Black Spirituality," in *Spiritual Traditions for the Contemporary Church*, ed. by Robin Maas and Gabriel O'Donnell, O.P. (Nashville: Abingdon Press, 1990), 332–333.

[5] Chris Nwaka Egbulem, O.P., "African Spirituality," in *The New Dictionary of Catholic Spirituality*, ed. by Michael Downey (Collegeville, MN: Liturgical Press, 1993), 17–21.

part of that spiritual gift that Pope Paul VI challenged all Africans to give to the whole Catholic Church. Challenging the church of Africa to open itself up to the breadth of the Catholic tradition, he called on Africans to let themselves "be capable of bringing to the Catholic Church the precious and original contribution of 'negritude.'"[6]

The Seven Black Values

African American Catholics sought their connection with what was considered African values in a program known by its Swahili title as the *Nguzo Saba* (Seven Black Values). The original Swahili names are the following:

> *umoja* (unity)
> *kujichagulia* (self-determination)
> *ujima* (collective work and responsibility)
> *ujamaa* (cooperative economics)
> *nia* (purpose)
> *kuumba* (creativity)
> *imani* (faith)

Although these values, with the exception of *imani* (faith), have seemingly very little religious content, some African American Catholics have formulated their own religious meanings. For example, *kujichagulia*, which means self-determination, is connected with the Gospel of Luke 9:51–53, where Jesus turns his face resolutely towards Jerusalem. Another Scripture passage connected with self-determination is Sirach 15:14: "When God in the beginning, created man, he made him subject to his own free choice." This text is especially connected with the vocation awareness aspect of the youth retreats associated with this self-determination.[7]

---

[6] Pope Paul VI, "To the Heart of Africa," *The Pope Speaks* 14 (1969): 214–220, esp. 219.

[7] See the leaflet "Celebrating African American History Month Resource Packet" (Louisville: Office of Multicultural Ministry of the Archdiocese of Louisville, 1999). One of the first Catholic efforts to utilize the Seven Black Values for a Black Catholic concept of spirituality is found in A. M. McKnight, C.S.Sp., "A Black Christian Perspective of Spirituality," in *Theology: A Portrait in Black, Proceedings of the Black Catholic Theological Symposium*, no. 1 (Pittsburgh: Capuchin Press,

Many African American Catholic programs do have the merit of making this connection between the *Nguzo Saba* and Scripture. Still, this list of Black values is neither African in origin nor religious in its original meaning. The credit for the *Nguzo Saba* goes to Maulana Karenga,[8] head of the Black Studies Program at California State University at Long Beach, California, and director of the African American Cultural Center in Los Angeles. In the 1960s, in the wake of the Black Power movement and the resurgence of Black pride and African culture, Karenga began an intellectual movement known as *Kawaida* (tradition) made up of pan-Africanist thought and socialist ideals. The Black values would serve as the undergirding of this Black nationalist, cultural movement of *Kawaida*.[9] Karenga created *Kwanza*, modeled after a hypothetical African harvest festival. *Kwanza* is celebrated from December 26 to January 1. One Black value is celebrated each day. Special kits are sold with black, green, and red candles and programs. *Kwanza* does not pretend to have any connection with Christmas as a religious celebration.

Is There a Christian Value?

Perhaps it is time for Black Catholics to ask themselves whether Karenga's Seven Black Values are the final word on what Black spirituality should be. Should not there be a more transcendent dimension to Black spirituality? Where is the hunger for God that calls us to enter into the dark cloud of Mount Sinai, where, like Moses, we come face to face with God? Where is that hunger for God that brought Saint Moses the Black to convert from a life of banditry to one of a monk and a priest in the Egyptian desert,

---

1980), 103–112. In this article, McKnight indicates that all spirituality must find its roots in Christ but that Black spirituality is "wholistic." This means that it must include the horizontal dimension of concern for one another as Blacks. Our struggle for liberation is not centered in ourselves. In this way the *Nguzo Saba* should serve as a way to live our Christian life in a way that leads to unity and service.

[8] Karenga was born Ronald McKinley Everett in 1941. See Jack Salzman, David L. Smith, and Cornel West, eds., *Encyclopedia of African-American Culture and History* (New York: Macmillan Library Reference, 1996), s.v. "Karenga, Maulana (Everett, Ronald McKinley)."

[9] *Encyclopedia of African-American Culture and History*, s.v. "Kawaida."

becoming one of the first generation of Christian monks and one of the first Black saints.[10]

John Mbiti once said that "Africans are notoriously religious."[11] Africans are also notoriously spiritual. This desire for the spiritual was not lost in the Middle Passage; the same characteristic is found among African Americans. It is from this fund of religious spirit that we may find some of the spiritual values that comprise African American Catholic spirituality.

African American Catholic Spirituality: The Virtues

When we talk about values, we are really talking about behavior. Certain kinds of behavior are seen as good. The continual effort to practice more perfectly this good behavior is to acquire a habit of goodness. This habit is what the Scholastic theologians called *virtue*. There are different modes of good behavior, and there are different virtues. The virtues are common to all, but each culture places its own value on each virtue. To live out these virtues in the face of opposition and great hardship is to practice heroic virtue. Those who do so are the saints. That is why a review of the saints of a given people or nation at a particular time in history gives us a picture of a people's spirituality.

What are the virtues that typify the spirituality of a Black people? One such virtue is hospitality, which comes out of a sense of community. One cannot live long in Africa without learning that courtesy and politeness are deeply ingrained in the African cultural systems. That courtesy arises from the virtue of hospitality. It is the way Africans learn to relate to others with respect and dignity and contributes to the African respect for the elders. The virtue of hospitality gives rise to magnanimity or generosity, which are clearly important in the African folktales. Ultimately, hospitality, generosity,

---

[10] Saint Moses the Black died around 407 in the Desert of Scete. See Jean-Claude Guy, S.J., *Les Apophtegmes des Peres, Collection Systematique*, chap. I-IX, in *Sources Chretiennes*, 387 (Paris: Les Editions du Cerf, 1993), 68–70.

[11] John S. Mbiti, *African Religions and Philosophy* (London: Heinemann, 1969), 1.

and courtesy find their origins in love. The sense of mystery, of God's presence, and of God's power are all the result of reverence—the habit of prayer—which is one of the important aspects of African American spirituality. This sense of prayer, manifested both in the liturgical worship and in private prayer, is evident in Africa both in dance and in the action of full-length prostration before the Blessed Sacrament.

In the same way, African American spirituality is grounded in the experience of prayer. I had the opportunity to participate in a retreat for Black Catholics in the United States. The theme was prayer. Without any prompting or display of reticence, fifty to sixty laypersons began to speak with enthusiasm about the meaning of prayer, about their parents who showed them how to pray, about the place of prayer in their daily lives, about the necessity "to season all things with prayer," about the place of touching others and holding others as we share with others in prayer, and about the importance of surrendering one's whole self to God in prayer.[12] On another occasion, a ninety-year-old nun from Louisiana described how her Catholic grandmother, a slave, always had her rosary in hand. She prayed the rosary throughout the day and was never found without it. Other nuns in Louisiana explained how their parents, all Catholics, would go into the woods and sing and pray together. In Louisiana, where Black Catholics were segregated within the parish church, a place apart for shared prayer was important.

One salient feature of African American Catholic spirituality is the place of Scripture. Both Black Protestants and Black Catholics utilized Scripture in talks and everyday language. At the Black Catholic Lay Congresses, held from 1889–1894, Black laymen wove allusions to Scripture into their speeches, which Black speakers today would not do. At the 1890 congress held in Cincinnati, William S. Lofton, a Black dentist from Washington, D.C., spoke about the need for Catholic education for Black youth. In speaking about racial prejudice in this country, he used the following examples:

---

[12] Cyprian Davis, O.S.B., "Black Spirituality: A Roman Catholic Perspective," *Review and Expositor* 80 (1983): 97–108, esp. 104–106.

Our efforts would ... [seem] ... so fruitless as to provoke only the ridicule of our enemies. But our daily experience, the unquestionable testimony of historians of all ages, and above all the Old and New Testaments, bear witness to the fact that the infinitely perfect God delights to overcome the strong with the weak, the wise with the simple, and if we provoke the sarcastic ridicule of our enemies, let us call to mind the victory of a David over a Goliath.[13]

Addressing the Fourth Black Catholic Congress in 1893, James Spencer of Charleston, South Carolina, spoke on the necessity for Black parish churches separate from White parishes, but he concluded with a plea for unity:

Differing in language, in habit and in taste, we are all united in the bonds of a common religion, having one Lord, one faith, one baptism, one God and Father of all, who is above all and through all and in us all.[14] ... and [we shall] join in one grand chorus, [in] the beautiful words of Ruth: "Be not against me or desire that I should leave thee and depart, for withersoever thou shalt go I will go, and where thou shalt dwell, I also will dwell; thy people shall be my people, and thy God my God. The land that shall receive thee dying, in the same will I die, and there shall I be buried."[15]

Finally, when Charles Butler addressed the Columbian Catholic Congress in Chicago in 1893 in a talk entitled "The Future of the Negro Race," he too used Scriptural allusions to explain the present situation of the African American. "The history of the [Negroes'] sufferings has been recorded by Him who knows the secrets of all hearts. Their sufferings were not unlike the sufferings of the Israelites of old, who were held in bondage for 400 years." He spoke of the mass movement of Blacks to the North as an "exodus" because "[the Negroes] were willing to endure any hardship short of death to reach a land where, under their own vine and fig trees, they could enjoy the life our Creator intended for them."[16]

---

[13] *Three Catholic Afro-American Congresses* (Cincinnati: American Catholic Tribune, 1898; reprint, New York: Arno Press, 1978), 95.
[14] Eph 3:5–6.
[15] Ru 1:16–17; *St. Joseph's Advocate*, 12th year (1894): 634.
[16] *The World's Columbian Catholic Congresses* (Chicago: J. S. Hyland, 1893), 123.

Saints Among Us

One of the contributions made to the American Catholic Church by African American Catholics has been the gift of holiness.[17] Pope John Paul II has beatified and canonized almost a dozen African men and women who lived lives of heroic charity and extraordinary faith. Saint Martin de Porres, canonized by Pope John XXIII in 1962, lived and worked in Lima, Peru, where he died in 1639. He was a man who displayed immense charity in a life of service and in his profession of healing given freely to all who asked. He was a servant in the Dominican convent there. Dispensing alms, healing, and aid, he reached out to all with humor, concern, and love. Two centuries later in New York City, a former slave from Haiti, the Venerable Pierre Toussaint, who died in 1853, left the memory of unceasing charity shown to others—to homeless Black orphans, to the aristocratic women whose hair he dressed, to the many people to whom he gave a home, a refuge, and money. He did it with humor and grace. All revered him as a saint.

Likewise, two Black American women have had their causes for sainthood introduced in Rome. One, Elizabeth Lange, founded the Oblate Sisters of Providence in 1829 in order to begin a school in Baltimore for the education of girls and later for boys. She founded a community that became the home for the Baltimore Black Catholic community. Service to others was the keynote of the life of Henriette Delille, a free woman of color in New Orleans, who began her community of pious women in the 1840s to serve aged ex-slaves thrown on the mercies of a society that had no place for them. Henriette's community cared for them and many others who found an asylum known as the hospice of the Holy Family, which eventually became the name of the growing community of religious women—the Sisters of the Holy Family. Their service was to the poor, their teaching for young girls of color, and their courses in catechetics for the slaves.

---

[17] Editor's note: This survey of U.S. Black canonization causes was accurate at the time the essay was originally published in 2001. Since this time, additional causes have begun. See Cecilia A. Moore's "Writing Black Catholic Lives: Black Catholic Biographies and Autobiographies," found later in this volume.

Conclusion

Is this Black Catholic spirituality, homegrown on American soil, significantly different from the spirituality of White American Catholics? Probably not, but looked at in another way, the answer is a resounding "yes." Daniel Rudd thought that Black Catholics had a call to be a "leaven" among Black Americans. As Catholics in what many thought to be a White church, they had a particular burden to bear. As Catholics, they were often neglected; as enslaved, they helped build a church; as parishioners they were forced to the back of the same churches. Still, as Catholics they sang their own songs, prayed in their own cadenced phrases, and practiced their own virtues. They found their own space in a sometimes-hostile brand of Catholicism, into which their own spirit was bathed with God's grace and thereby enriched the spirituality of the Catholic Church in America today.

"Gonna Move When the Spirit Say Move": A Black Spirituality of Resistance and Resilience

C. VANESSA WHITE

I'm Gonna Move When the Spirit Say Move
I'm Gonna Move When the Spirit Say Move
When the Spirit Say Move, I'm Gonna Move, O Lord
I'm Gonna Move When the Spirit Say Move.
—African American spiritual

BLACK PEOPLE[1] are a Spirit-filled people. Sister Thea Bowman wrote that black spirituality is at the same time a response to and reflection on black life.[2] It transcends regional differences and socioeconomic backgrounds. Black spirituality has been instrumental through its spiritual and cultural elements for black people to liberate themselves from the internal tyrannies that sequester the soul and destroy the mind.[3] This sense of the Spirit has helped black people survive centuries of oppression, discrimination, alienation, human devaluation, Jim Crow law, lynching, flogging, murder, police beatings and killings, as well as a history of inadequate health care and poor educational systems.

To understand black people, one must understand their spirituality, which is a response to and a reflection on black life and

---

[1] Throughout this text I will use both the term "black" and African American to identify persons whose ancestor were taken from Africa, endured the Middle Passage, were brought to the United States, and then sold into enslavement.
[2] Thea Bowman, F.S.P.A., "Spirituality: The Soul of the People," in *Sister Thea Bowman: Shooting Star* (LaCrosse, WI: Franciscan Sisters of Perpetual Adoration, 1999), 39, reprinted from *Tell It Like It Is: A Black Catholic Perspective in Christian Education* (Oakland, CA: National Black Sisters Conference, 1983).
[3] Carlyle Fielding Stewart, *Soul Survivors* (Louisville, KY: Westminster John Knox Press, 1997), 23.

culture.⁴ This culture and spirituality are rooted in African heritage and colored by the Middle Passage from Africa to America, slavery, the Caribbean and Latin experience, segregation, integration, and the ongoing struggle for liberation. Ingrained in the fabric of black life, it is at once God-awareness, self-awareness, and other-awareness.⁵ As Diana Hayes writes, "African American spirituality is grounded in a devotion to the Holy Spirit and her ability to create possibility in the face of denial.... It is a spiritual story of hope in the face of despair, of quiet determination in the face of myriad obstacles, of a quiet yet fierce dignity over against the denial of humanity."⁶ Ultimately, African American spirituality is one of resistance and resilience.

Cyprian Davis, O.S.B., noted that the context of black spirituality is the African experience lived out in America, an experience of marginalization and devaluation, which shaped the African American religious experience.⁷ To understand this spirituality, it is useful to consider three perspectives regarding these experiences and their effects on the psyche and spirit of this people: W. E. B. Du Bois; Jamie T. Phelps, O.P.; and Paul Gilroy. All three express, in their own unique way, the tension of merging African and Western culture in modernity and post-modernity, providing a lens to journey into the spirituality of black people.

W. E. B. Du Bois, founder of the National Association for the Advancement of Colored People (NAACP) and a leading twentieth-century African American intellectual, stated:

> The Negro is a sort of seventh son, born with a veil and gifted with second sight in this American world—a world that yields him no true self-consciousness, but only lets him see himself through the revelation of the other world. It is a peculiar sensation, this double consciousness, this sense of always looking at one's self through

---

4   Bowman, "Spirituality: The Soul of the People."
5   Bowman, "Spirituality: The Soul of the People," 40.
6   Diana Hayes, *Forged in the Fiery Furnace: African American Spirituality* (Maryknoll, NY: Orbis, 2012), 3.
7   Cyprian Davis, O.S.B., "Some Reflections on African American Catholic Spirituality," *U.S. Catholic Historian* 19, no. 2 (Spring 2001), 8.

the eyes of others, measuring one's self through the eyes of others, measuring one's soul by the tape of a world that looks on in amused contempt and pity. One ever feels the twoness—an American, a negro, two souls, two thoughts, two unreconciled strivings, two warring ideals in one dark body, whose strength alone keeps it from being torn asunder.[8]

Jamie T. Phelps, O.P., a womanist, systematic theologian, built upon Du Bois' insights in considering African American Catholics:

African American Catholics experience a double invisibility, marginalization and devaluation. In the Black world we are marginalized because of our religious identity as Catholics, and in the Catholic world we are marginalized because of our racial identity as African Americans.... Black Catholics simply wish to make it possible to be Black, Catholic and American without being cursed and spit upon, devalued and marginalized by other Blacks, Catholics or Americans.[9]

Paul Gilroy expressed how African Americans' struggle for personhood in the nineteenth and twentieth centuries shaped their psyche. He explained their tension to survive as persons of value:

They had to fight—often through their spirituality—to hold on to the unity of ethics and politics sundered from each other by modernity's insistence that the true, the good and beautiful had distinct origins and belong to different domains of knowledge.[10]

These writers articulated particular aspects of black spirituality, especially the reality of marginalization in the United States, but how is black spirituality further defined and expressed? The following helps define and express black spirituality through examining five key characteristics.[11]

---

[8] W. E. B. Du Bois, *The Souls of Black Folk* (New York: New American Library, 1903, 1969), 45.
[9] Jamie T. Phelps, O.P., "African American Catholics: The Struggles, Contributions and Gifts of a Marginalized Community," in *Black and Catholic: The Challenge and Gift of Black Folk* (Milwaukee: Marquette University Press, 1997), 21, 18.
[10] Paul Gilroy, *The Black Atlantic* (Cambridge, MA: Harvard University Press, 1993), 39.
[11] *"What We Have Seen and Heard": A Pastoral Letter on Evangelization from the Black Bishops of the United States* (Cincinnati: St. Anthony Messenger Press, 1984), 9.

Characteristics of African American Spirituality

1. God-Centered: God of Our Mind

God is central in the lives of many people of African descent. God is one who is both immanent and transcendent. God dwells within as well as he sits on the throne. As Diana Hayes states, the immanent God loves and nurtures us like a parent bending low over a child, even as the transcendent God judges those who oppress us and call us forth into freedom.[12] Black people's relationship with Jesus is an example of this personal and immanent God. It is not uncommon for black people's first thought in the morning to be, "Thank you, Jesus." Diana Hayes writes,

> Jesus as immanent humanity is brother, sister and friend; he is in all ways one with us, walking and talking with us, sharing our journey and carrying our burdens, and suffering the pain of our oppression and rejection, yet as transcendent Son of God, he will come forth in glory to lead us to the Promised Land.[13]

The ancestors, grandmothers, grandfathers, aunts, and uncles testified to God's power in their lives. Such phrases as "God, don't ever change" and "There will always be God" infuse their language and speak of black people's concept of God. African Americans have always relied on God's sanctity, mercy, and transformation.[14] This firm belief in God led to mercy for white racists and acceptance of discriminatory practices within the Catholic Church.

The black bishops' 1984 pastoral initially shared with the broader Church four components of African American spirituality: contemplative, holistic, joyful, and communitarian. The characteristics that I list in this essay were first published in C. Vanessa White, "Fruits of the Spirit: Five Spiritual Gifts of African American Catholics," *U.S. Catholic* (August 2002), 40-41.

[12] Diana Hayes, *And Still We Rise: An Introduction to Black Liberation Theology* (New York: Paulist Press, 1996), 171-172.

[13] Hayes, *And Still We Rise*, 172.

[14] Stewart, *Soul Survivors*, 26.

2. Biblically-Rooted: People of the Book

Cyprian Davis taught that black spirituality is a spirituality of the Word.[15] Any serious discussion of African American spirituality must consider the importance of Christian scripture in the identity, formation, and empowerment of black life.[16] African Americans have a personal relationship with Sacred Scripture; their sense of self is based on their understanding and integration of the Word. Even during enslavement, the Bible was not foreign to them. The stories were told and retold in sermons, spirituals, and shouts.[17] The Bible provided a language for African Americans to articulate their thoughts, ideas, and feelings about their lives and their lives in God, who was for them very present in their daily journey.[18] The Bible has had both a liberating and humanizing function in African American life while also remaining a reliable source of inspiration for black survival.[19] Personal relationships with God and love for Scripture have been important for African American families' ecumenical character, bridging the religious gap in families with multiple faith traditions (where the same family could have members who are Catholic, Baptist, Lutheran, A. M. E. Zion, Apostolic, Pentecostal, among others).

3. Joyful, Contemplative, and Holistic: Full of the Spirit

Joy is a hallmark of black spirituality.[20] As a fruit of the spirit, joy among peoples of African descent has sustained them even during the most difficult times. African American people are able to experience joy even and in the midst of suffering. Funerals in the black community are sorrowful experiences as well as celebrations because the person has finally "made it over." While not negating suffering, it focuses on hope in Jesus Christ.

---

[15] Cyprian Davis, O.S.B., "The Black Contribution to a North American Spirituality," *New Catholic World* 225 (July/August, 1982): 183.
[16] Stewart, *Soul Survivors*, 10.
[17] "What We Have Seen and Heard," 4.
[18] Michael I. N. Dash, "The Bible in African American Spirituality," *Good News Bible with Deuterononicals/Apocrypha: Jubilee Edition* (New York: American Bible Society, 2002), 311.
[19] Stewart, *Soul Survivors*, 11.
[20] "What We Have Seen and Heard," 9.

As black spirituality is holistic, feelings are not separate from intellect, and the heart is not separate from the soul. Black people use their entire bodies to express their love of God; their joy is expressed in movement, dance, song, art, sensation, thanksgiving, and exultation. As noted by the black bishops, "Divisions between intellect and emotion, spirit and body, action and contemplation, individual and community, sacred and secular, are foreign to us."[21]

African American people are also a contemplative people, having an awareness of God's presence not through thought but through love.[22] God's presence is experienced at all times and in various ways. It is not uncommon to hear of "resting in the Lord" or observe elders rocking or humming in deep prayer. These indescribable moments of deep spiritual abiding bear the marks of contemplative practice.[23] Lifted up by God's presence, African Americans respond by surrendering and basking completely in marvelous mystery, whether in church on bended knee or at home in labor or at rest.[24] Today we live in a time of great noise and busyness. The emergence of cell phones, Zoom meetings, and the deluge of emails shape an environment that disrupts the ability to listen and dwell in God's Spirit. The lack of contemplative abiding has created a restless longing in black people.[25]

It is not uncommon to hear those in the African American community speak of being led by the Spirit, which propels them in their actions and decisions. During worship and prayer, they are frequently moved to tears, shouts, and raised hands, which attest to the deep joy and peace felt through the dwelling of God's Spirit. The

---

[21] "What We Have Seen and Heard," 8.
[22] William H. Shannon, "Contemplation, Contemplative Prayer," in *The New Dictionary of Catholic Theology*, ed. by Michael Downey (Collegeville, MN: Liturgical Press, 1993), 209.
[23] Barbara A. Holmes, *Joy Unbearable: Contemplative Practices of the Black Church* (Minneapolis, MN: Fortress Press, 2004), 7.
[24] United States Conference of Catholic Bishops, Secretariat for Black Catholics and Secretariat for the Liturgy, *Plenty Good Room: The Spirit and Truth of African American Catholic Worship* (Washington, DC: USCC Publishing, 1990), no. 49.
[25] Holmes, *Joy Unbearable*, 2.

impulse in black spirituality to abandon oneself to the divine will and the indwelling Spirit lends itself to a particularly intimate experience of God.[26] Black spirituality has taught black people what it means to "let go" and "lean on the Lord."

4. Person and Community Focused: All are Welcome

In West African tradition, the "I" is defined by the "we" so that individual identity is found in the context of community. This is expressed in the saying, "I am because we are; and because we are, I am."[27] This is evident in black churches through worship and celebration. Because hospitality and community are gifts of black folk, one cannot enter an authentically black church and not feel that all are welcome in the House of God, and no one stands alone in prayer. This communal aspect of black spirituality shapes the community and, in turn, is shaped by the community.[28]

A story told about Thea Bowman illustrates this communal aspect of African American spirituality.[29] A white seminarian ministering in the black community asked Sister Thea, "Why is it when someone in the black community gets a new car, the people in the neighborhood or community seem to be so happy about it?" Thea answered, "Because if they have a car, then I have a ride." This shared joy is evident today in the African American community.

This person- and community-centered component shape the African American sense of human life's sacredness.[30] Because all human life is sacred and the individual and community are interdependent, it is everyone's responsibility to become good representatives

---

[26] Jamie T. Phelps, O.P., "Black Spirituality," in *Spiritual Traditions for the Contemporary Church*, ed. by Robin Maas and Gabriel O'Donnell (Nashville, TN: Abingdon Press, 1990), 334.
[27] Flora Wilson Bridges, *Resurrection Song: African American Spirituality* (Maryknoll, NY: Orbis, 2001), 108.
[28] Phelps, "Black Spirituality," 342.
[29] Sister Eva Lumas, S.S.S., shared this story at a catechetical seminar at St. Sabina Catholic Church in Chicago over thirty years ago.
[30] Peter Paris, *The Spirituality of African Peoples: The Search for a Common Discourse* (Minneapolis, MN: Fortress Press, 1995), 135.

of their respective communities. A common caution is to avoid bringing shame onto the community (or, more recently, to be "a credit to the race").

5. Justice and Liberation Oriented: Called to Do Justice

African American spirituality leads to freedom. The journey to a closer union with God brings not only personal freedom and authenticity but also invokes a community striving for liberation from all forms of oppression. It leads to prophetic action for justice that requires liberation from sin and its effects.[31] In all human activities, African peoples have been concerned primarily with two forms of justice: (1) individual obligations to the community as mediated through dealings individuals have with one another; and (2) community obligations to itself and its members.[32]

The community- and person-focused nature of African American spirituality profoundly affects how black people treat each other, infusing a sense of social concern and a spirituality moving the person and community to action. Connecting this justice instinct to the Christian message, Jamie Phelps noted:

> Not all black Christians embrace this universal and community centered understanding of the meaning of Jesus' life. They, like some other Christians, believe that the life and death of Christ have nothing at all to do with the ecclesial and social structures of human society, even when these structures suppress the spirit of love, truth, and liberation given to each person and community for building up and preparing God's kingdom.[33]

The absolute criterion of African American spirituality's authenticity is its impact on the quality of the believer's life.[34] The question becomes, do the actions of the community lead to right relationships? Does the person act right and call others to be right?

---

[31] Phelps, "Black Spirituality," 344.
[32] Paris, *The Spirituality of African Peoples*, 152.
[33] Phelps, "Black Spirituality," 345.
[34] Phelps, "Black Spirituality," 344.

Do the person and community struggle for the liberation of oppressed races and nations?[35] In committing to liberation and justice, those imbued with the Spirit must stand for the truth. The sense of right relationship inspires African Americans to do right, act right, and be right. They must walk the path of Jesus, a man of justice who announced the gospel to the poor, oppressed, and marginalized in society and who set the captives free. They must promote justice not only from the pulpit, but in the schools, in their homes, and throughout the world.

Spiritual Foundations of African American Liturgy

Liturgy that does not have meaning for the community is dead. For African American liturgies to express and nourish black people's spirituality, a central focus must be to help translate the absurdities and atrocities of their experience into vital, real, and meaningful idioms.[36] They should facilitate the discovery of new insights and meanings while also challenging the community to live life anew as Christ's disciples so that they recognize themselves in him. If liturgy does not address the Spirit of God, the Catholic faith, and the lived experience of African American people, then it does not transform and liberate. The liberating power of black liturgy lies in its ability to translate black life into meaningful texts of praise, spirituality, and human empowerment.[37]

The liturgy's quality is also important to African Americans. Father Clarence Rivers stated that liturgists and clergy need to be "more concerned with making this particular celebration the best possible celebration for the people involved."[38] But good liturgy is a challenge for more than the celebrant; as Melva Wilson Costen writes, "No participation in ritual action, whether culturally understood or borrowed from other cultures, can be renewing if the intent

---

[35] Jamie Phelps, Lecture at the Institute for Black Catholic Studies, Xavier University of Louisiana, New Orleans, 2000.
[36] Stewart, *Soul Survivors*, 112.
[37] Stewart, *Soul Survivors*, 112.
[38] Clarence J. Rivers, *Soulful Worship* (Washington, DC: National Office for Black Catholics, 1974), 22.

of the Christ event is not rooted in a true desire of the worshipper to be transformed."[39]

Black Religious Expression

In understanding the liturgy's role, it is important to highlight the embodiment of black religious expression in worship's primary components: prayer, preaching and storytelling, music, and movement. Because all the sounds of a people comprise their oral tradition, when recalling faith stories and the people's history, the black person's main mode of communication has always been the oral-aural tradition.[40] Clarence Rivers stated that the term oral-aural might mislead because in these cultures all the senses are engaged without the eyes' dominance.[41] Rivers further explained the particularity of the oral-aural tradition:

> A people whose roots are in a "literate" tradition will tend to listen *to* music. Their other senses are restrained by the tendency of the eye toward uninvolved observation and detachment. Whereas a people whose roots are in an oral tradition have no such restraints and they will inevitably tend to merge with music, to become involved with it, to dance. And if not to actually dance, then at least to give oneself over entirely to the sentiment of the song.[42]

This does not negate the written word but brings attention to a preferred mode of expression. Oral people's language tends to be poetic, which is seen in African American religious experience. The relationship between the African American's oral-aural tradition in liturgy and in religious expression is examined in the following section.

1. Prayer and Ritual

Prayer in the black community connects the individual and the community with the divine. It assumes that God is just and loving

---
[39] Melva Wilson Costen, *African American Christian Worship* (Nashville, TN: Abingdon Press, 1993), 128.
[40] Bowman, "Spirituality: The Soul of the People," 85.
[41] Clarence Joseph Rivers, *The Spirit in Worship* (Cincinnati: Stimuli, 1978), 21.
[42] Rivers, *The Spirit in Worship*, 21.

and the human dilemma is that we cannot always experience and see God's justice and love.[43] Black people would have perished in despair long ago on the slave ships, in the fields, and during the times of lynching, but prayer provided a common source for hope.[44] Their prayer tradition has been one of spontaneity. From deep in the soul, prayers are personal conversations that individuals and the community have with God.[45] Prayers do not have to be written to be invoked, as is evidenced in many black Catholic churches during the prayers of the faithful when intentions are elicited from the assembly. The community participates in the prayers whether vocally, swaying, raising hands, or nodding heads.

As a vital force of liberation that allows free expression of the mind, soul, and heart, black prayer is part of the spiritual empowerment process of African Americans.[46] Through prayer, the individual and community gain a power that propels them forward, believing that "they can do all things through Christ" (Phil 4:13). The prayer tradition expresses the ultimate faith the individuals and community have in God's action.

Ritual is of particular importance in the worship experience of black people, as seen in preaching, ushers, church nurses, deacons, banquets, altar calls, and protocol. Through these, the black personality experiences the specialness of the "holy."[47] In black Catholic communities today, that sense of ritual is found in liturgies and fraternal organizations, such as the Knights of Peter Claver and its Ladies Auxiliary, where ritual remains important.[48]

---

[43] James Melvin Washington, ed., *Conversations with God: Two Centuries of Prayers by African Americans* (New York: Harper Collins Publishers, 1994), xvi.
[44] Stewart, *Soul Survivors*, 116.
[45] Washington, *Conversations with God*.
[46] Stewart, *Soul Survivors*, 116.
[47] Nathan Jones, *Telling the Old, Old, Story: Education Ministry in the Black Community* (Winona, MN: St. Mary's Press, 1982), 48.
[48] The Knights of Peter Claver, a black Catholic national fraternal organization, was founded in 1909. Its motto is "Love through Christian Service."

2. Preaching and Storytelling

African American people know how to tell a story, a gift traceable to slave times, as evidenced in African American folktales and the earlier African tradition of the *griot* (storyteller). The *griot* and the elders were custodians of the collective story, the history, the customs, and the values of the people. Storytelling is still alive today, as witnessed in the home-going service for a beloved family member. The grandmothers, grandfathers, aunts, and uncles tell the "old, old story" of the family to bring it alive for a new generation.

The oral-aural tradition's importance in the African American community makes the preacher's role vital to the worship experience. Preaching must be carried out in the idiom, style, and worldview of a particular people to have meaning.[49] To be effective, a preacher must have a relationship and knowledge of the community's spirituality, give sermons that frequently allude to and are rooted in scripture, and employ a style that includes tonal quality, rhythm, and "call and response."[50]

3. Music

Music is among the most visible expressions of African American spirituality, a living repository of their thoughts, feelings, and will.[51] The first published liturgical document in the African American community was a hymnal. In 1801, Richard Allen, founder of the African Methodist Episcopal Church, published *A Collection of Hymns and Scriptural Songs from Various Authors*, used by enslaved persons and fugitives in worship.[52] Sacred song preserved the

---

[49] Henry Mitchell, *Black Preaching: The Recovery of a Lost Art* (Nashville, TN: Abingdon Press, 1993), 11.

[50] "Call and response" is a form of response to the black preaching style. It allows the community to participate in the preaching with an oral affirmation, such as "Amen," "Thank You, Jesus," or "That's all right" (to name but a few). See Evans E. Crawford with Thomas H. Troeger, *The Hum: Call and Response in African American Preaching* (Nashville, TN: Abingdon Press, 1995).

[51] Bowman, "Spirituality: The Soul of the People," 87.

[52] Wilson Costen, *African American Christian Worship*, 94.

memory of African religious rites and symbols, holistic African spirituality, and rhythms, tones, and harmonies that communicated their deepest feelings across barriers of region and language.[53] Song invites the Holy Spirit to manifest in the midst of the worshipping community.[54] Black sacred song is real, spirit-filled, life-giving, and participatory, through which the worshipping community is not passive but active.[55]

Spirituals were the first African American musical form used by black Catholic communities. Spirituals form a cultural touchstone that reaches back to the roots and early manifestations of the U.S. black religious experience.[56] Their biblical character makes them a desirable expression of Black Catholic worship.[57] Black sacred song has been the source and expression of black faith and devotion, and whether it is folk or composed, rural or urban, traditional or contemporary, it truly is the song of the people.[58]

4. Movement and Dance

Like music, movement, specifically dance, has significant value in the black religious tradition. Traditional West African religions were often defined as dance religions. Within black religious expression, the importance of movement to express faith is evident. The raising and clapping of hands, the stomping of feet, and the overall sense of spiritual abandonment are more clearly seen and experienced in the black church tradition than in other traditions. When the Spirit of the Lord takes hold through music, it is difficult for the

---

[53] Sister Thea Bowman, F.S.P.A., "The Gift of African American Sacred Song," in *Lead Me, Guide Me: The African American Catholic Hymnal* (Chicago: G.I.A. Publications, 1987), 4; Sister Thea Bowman, F.S.P.A., *Readings in African American Church Music and Worship* (Chicago: G.I.A. Publications, 2001), 210.
[54] Phelps, "Black Spirituality," 343.
[55] Bowman, *Readings in African American Church Music and Worship*, 211.
[56] Leon Roberts, "Development of African American Liturgical Music," in *Western Journal of Black Studies* 7, no. 3 (1983): 153, as cited in Mary E. McGann and Eva Marie Lumas, S.S.S., "The Emergence of African American Catholic Worship," *U.S. Catholic Historian* 19, no. 2 (Spring 2001): 33.
[57] *Plenty Good Room*, nos. 61–62.
[58] Bowman, "The Gift of African American Sacred Song," 4, 5.

black person not to express the inner workings of spirit and song through movement.

The power of black religious expression was demonstrated in 1990 when Sister Thea Bowman, one of the founding faculty members of the Institute for Black Catholic Studies at Xavier University of Louisiana, was suffering from cancer and could not teach. Being mostly bedridden and often too weak to speak, the entire Institute, including faculty and students, traveled to Canton, Mississippi, to be with Sister Thea. For over two hours, students and faculty poured out their love for Sister Thea through prayer, song, dance, poetry, storytelling, and preaching. When they arrived, Sister Thea could not sing and could barely sit up because of the pain, but after the presentation she shared her gift, singing the spiritual "Done Made My Vow to the Lord." This was a testament to the beauty and power of black religious expression and its connection to the spirituality of black folk.[59]

Conclusion

African American spirituality is the essence of African American culture and religion and has furthered the struggle for freedom. Unfortunately, as we move into the new millennium, black people's detachment from their spiritual roots has contributed to disconnectedness, isolation, and hopelessness. Having had to confront the recent killings of African Americans by police, the spread of the coronavirus that has disproportionately impacted the black community, and an increasingly evident political and racial divisiveness, there has emerged among black people a fatigue, impacting both spiritual and physical health.

What is needed at this time is a *Sankofa* moment. *Sankofa*, as a word and Adinkra symbol, emerged from Ghana, West Africa, meaning, "fetch back to get it." As black people journey towards wholeness, retrieval of those spiritual gifts that previously sustained the

---

[59] C. Vanessa White, interview with John Feister, for his book: *Sr. Thea's Song: The Life of Thea Bowman* (Maryknoll, NY: Orbis, 2012).

black community is necessary. The example of the six holy men and women of African descent from the United States, whose causes for sainthood have been opened by the Catholic Church, might provide a guide for this *Sankofa* moment.[60] Their lives and spiritual stories highlight the spiritual characteristics of black spirituality, a spirituality of resilience and resistance.

---

[60] The six men and women are Servant of God Mother Elizabeth Lange, foundress of the Oblate Sisters of Providence; Venerable Pierre Toussaint, a lay man and philanthropist; Venerable Henriette Delille, foundress of the Sisters of the Holy Family; Venerable Augustus Tolton, the first recognized black priest in the United States; Servant of God Julia Greeley, a lay woman devoted to the Sacred Heart of Jesus; and Servant of God Sister Thea Bowman, a Franciscan sister who promoted justice and inculturation.

Thank God We Ain't What We Was: The State of the Liturgy in the Black Catholic Community

CLARENCE JOSEPH RIVERS*

WITHIN THE RECENT PAST I have been asked to deliver a State of the Liturgy address for three different Black Catholic gatherings. The fact that such an address has been requested from three distinct and independent sources is an indication that there is a general concern. If nothing were being done, the question would not be asked for the answer would be known. If what is being done were adequate or better, the questions would not be asked. The asking of the question by different sets of people is an indication that the State of Liturgy within the Black Catholic community is somewhere between where it started and where it ought to go. The famous words of an unknown Black preacher express well my own conviction about this state:

> "We ain't what we want to be.
> We ain't what we gonna be.
> We ain't what we ought to be.
> But thank God we ain't what we was."

To borrow a phrase from the preacher, "What was we?" We "was" a people whose culture was considered inferior, second class, at best, and inadmissible in tasteful worship. To understand the inferior, "second class" position, and the unacceptability of Black culture within the Roman Catholic Church, one must understand the inferior, "second class" position of Black people within white, Euro-American society, including the Catholic Church. Doctrinally the Church is not supposed to be Black or white, Greek or Jew, slave or

---

* This essay was first published in *U.S. Catholic Historian* 5, no. 1 (1986): 81–89.

free; but as a matter of fact, the Roman Catholic Church in the United States has been and is radically white, and frequently seems determined to remain so, to the detriment of its Catholicity.

But Europeans did not always think of Black African society and culture as inferior. They knew that Blacks were among the leadership of their Moslem conquerors, especially in Spain. And when during the fifteenth century Europeans contacted Black, sub-Saharan Africa, the first European explorers of that century spoke admiringly of the civilization found there. The king of Portugal and the king of Kongo addressed correspondence to one another as fraternal equals; and a relative of one African king was ordained a bishop. It was not until their own "economic necessity" dictated otherwise that the Europeans began to look upon the sub-Saharan Africans as barbaric and savage. It seems that the Europeans could not in conscience despoil and enslave the Africans unless they could tell themselves that the Africans were uncivilized and without culture. And so began the European-American myth of African inferiority.

To compound this tragedy, oppressed Blacks (as any oppressed people will do) began to accept their oppressors' view of them. This is one aspect of the phenomenon of self-hatred. It begins with the oppressed wanting to be in the privileged position of the oppressor and unlike themselves, the oppressed. Where I was born, in Selma, Alabama (it would have been the same anywhere else), one did not have to be told that to be white was better than to be Black. It was an observable "fact." White men drove the garbage trucks, Black men had to handle the garbage. White people of even modest means had Black people doing their housework for them; the reverse was never true. White people of whatever age invariably addressed Blacks of whatever age on a first name basis; while Black people of whatever age always addressed white people of whatever age by the deferential "sir" or "ma'am." And so Black boys and girls dreamed of living in houses like white folks lived in (and that was okay); but they also dreamed of looking like white folks (and that was not okay). They longed to have "good hair" (straight hair) instead of "bad hair" (kinky hair), and longed to have light skin. And Blacks spent fortunes on hair straighteners (that were never really adequate) and skin bleaches (that never worked at all). And these devices were used not for mere cosmetic reasons (which would have been okay), but were an attempt to be "better" than Black, an attempt to be white, an attempt to be other than themselves.

Then, to compound and reinforce this sad state of affairs, religious missionaries and other white people, who wanted to do good for Blacks, strove mightily to teach Black people to sing, to speak just like white people; and they never ceased preaching to other never-quite-believing whites that all people were just alike, i.e., just like whites, and that any apparent difference could be readily explained away. And some Blacks (relatively few in number) became converts to white churches like the Catholic Church as a way of "social climbing" to get away from the obvious cultural blackness of the traditional Black churches.

But during all this time, from the fifteenth to the twentieth century, the seeds of Black dignity and self-esteem remained planted in the souls of Black folk and were nurtured there by the refreshing waters of Black religion. Even though, at some surface level many Blacks could even be led to admit that the culture of white religion was "superior" to their own; nonetheless, at the same time, at a deeper level it did not escape them that the "superior" culture of white religion did not satisfy their souls. And therefore the masses of Black folk remained in their own Black cults and churches. (In this connection it is interesting to note the growing conviction of Black church scholars, that the most significant of the Afro-American churches did not and do not receive their primary thrust from European Christianity but from our traditional African religion.) In the Black cults and churches, Black self-identity was maintained; and there the doctrinal seed of their somebodiness was watered; and there this need sprouted, flourished, and blossomed into the Black pride renaissance of the sixties. Then kinky hair was no longer considered "bad hair," but appreciated for its ability to be developed into "bushes" and "naturals" and "Afros." And "Black-is-beautiful" became the slogan-prayer of many who desperately hoped that it really was.

Only if we can understand this history can we understand the problem of Black culture within the Catholic Church. Only if we can understand that European-American society consciously or unconsciously fabricated the myth of African subhumanity to justify its own inhumanity; only if we can understand that oppressed Black people developed the affliction of self-hatred; only then can we understand why Black culture has been unrecognized by the white churches and has been frequently rejected even by Blacks within the white churches. To consider the problem of Black culture within the Catholic Church as merely or even primarily a question of aesthetic preference is a failure to understand history.

Before the pioneering work that we, somewhat unwittingly, began to develop at St. Joseph's Church in Cincinnati between the years 1956 and 1964, it can scarcely be said that the Roman Catholic Church in the Black community was on the road at all, on the way at all. Our liturgical pilgrimage had not even begun. In fact, the only effort that I know of, that attempted, before that period, to bring together Black culture and Catholic worship within the United States was that of a particular religious sister from somewhere, I believe, in Oklahoma. She attempted to cover the language of the Latin Mass with unadapted melodies from the Negro Spirituals. I remember the *Kyrie* was sung to the exact tune of "Nobody Knows The Trouble I See." The melody was an ill-fitting garment for the words. However noble the idea behind the effort, the effort itself was less than successful. But I do remember someone saying around that time that Sister might well have been more successful had she tried to adapt the basic style and the various elements of Black music to the needs of our liturgical texts without forcing, as it were, a shotgun wedding of existing melodies with incompatible texts. That admonition stayed with me for some time and was one of the influences that directed me when I first began to compose, after being challenged to do so by Father Boniface Luykx and was encouraged to do so in the context of St. Joseph's Parish.

But when I began to compose, in spite of the fact that there was a great musical vacuum in the Church and that significant numbers of people were open to and indeed did accept this "new music," there were also some negative reactions. A priest well-known in church music circles in those days is reported to have intoned the beginning of "God Is Love" and then fallen to one knee, Jolson-like,[1]

---

[1] Editor's note: A reference to Al Jolson, a popular U.S. singer, comedian, and actor of the 1920s through 1940s.

and crooned "Mammy." The "Music Overseer" of the Diocese of Peoria, Illinois, at that time sent out a letter saying that he thought that music of "particular ethnic origin" was not suitable for the liturgy. And even an archbishop of Cincinnati forbade Negro Spirituals to be sung at Mass in our cathedral on the specious rubrical grounds that they were secular music.

But in spite of these obstacles, the revolution would not be stopped. Typical of the failure of the establishment to stop the revolution was a situation related to me in a letter from a Marianist brother in Cleveland. He wrote, "Your music has been banned in our diocese, but now it is creeping back in as an 'abuse'!" In a similar vein, I received a letter from a gentleman in Washington, D.C., who wrote that it was interesting to see in his church the people who had to bite their lips to keep from singing; and he related the story that one woman when asked what she thought of the music admitted that she did not like it, but marveled at the fact that nonetheless it seemed to make people nicer to each other in the parking lot after Mass. The revolution would not be stopped! The probing, and the prodding, and the pushing of the Spirit was at work within the Church; and the Spirit, free like the wind, freely blew where it would.

Then with the official proclamation of the Second Vatican Council there were no longer any official grounds for the prohibition of various kinds of music, particularly Black religious music, from being properly appropriated and appreciated within the Church. At first there was an unlooked for but altogether explainable reaction to my introducing Black-flavored music into Catholic worship. In August of 1964 when the first Mass in English was celebrated at Kiel Auditorium [in St. Louis, Missouri] at the Annual Convention of the Liturgical Conference, I was invited to lead the congregation in singing "God Is Love" as one of the communion hymns. Much to my surprise the song stirred and stimulated this crowd of 20,000 people, 99.44/100% white. Within a short time, the questions came pouring in: Did Father Rivers think that the white people could do the same kind of thing with their folk traditions? "Of course," I responded naively, but nonetheless truthfully, "why not?" And the Folk Music movement in the Church-at-large was on. Ray Repp came to me. I encouraged him. Joe Wise and I became friends, and I encouraged him. Strangely, as I have said before, my efforts to bring Black music into the Church had not at first stimulated a Black renaissance in the Church. White Catholics, considering it music for Blacks, wanted a "folk" music of their own; and Black Catholic flocks or their clerical shepherds, it seems, were not ready for a Black folk music. Around that time, in the early sixties, I was invited to St. Peter Claver Church in Baltimore to share in a very small way some of my music with that congregation. A young girl asked me, "Why are we going backward to that kind of stuff?" At this time, in the early sixties, most of the invitations I received to lecture about or to give informed concerts of my music came from white Protestant-affiliated colleges, and from a few liberal white parishes. During this period when I was still a full-time teacher in the Archdiocese of Cincinnati and could afford to offer my services for free-will offerings, and sometimes received only travel expenses back and forth, I received only one invitation from a Black parish and it was from the above-mentioned parish in Baltimore.

In the late 1960s, however, the Black renaissance reached within the walls of the Catholic Church. Beginning with the declaration of the Black Catholic Clergy Caucus in 1968 that the Roman Catholic Church was a white racist institution, a more organized Black Catholic movement within the Church culminated in the establishment of the National Office for Black Catholics. Only then did I begin receiving invitations from Black Catholic parishes.

A few churches in various cities began to form Gospel choirs and specialized in Black music at Mass. Some did very well and some did very poorly, but the fact that we were doing anything at all could evoke the sentiment, "Thank God We Ain't What We Was!"

The more I worked with music and worship, the more I began to perceive that within the Western mind there was a dichotomy between music and prayer, between music and worship. Instead of singing the Mass, we sang at Mass; and unmindful of the axiom that "He who sings well prays twice," some people, particularly clergy, insisted that we should not hold up the prayers of the Mass with too much singing. As a consequence, we would sing one or two verses of a hymn leaving the rest of the song behind—even though the rest of the song may have been needed to make complete sense. Because of a lack of a sense of artistic integrity, many parishes fell into (and some are still in) the four-hymn syndrome. That is, they would sing a hymn at the beginning of Mass, one at the Offertory, one during Communion, and one at the end of Mass. Many parts of the Mass that needed to be sung, like the "Holy, Holy, Holy" and the "Lamb of God" and the "Allelujah" verse and other acclamations were left unsung, and unsung they made no more sense than reciting, "Happy Birthday to you, Happy Birthday to you, Happy Birthday Dear Melvin, etc." It was within the general context of the Church's groping to integrate the music with the rest of worship that I came to understand that it was not enough for us to introduce Black music into the liturgy but that it was necessary to bring the whole range of Black culture to bear on our worship efforts. In practice it meant that we needed to bring a more poetic quality to our prayers and our preaching; and we needed to perform spoken prayers and sermons in a way that a sense of poetry demanded.

The lack of poetry either in active performance or in written composition has led to ineffectual proclamation of the Word and to aesthetic incoherence in the Liturgy. Black music separated from Black prayer styles and Black preaching styles disjointed the Liturgy. And the presidential prayers of the Mass, especially the Eucharistic prayer, the readings, and the preaching paled, as it were, into insignificance alongside the soul-touching music that was now being sung. The spoken prayers, the reading, and the preaching became dead spots, stopping the dramatic movement, the flow of the service. And this imbalance led misguided people to express the view that the music should somehow be suppressed or held back in order to give the other parts of the Mass a chance to be heard. But the solution did not and does not lie in that direction. Very opposite is the case. The other parts of the Mass need to be brought up to the relative level of excellence that we are beginning to achieve in our musical performances.

As recently as two years ago, a Cincinnati priest voiced the opinion that the director of music was de facto more the president of the assembly at a particular Mass in our cathedral than was the principal concelebrant. Again, the implication was that the music director should have been more restrained so that the presiding concelebrant might have a chance. But I reminded our liturgical commission, when this came up, that in the traditional Black churches, no matter how strong the music, the spoken prayer events and the preaching events still maintained their proper force and power within the service and no one doubted that the preacher was the president of the assembly even though the only thing he may have done during the service was to preach.

Again, it was this dichotomy between relatively excellent performance in music and absolutely lousy performance in spoken prayer and reading and preaching that led some specialists in Black culture to wonder if it were really possible to combine Black culture and Catholic worship. One such person was Dr. [Maurice Henderson] McCall, on the faculty of Cincinnati Conservatory of Music. But Dr. McCall changed his mind after he first heard preaching and praying in a Roman Catholic context that was Black-influenced. When he finally heard a Eucharistic prayer based on the style of traditional Black prayer, he told me that now he knew that what we were trying to achieve was a real possibility. I was then more convinced than ever that our problem now lay not in dealing primarily with music but even more so with the other elements of the Mass.

And that is where we are today. We have not yet found a way to train our preachers and our readers and our prayers so that they would become fit instruments of the Holy Spirit; and, until the Mass as a whole becomes an effective channel of the Spirit and leads to our ongoing metanoia or conversion, to spiritual growth and inspiration, the Mass as a whole will be inauthentic. And I lay before you the proposal that we bring our collective imaginations together to solve this problem, as an artistic and cultural one, rather than merely trying to discover new rationales and a new theology, which, when discovered, will presumably automatically trigger a change.

The African American Catholic Hymnal and the African American Spiritual

M. SHAWN COPELAND*

Introduction: Aesthetic Inculturation

IN THE PAST FOUR DECADES African American Catholics have done a good deal to animate and direct the inculturation of our faith and to transform and shape various aspects of our celebration of the Eucharistic liturgy, our preparation for and reception of sacraments, our private and communal prayer, and, thus, our spirituality. The fine start on this endeavor owes much to the National Office for Black Catholics (NOBC), particularly, the untiring and imaginative leadership of Marianist Joseph Mary Davis, its first executive director, and Clarence Joseph Rivers, the doyen of Black Catholic liturgists. In the mid-1970s and early 1980s, through annual workshops, conferences, and the publication of its journal, *Freeing the Spirit*, as well as occasional monographs, the NOBC's program for Culture and Worship constructed a platform for the work of Black Catholic composers and liturgists such as Rivers, Rawn Harbor, Leon Roberts, Marjorie Gabriel-Burrow, Grayson Brown, Avon Gillespie, Eddie Bonnemere, and Ray East. These men and women molded and directed an African American renewal of Catholic worship, ritual, and forms of prayer. Thus, at least, to date, we may conclude that the primary impact of inculturation for African American Catholicism has been aesthetic, and the publication and widespread use of *Lead Me, Guide Me: The African American Catholic Hymnal* is a singular example of this impact.[1]

---

* This essay was first published in *U.S. Catholic Historian* 19, no. 2 (Spring 2001): 67–82.
[1] *Lead Me, Guide Me: The African American Catholic Hymnal* (Chicago: G. I. A. Publications, 1987).

There were, perhaps, two proposals for a hymnal reflective of the spiritual, that is religious and cultural, sensibilities of Black Catholics. Avon Gillespie prepared a proposal for a hymnal in 1978. Three years later, Father James T. Menkhus, an associate pastor of St. Martin's in Baltimore, Maryland, recognized the need for liturgical and devotional music reflective of his congregation.[2] In 1983, the National Black Catholic Clergy Caucus authorized the development of a hymnal and formed a committee whose membership included professional musicians and liturgists as well as men and women who represented the commonality and plurality of the Black Catholic experience.[3]

In 1987, *Lead Me, Guide Me* was published by the Gregorian Institute of America, the major U.S. Catholic music publisher. The hymnal takes its name from a well-known hymn much beloved by Black Catholics, "Lead Me, Guide Me," composed in 1953 by Black gospel songwriter Doris Akers. It was dedicated to Father Clarence Rivers. Between its red, black, and green covers, *Lead Me, Guide Me* embraces the signature music of the twin heritages of Black Catholics: spirituals and Gregorian plainchant. Also included are gospel compositions, traditional and contemporary Catholic hymns in English and Latin, hymns composed by Dr. Isaac Watts and adapted to a Black idiom, and African American freedom songs.

As an aesthetic achievement of African American Catholic inculturation, *Lead Me, Guide Me* was "born of the needs and aspirations of Black Catholics for music that reflects both our African American

---

[2] Jon Michael Spencer, *Black Hymnody: A Hymnological History of the African-American Church* (Knoxville: University of Tennessee Press, 1992), 193.

[3] Bishop James Patterson Lyke and Father William Norvel list the following, along with the organization that each person represented, as members of the Black Catholic Hymnal Committee: Father Arthur Anderson, O.F.M, coordinating assistant; Edmund Broussard, Knights of Peter Claver and Ladies Auxiliary; Marjorie Gabriel-Burrow, National Association of Black Catholic Administrators; Bishop Wilton D. Gregory, the National Black Catholic Clergy Caucus; Avon Gillespie, who had developed a proposal for a hymnal in 1978; Rawn Harbor and Leon Roberts, the National Association of Black Catholic Musicians; Ronald Sharps, the National Office for Black Catholics; Brother Robert Smith, O.F.M. Cap., the National Black Seminarians Association; and Sister Laura Marie Kendricks, H.V.M., the National Black Sisters' Conference. See "Preface," *Lead Me, Guide Me*.

heritage and our Catholic faith."[4] Still, beyond this crucial existential, there is a larger social and cultural setting to take into account. To appreciate the hymnal, we need to look to the confluence of three events: the Civil Rights movement of the 1960s, the Black Arts movement, and the Second Vatican Council. For Black Catholics, these events are nearly inseparable. The 1954 Supreme Court order to desegregate schools injected the Civil Rights movement with a new fervor and momentum that spilled over first into the Montgomery bus boycott of 1955, then into the sit-ins and freedom rides that took up the dangerous and daring struggle against legalized White racist regimes in the South. In the painful contest between King's Gandhian nonviolence and the students' angry cry for "Black Power," Black artists recognized the profound, even metaphysical, meaning of cultural self-determination. These artists grasped the need to reconnect aesthetics and ethics and refused to separate art from the whole of Black life, especially during that period of urban rebellion and social turbulence. Indeed, writer Larry Neal declared, "Black Art is the aesthetic and spiritual sister of the Black Power concept."[5]

Finally, in a number of ways, the Second Vatican Council enabled Black Catholics to enter deeply, fully, and authentically into the retrieval and appropriation of their culture and history, to protest and act on behalf of social justice, and to understand these activities as a liberating praxis. The council's impact on African American Catholics came through its repudiation of the Church's insularity and its identification with the world;[6] its insistence that the laity have a "special and indispensable role in the mission of the Church" and must not be deprived of "their rightful freedom to act on their own initiative";[7] its public affirmation of Catholic respect

---

    4   "Preface," *Lead Me, Guide Me*.
    5   Larry Neal, "The Black Arts Movement," in *Within the Circle: An Anthology of African American Literary Criticism from the Harlem Renaissance to the Present*, ed. by Angelyn Mitchell (Durham, NC: Duke University Press, 1994), 184.
    6   Vatican II, *Gaudium et Spes*, December 7, 1965, https://www.vatican.va/archive/hist_councils/ii_vatican_council/documents/vat-ii_const_19651207_gaudium-et-spes_en.html.
    7   Vatican II, *Apostolicam Actuositatem*, November 18, 1965, http://www.vatican.va/archive/hist_councils/ii_vatican_council/documents/vat-ii_decree_19651118_apostolicam-actuositatem_en.html, nos. 1, 24.

for individual conscience and religious freedom; and its serious interest in the contemporary problems of the day—the economic and political exploitation of peoples and countries of the so-called third world, the threat of nuclear war, disregard for the sanctity of human life, racism, and unbridled technological innovation.

Since the influence of the Second Vatican Council on Black Catholics has been a topic of frequent treatment, this article will sketch the Civil Rights movement and the Black Arts movement—social and cultural forces that made *Lead Me, Guide Me* possible, perhaps, even, necessary.[8] I will then turn to the inclusion of sixty-three African American spirituals in the hymnal, which is one more sign of Black Catholic self-affirmation of Black identity. A brief history of the spirituals may assist readers unfamiliar with their composition and dissemination. Finally, the article concludes with some sightings of the spirituals in Black Catholic life.

Black Catholic Identity and Civil Rights

With the exception of the Supreme Court's 1896 decision of *Plessy* v. *Ferguson*, perhaps, no judicial ruling on the civil rights of African Americans matches the significance of the Supreme Court's 1954 opinion in *Brown* v. *Board of Education of Topeka*. The *Plessy* decision admitted the inscription of the "separate but equal" doctrine onto the Constitution. By the end of the century, most of the Southern states had expanded their segregation regulations and passed Jim Crow laws, so that by 1908 streetcar segregation was common. Historian C. Vann Woodward observed that by the 1950s, law and/or custom had created and sanctioned "a racial ostracism that extended to churches and schools, to housing and jobs, to eating and drinking . . . all forms of public transportation, to sports and recreation, to hospitals, orphanages, prisons, and asylums, and ultimately to funeral homes, morgues, and cemeteries." This condition of segregation was held to be a "final settlement," a "permanent

---

[8] See Melva Wilson Costen, "Published Hymnals in the Afro-American Tradition," *The Hymn* 40, no.1 (January 1989): 17; also William Farley Smith, review of *Lead Me, Guide Me: The African American Catholic Hymnal*, *The Hymn* 40, no. 1 (January 1989): 13–14.

system" beyond alteration or change.[9] John Hope Franklin concluded his study of the history of legalized segregation in the United States in these words:

> The law had created two worlds, so separate that communication between them was almost impossible.... The wall of segregation had become so formidable, so impenetrable, apparently, that the entire weight of the American tradition of equality and all the strength of the American constitutional system had to be brought to bear in order to make even the slightest crack in it.[10]

The Supreme Court's unanimous reversal of the *Plessy* decision in 1954 ignited the embers of the Civil Rights movement of the 1950s and 1960s and led to a response that the Court might *not* have intended. Standing on more than 350 years of protest, prayer, and hope, Black Americans "took the Supreme Court decision and made of it a heroic declaration of equality."[11] They understood the Court's decision as the fulfillment of an overdue promise and concluded that if segregation in education was wrong because of the invidious inequalities inherent in its very existence, then segregation itself was wrong and every manifestation of it ought to be abolished. Men, women, university students, and even children picked up the struggle for freedom with prayerful and bold courage.

Flush with the success of the Montgomery bus boycott, African Americans began campaigns of massive civil disobedience, refusing to tolerate any longer the abuses of White American racism. The freedom riders, young African American college students and their White counterparts, were notable in their commitment. Both Bernice Johnson Reagon and Robert Moses have written of how these young people set aside their studies to serve as sit-in leaders, voter

---

[9] C. Vann Woodward, *The Strange Career of Jim Crow*, 3rd rev. ed. (New York: Oxford University Press, 1974), 7.
[10] John Hope Franklin, "History of Racial Segregation in the United States," in *The Black Community in Modern America*, vol. 2 of *The Making of Black America*, ed. by August Meier and Elliott Rudwick (New York: Atheneum, 1969), 12–13.
[11] Albert B. Cleage, Jr., "The Black Messiah and the Black Revolution," in *Quest for a Black Theology*, ed. by James J. Gardiner and J. Deotis Roberts Sr. (Philadelphia: United Church Press, 1970), 2.

registration organizers, office workers, and tutors in segregated rural and urban communities. In Mississippi, for example, local leaders like Amzie Moore, Reverend George W. Lee, C. C. Bryant, Jack Smith, and E. W. Steptoe instructed these young people in the critical reading of people and situations, supported them, housed them, fed them, nursed their wounds from beatings, and arranged their bail on arrest.[12] Already, Thurgood Marshall had made the NAACP (the National Association for the Advancement of Colored People) a household word. During these years, the nation became acquainted with grassroots Black organizations such as the Southern Christian Leadership Council (SCLC), the Congress on Racial Equality (CORE), and the Student Nonviolent Coordinating Committee (SNCC). However, these groups still maintained the gender line; the movement was clerical and male and could deal but haltingly with the leadership of plain-speaking, self-confident women like Ella Baker.

While Catholic participation in the Civil Rights movement would come later, Moses recalls "Father John LaBauve, a Catholic priest in Mound Bayou [Mississippi] whose parish home Amzie [Moore] had used for voter registration workshops, [and who] had been transferred out of the Delta."[13] Catholics would be galvanized after the March on Washington in August 1963, the dreadful Sunday bombing of Birmingham's Sixteenth Street Baptist Church in September 1963 in which four young girls were killed, and the March 1965 march on Selma. Catholic participation in the interracial Selma to Montgomery marches was captured in a widely reprinted photograph featuring approximately a dozen priests in collars, including Black Catholic priest George Clements of the Archdiocese of Chicago, and four religious women in full habit, including Black Catholic Franciscan Sister of St. Mary, Antona Ebo.

---

[12] Bernice Johnson Reagon, "Let the Church Sing 'Freedom,'" *Black Music Research Journal* 4 (1987): 105; also Robert P. Moses, *Radical Equations: Math Literacy and Civil Rights* (Boston: Beacon Press, 2001), 23–57.

[13] Moses, *Radical Equations*, 44.

The Black Arts Movement

In the murky political environment spawned by the assassinations of President John F. Kennedy, Malcolm X, Dr. Martin Luther King Jr., and Senator Robert Kennedy, the "aesthetic of integration" that King had charted in his "I Have a Dream" speech began to cede to an "aesthetic of separatism" promulgated by the Black Arts movement.[14] This was a defensive posture and protested the daily structural and systemic violence of anti-Black racism in America. The event considered to be the generative idea behind the Black Arts movement is the 1964 founding of the Black Arts Repertory/Theatre School in New York. This endeavor was led by dramatist, critic, and poet LeRoi Jones (Amiri Baraka) along with several other Black artists. The theatre took its program of plays, concerts, and poetry readings to Harlem, Larry Neal wrote, with the intention of "shatter[ing] the illusions of the American body politic, and awaken[ing] black people to the meaning of their lives."[15] Although short-lived, the theatre inspired the formation of Black art groups in Los Angeles, Detroit, Chicago, Jersey City, New Orleans, Philadelphia, and Washington, D.C. The Black Arts movement was also the force behind the call for Black studies programs which spread to many of the nation's college campuses.

LeRoi Jones, Larry Neal, Hoyt W. Fuller, Addison Gayle Jr., Don L. Lee (Haki Madhubuti), and Ron Karenga were among the chief architects of the movement. Lee, in particular, acknowledged the talent and contributions of Black female artists like Gwendolyn Brooks and Mari Evans. For the most part, however, like the Civil Rights movement, the Black Arts movement stayed wide of the gender line.

Gayle's collection, *The Black Aesthetic*,[16] functioned as a kind of manifesto of the movement, although at least one earlier collection,

---

[14] Angelyn Mitchell, introduction to *Within the Circle: An Anthology of African American Literary Criticism from the Harlem Renaissance to the Present*, ed. by Angelyn Mitchell (Durham, NC: Duke University Press, 1994), 9–10.
[15] Neal, "The Black Arts Movement," 188.
[16] Addison Gayle Jr., *The Black Aesthetic* (New York: Doubleday, 1971).

Anger, and Beyond,[17] challenged Black writers to place their creative imagination at the service of the freedom and dignity of Black people. In his introduction to *Anger, and Beyond*, Herbert Hill declared:

> In the future, Negro authors will not be writing as some did in the past, to please or titillate white audiences; they will not be telling of quaint and amusing colored folks or of exotic sensual Negroes who exist only in the fantasies of white people living in a society tragically obsessed by race and color.[18]

Black writers, Hoyt Fuller argued, did not reject universals, but rather the "assumption that style and language and concerns of [whites] establish the appropriate limits and frame of reference for black [art] and people."[19]

The most enduring slogan of the Black Arts movement was "Black is Beautiful," and it was shouted with relish at every opportunity. James Brown's recording of "Say It Loud, I'm Black and I'm Proud" was a popular standard. This aesthetic affirmation signified the release of women and men from centuries of oppression and self-hatred and the repudiation of any type of imitation of whites as a standard for life and art. To accept that "Black is Beautiful," Gayle asserted, was the first step in recovering from the "cultural strangulation" of Black life and Black art under the dominant White aesthetic and constructing a new and Black aesthetic.[20] Finally, one of the chief aims of the Black Arts movement was to reconnect aesthetics and ethics. To effect this, Neal argued that the Black artist must take the perspective of the oppressed: "In a context of world upheaval, ethics and aesthetics must interact positively and be consistent with the demands for a more spiritual world."[21]

---

[17] Herbert Hill, ed., *Anger, and Beyond* (New York: Harper & Row, 1966).
[18] Hill, *Anger, and Beyond*, xxii.
[19] Hoyt W. Fuller, "Towards a Black Aesthetic," in *Within the Circle: An Anthology of African American Literary Criticism from the Harlem Renaissance to the Present*, ed. by Angelyn Mitchell (Durham, NC: Duke University Press, 1994), 203.
[20] Addison Gayle Jr., "Cultural Strangulation: Black Literature and the White Aesthetic," in *Within the Circle: An Anthology of African American Literary Criticism from the Harlem Renaissance to the Present*, ed. by Angelyn Mitchell (Durham, NC: Duke University Press, 1994), 212.
[21] Neal, "The Black Arts Movement," 186.

The Black Arts movement called for a disengagement with the aesthetic values of White America. Black dramatists, critics, poets, and novelists sought a distinct standard for themselves, their art, and their people. They found its characteristic features of authentic self-regard, disciplined improvisation, polyrhythms, asymmetry, intensity, irony, and sarcasm in music—in particular, jazz. A generation later, Cornel West would make the same assessment and measure his own *oeuvre* by that of John Coltrane.

It is not possible to say with complete confidence just which Black Catholics were reading these critics, dramatists, and poets; if the regular gatherings of Black religious and clergy in Detroit and Chicago in the late 1960s and early 1970s can be taken as some measure, there were quite a few. Black Catholics have never been complete strangers to their culture, but the early contributions of Father Clarence Rivers, Father (now Bishop) Moses Anderson, S.S.E., Cyprian Rowe, and Sister Francesca Thompson, O.S.F., and then later those of Sister Thea Bowman, F.S.P.A., Father Joseph A. Brown, S.J., and Sister Eva Regina Martin, S.S.F., would reveal deep, critical immersion and appropriation of the wealth of African and African American literary, musical, historical, and material culture.

Spirituals: The Songs of an Enslaved People

I cannot say precisely when I first heard a spiritual, but I will forever associate the experience with my grandmother's singing on Sunday mornings after Mass. My maternal grandmother, Mattie L. Hunt Billingslea, was the last of eight children born to James and Mary (nee Hunt) Hunt in Macon, Georgia, early in the last century. Not long after the First World War, her widowed mother and enterprising brothers moved their family to Detroit, Michigan. Although the family attended Quinn Chapel African Methodist Episcopal Church, sometime in the 1940s my grandmother became a Catholic. She was baptized in Sacred Heart Church, one of the three or four churches in the archdiocese that seem to have been reserved for Black Catholics. In my childhood we were members of Holy Ghost parish, whose small, segregated, and demanding elementary school I attended. Each Sunday, one of the Spiritans (we knew them as Holy Ghost Fathers) celebrated the children's Mass. It was no different than the earlier or later Masses, but the priest would step away from the lectern (pulpit would be much too pretentious to describe the outfitting of our basement mission church), stand close to the communion rail, and explain the gospel directly and simply, but not, I think, condescendingly. Although my grandmother already would have heard Mass, when I returned home, I was expected to summarize the gospel and give something of the homily. What I remember so well is that very often when I opened the front door, her rich alto would be raised in a spiritual. Much later, when I heard other Black Catholics tell similar stories, I recognized such singing of spirituals as a conserving, healing, even compensatory religious and psychic practice.

The spiritual, created by enslaved women and men, is rivaled, perhaps, only by jazz as the most widely known of all African American musical genres.[22] While it is difficult to date with any precision the origin of these songs, historians Miles Mark Fisher and Dena J. Epstein argue that the spirituals can be traced to the early eighteenth century.[23] Certainly the brutal social conditions (legalized and perpetual servitude, racial stigma, physical abuse, and alienation) of their composition were already in place by that time. Reports about the distinctive singing and dancing of the enslaved people drifted northward only gradually through travelers' chronicles, newspaper and journal articles, diaries of missionaries and teachers, novels, and the speeches and narratives of fugitive slaves.[24]

---

[22] John Lovell Jr., *Black Song: The Forge and the Flame—The Story of How the Afro-American Spiritual Was Hammered Out* (1972; reprint, New York: Paragon, 1986), 400. This work treats more than 375 years of the history of the African American spiritual; it is steeped in the flavoring of six thousand songs and refers to or cites directly more than five hundred of them. Other scholarly studies of the spirituals include Howard Thurman, *Deep River and The Negro Spiritual Speaks of Life and Death* (Richmond, IN: Friends United Press, 1975); James H. Cone, *The Spirituals and the Blues: An Interpretation* (Westport, CT: Greenwood Press, 1972); LeRoi Jones, *Blues People: The Negro Experience in White America and the Music That Developed from It* (New York: William Morrow, 1963); Jon Michael Spencer, *Protest and Praise: Sacred Music of Black Religion* (Minneapolis: Fortress Press, 1990).

[23] Miles Mark Fisher, *Negro Slave Songs in the United States* (New York: Citadel Press, 1953); Dena J. Epstein, *Sinful Tunes and Spirituals: Black Folk Music to the Civil War* (1977; Urbana: University of Illinois Press, 1981).

[24] Epstein, *Sinful Tunes and Spirituals*, 161–183, 215–237, 241–302.

Anglo-American and European visitors to the antebellum South were struck by the singing and dancing of the enslaved peoples. Many dismissed the songs as "uncouth barbarism, [while] others were stirred by the vigor of the dancing and the weird sadness of the songs."[25] To be sure, Southerners had mentioned the singing and dancing of the enslaved peoples, but usually as evidence of the Africans' contentment with their condition. The White men and women of the South deemed it "bad policy to give slaves credit for any type of cultural achievement."[26]

Because of their biblical content, the spirituals are associated with the Christianity of the enslaved Africans, but the Middle Passage did not completely eradicate religious practices, aspects and apprehension of material culture, social and religio-cultural beliefs, and cognitive orientations or ways of thinking about reality, life, and relationships.[27] The traditional religions of Africa formed the first stratum of the religio-cultural world of the enslaved peoples. These religions were, and remain, highly particular rather than universal. Yet, beneath the diversity of so many peoples, common modes of perception, common values, and common patterns of ritual can be discerned. For Africans, religion permeated every domain of human life. The whole of the universe radiated and mediated forces of the sacred—the supreme Deity, the divinities, and the spirits. There was no "formal distinction between the sacred and the secular, between the religious and non-religious, between the spiritual and the material areas of life."[28] Thus, religion occupied the whole person and the whole of a person's living. The most ordinary and the most extraordinary tasks and activities of daily life, human relationships, social

---

[25] Sterling Brown, "The Spirituals," in *The Book of Negro Folklore*, ed. by Langston Hughes and Arna Bontemps (New York: Dodd, Mead and Company, 1958), 279.
[26] Lovell, *Black Song*, 400.
[27] Joseph E. Holloway, ed., *Africanisms in American Culture* (Bloomington: Indiana University Press, 1990), 2–13; Albert Raboteau, *Slave Religion: The 'Invisible Institution' in the Antebellum South* (New York: Oxford University Press, 1975), 5–7; Martha Washington Creel, *"A Peculiar People": Slave Religion and Community-Culture Among the Gullahs* (New York: New York University Press, 1988), 29–50.
[28] John Mbiti, *African Religions and Philosophies* (Garden City, NY: Doubleday/Anchor, 1970), 2.

interactions, and natural phenomena were suffused with religious understandings and meanings.

In addition to a supreme Deity and various lesser divinities or gods, Africans had to take into account their ancestors. These honored dead, both those who died long ago and the deceased of more recent memory, remained, even in death, most intimately connected to the living. Because they are believed capable of intervening in daily affairs—bestowing blessing or meting out punishment—the ancestors had to be ritually venerated according to custom.[29]

In traditional African religions, there were no sacred scriptures to be proclaimed and exegeted, no creeds to be studied and memorized, no dogmas to claim assent and observance. Religion "is written not on paper but in people's hearts, minds, oral history, rituals and religious personages like priests, rainmakers, officiating elders and even kings."[30] Ritual and ceremonial practices were central to marking rites of passage or initiation, funerals, births, and coronations or installation of chiefs. Singing, dancing, drumming, and creating and reciting poetry were essential, interrelated components of these rituals.

Still, the Christianization of the enslaved Africans remains a disputed issue. Scholars cannot isolate each discrete moment from authentic efforts to evangelize and catechize enslaved Africans to the appearance of Black Christian churches. What we know unequivocally is this: Anglo-American Christianity, as the preaching of salvation in Jesus of Nazareth, had a decisive impact on the enslaved peoples. In turn, these men and women shaped and "fitted" Judeo-Christian practices, rituals, symbols, myths, and values to their own particular social experiences, religio-cultural expectations, and personal needs; these traditions helped the slave community to form an image of itself.[31] At the same time, because so very much of the intimate life of the enslaved peoples was hidden from

---

[29] E. Bolaji Idowu, *African Traditional Religion: A Definition* (Maryknoll, NY: Orbis Books, 1975), 184.
[30] Mbiti, *African Religions and Philosophies*, 5.
[31] Raboteau, *Slave Religion*, 213.

the master class—indeed from nearly all Whites—it is not possible to pronounce with certainty the burial of the gods of Africa and the complete disappearance of the traditional religions that honored them. When enslaved Africans moaned:

> I've been 'buked an' I've been scorned,
> Dere is trouble all over dis worl',
> Ain' gwine lay my 'ligion down, Ain' gwine lay my 'ligion down,

we can never be completely sure *which* religion they were refusing to surrender.

Most historians and cultural anthropologists would agree that on plantations, religion was the sphere in which the enslaved Africans generally were able to exercise some measure of autonomy and freedom in intelligence, action, and creativity; still, they did so often at the risk of grave punishment. The attitudes and practices of slaveholders regarding the religious activities of slaves have been well documented. On some plantations the enslaved peoples were permitted to hold independent, and sometimes, unsupervised worship services; on other plantations they attended White churches, sitting or standing in designated areas. On still other plantations, the enslaved people were punished for praying and singing. Yet, from snatches of stories from the Scriptures, sermons, and their own critical reflections, the enslaved peoples fashioned "an inner world, a scale of values and fixed points of vantage from which to judge the world around them and themselves."[32]

Poet and literary critic James Weldon Johnson held that many spirituals were the work of highly gifted individuals whom he called in a celebrated poem "black and unknown bards."[33] Novelist and folklorist Zora Neale Hurston maintained that the spirituals were "Negro religious songs, sung by a group, and a group bent on expression of

---

[32] C. Johnson and A. P. Watson, eds., *God Struck Me Dead* (Philadelphia: Pilgrim Press, 1969), vii.

[33] James Weldon Johnson and J. Rosamond Johnson, *The Books of American Negro Spirituals*, 2 vols. (1925; 1926; 1969; reprint, New York: Da Capo Press, 1989), 11–12.

feelings and not on sound effects."[34] When asked about their method of composing their religious songs, enslaved men and women often replied: "De Lord jes' put hit en our mouf. We is ignorant, and de Lord puts ebry word we says en our mouf."[35] A former enslaved woman from Kentucky insisted that the spirituals were formed from the material of traditional African tunes and familiar songs:

> Us ole head use ter make 'em on de spurn of de moment, after we wressle wid de Spirit and come thoo. But the tunes was brung from Africa by our grandaddies. Dey was jis 'miliar song.... Dey calls 'em spirituals, case de Holy Spirit done revealed 'em to 'em. Some say Moss Jesus taught 'em, and I's seed 'em start in meetin'. We'd all be at the 'prayer house' de Lord's Day and de white preacher he'd splain de word and read whar Ezekiel done say: Dry bones gwine ter lib again. And, honey, de Lord would come a-shining thoo dem pages and revive dis ole [woman's] heart, and I'd jump up dar and den and holler and shout and sing and pat, and dey would all cotch de words... dey's all take it up and keep at it, and keep a-addin to it and den it would be a spiritual.[36]

Widespread "discovery" of the spiritual coincides with the Civil War and the inevitable close and direct contact between northern White soldiers and enslaved people, including Black soldiers. The most well-known record of such encounters is provided by Thomas Wentworth Higginson. A New Englander, Unitarian clergyman, and abolitionist, Higginson took command in November 1862 of the First South Carolina Volunteers, a regiment consisting largely of freed slaves from the Sea Islands.[37] In an article that he prepared for the *Atlantic Monthly*, Higginson commented on the men's singing of religious songs and offered an extended description of a shout.[38]

---

[34] Zora Neale Hurston, *The Sanctified Church* (Berkeley, CA: Turtle Island Foundation, 1983), 80.

[35] M. V. Bales, "Some Negro Folk Songs of Texas," in *Follow De Drinkin' Gou'd*, ed. by James Dobie (Austin: Texas Folklore Society, 1928), 85.

[36] Raboteau, *Slave Religion*, 244–245.

[37] Leon F. Litwack, *Been in the Storm So Long: The Aftermath of Slavery* (New York: Knopf, 1979; New York: Random House, 1980), 68–69.

[38] Thomas Wentworth Higginson, "Leaves from an Officer's Journal," parts 1 and 2, *Atlantic Monthly* 14 (November 1864): 521–529; (December 1864): 740–748.

The first attempt at a serious and systematic collection of songs composed by the enslaved peoples appeared in 1867. *Slave Songs of the United States* was compiled by three Northerners, William Francis Allen, Charles Pickard Ware, and Lucy McKim Garrison, who was the inspiration behind the effort.[39] In June of 1862, McKim accompanied her father, James Miller McKim, to the Sea Islands of South Carolina. James McKim was an agent of the Philadelphia-based Port Royal Relief Committee, one of several voluntary groups organized by Northern anti-slavery people to recruit teachers, missionaries, and administrators to work with the emancipated slaves and to raise money for their salaries and supplies of food, clothing, and equipment. Lucy accompanied her father on a three-week tour of inspection and acted as his secretary. Her "perceptive enthusiasm" for the music prompted her to transcribe what she heard.[40] From Philadelphia, daughter and father corresponded with John Dwight, editor of *Dwight's Journal of Music*, who published a small collection of the songs along with remarks by James McKim.[41] Lucy McKim's initial efforts to disseminate the religious and work songs of the enslaved people met with little public interest, but her collaboration with Allen and his cousin Ware, each of whom had begun to collect slave songs, bore fruit in a "book of permanent historical value."[42] However, the most definitive role in introducing the songs of the enslaved peoples to the world outside their tightly drawn circle of culture belongs to Fisk University.

In the decade following the Civil War, a number of church groups dedicated themselves to the education of the newly freed people. Fisk University, founded by the American Missionary Association of the Congregational Church, opened its doors in January 1866 to all students regardless of race. Although many of its teachers worked for little or nothing, by 1870 Fisk was on the verge of bankruptcy. George L. White, a teacher of music, suggested a concert

---

[39] William Francis Allen, Charles Pickard Ware, and Lucy McKim Garrison, comps., *Slave Songs of the United States* (1867; reprint, Bedford, MA: Applewood Books, 1995).
[40] Epstein, *Sinful Tunes*, 256, 288.
[41] Epstein, *Sinful Tunes*, 288.
[42] Epstein, *Sinful Tunes*, 303.

tour to raise funds and to publicize the school. Despite the opposition of the school's trustees, White formed a singing group of nine Fisk students, all but one former slaves. From 1871 to 1875, the group, which became known as the Jubilee Singers, gave concerts in northern cities as well as England, Scotland, and Germany, singing the spirituals they had learned from their enslaved parents.[43] The perseverance and simple goodness of these young men and women in the face of rejection, discrimination, mockery, and ridicule at home and abroad made them heroic; Fisk University's Jubilee Hall made them legendary.

In their original settings, the creation and singing of the spirituals were marked by flexibility, spontaneity, and improvisation. The pattern of call-response allowed for the rhythmic weaving or manipulation of time, text, and pitch, while the response or repetitive chorus provided a recognizable and stable foundation for the extemporized lines of the soloist or leader.[44] Hurston insisted that the spirituals are best appreciated when we imagine them, not concertized with dissonances "ironed out," but moaned in jagged irregular harmony, falsetto breaking in, and keys changing with emotion.[45] W. E. B. Du Bois called the spirituals "sorrow songs"[46] and, as such, perhaps, they are best understood when we imagine them in intimate mystical or ritual settings—cabins of rough wooden planks, "woods, gullies, ravines, and thickets" (aptly called brush arbors or hush arbors).[47]

The spirituals are inextricably bound to African American adaptations of religious rituals that invariably included hand clapping or the stomping of feet, which would have compensated on many

---

[43] Lovell, *Black Song*, 402–422; see also Andrew Ward, *Dark Midnight When I Rise: The Story of the Jubilee Singers Who Introduced the World to the Music of Black America* (New York: Farrar, Straus and Giroux, 2000).
[44] Portia K. Maultsby, "Africanisms in African-American Music," in *Africanisms in American Culture*, ed. by Joseph E. Holloway (Bloomington: Indiana University Press, 1990), 193.
[45] Hurston, *Sanctified Church*, 80.
[46] W. E. B. Du Bois, *The Souls of Black Folk* (1903; New York: Vintage Books/Library of America, 1990), 180.
[47] Raboteau, *Slave Religion*, 215.

plantations for the outlawed drum. However, the spiritual is linked most intimately to the staid shuffling of the *ring-shout*. A distinct form of worship, the ring-shout is basically a dancing-singing phenomenon in which the song is danced with the whole body—hands, feet, shoulders, hips. When the spiritual was sounded, the ring-shout would begin. The dancers formed a circle and moved counterclockwise in a ring, first by walking slowly, and then by shuffling—the foot just slightly lifted from the floor. Sometimes the people danced silently; most often they sang the chorus of the spiritual as they shuffled. At other times the entire song itself was sung by the dancers. Frequently, a group of the best singers and tired shouters stood at the side of the room to "base" the others, singing the body or stanzas of the song and clapping their hands. The dancing and singing would increase in intensity and energy and sometimes went on for hours.[48]

In creating the spirituals, the singers drew heavily and selectively on material "picked up . . . rather than read from" the Old and New Testaments. Nearly all slaveholders denied the teaching of even rudimentary reading and writing to enslaved Africans, and several Southern states made this law. Slaves caught writing could be penalized by having a forefinger cut from the right hand.[49]

Biblical places most conspicuous in the spirituals include the Jordan River, Egypt, the Red Sea, Canaan, and Galilee. The people of the Old Testament who appear with some frequency in the songs include Abraham, Jacob, Moses and the Israelites, Pharaoh, Joshua, David, Ezekiel, Jonah, Daniel, and the three Hebrew Children—Shadrach, Meshach, and Abednego. Jesus is highly featured, particularly his birth, crucifixion, death, and resurrection; also prominent are Mary, Jesus' mother; John the Baptist; the apostles John, Peter, Thomas, and Paul; Nicodemus; Mary and Martha of Bethany; Mary Magdalene; and Lazarus.[50]

---

[48] Raboteau, *Slave Religion*, 70–71.
[49] Lovell, *Black Song*, 257; see also Janet Duitsman Cornelius, *When I Can Read My Title Clear: Literacy, Slavery, and Religion in the Antebellum South* (Columbia, SC: University of South Carolina Press, 1991).
[50] Lovell, *Black Song*, 258, 260–261.

The vocabulary or rhetoric of the spirituals is intensely poetic and expressive, decorative and poignant. It is characterized by vivid simile, creative and effective juxtaposition of images, and metaphor. Grounded in the experience of oppression, this highly charged symbolic language is most fundamentally a rhetoric of survival and resistance. The spirituals are unambiguously clear that "none but the righteous shall see God" and that the wicked shall be punished, but never are these songs tainted by any scent of hatred or references to vengeance. The Christianity of the spirituals is a religion of reconciling redemptive love. These songs dug the foundation for the successive waves of the struggle for freedom and civil rights and watered the stream of cultural retrieval and reappropriation. The spirituals are songs sung in hope of liberation in the context of a wilderness, but one in which God is at work, daily, hourly, to bring justice to completion.

The Fusion of Black and Catholic Traditions: Lead Me, Guide Me

The publication of *Lead Me, Guide Me: The African American Catholic Hymnal* was welcomed by reviewers. Black Protestant hymnologists Melva Costen and Jon Spencer were quick to recognize the role of the Civil Rights movement and the Black cultural revolution in prodding Black Catholics to explore and embrace their identity.[51] Wendelin Watson commented on the fusion of the Black and Catholic aesthetic liturgical traditions:

> The very appearance of *Lead Me, Guide Me* is striking and makes a distinct statement regarding the strong African-American heritage of Black Catholics. It has a hardbound laminated cover in the colors of the Black American liberation flag—red, black, and green—which symbolize the Black heritage and solidarity with African peoples. The flags of many African countries are made up of these colors which symbolize the shed blood, the race/color, and the land of its peoples. The title, *Lead Me, Guide Me* appears at the bottom of the front cover in bright green letters

---

[51] Costen, "Published Hymnals in the Afro-American Tradition," 17; Spencer, *Black Hymnody*, 187.

against a black and red design characteristic of African kinte [sic] cloths.⁵²

Watson also noticed the use of Catholic symbols on the cover: on the front, the large capital letter *P*, evoking the Greek symbol, *chi-ro* used among early Christian communities to represent Christ, and, on the back, the stylized letter *M*, a Marian tribute.⁵³

One of the earliest attempts to incorporate spirituals into European American Christian liturgical traditions may well have occurred in 1934 through the work of an Episcopal priest at the "Negro mission" of St. Simon of Cyrene, near Cincinnati, Ohio. This successful effort was documented by Sister Esther Mary, N.C.T., in her article, "Spirituals in the Church."⁵⁴ In a lecture at the first meeting of the Black Catholic Theological Symposium, Rivers recalled a similar experiment, one not nearly so successful. Rivers commented on the attempt by a religious sister in Oklahoma to bring together Black culture and Catholic worship:

> [Sister] attempted to cover the language of the Latin Mass with unadapted melodies from Negro spirituals. I remember the *Kyrie* was sung to the exact tune of "Nobody Knows the Trouble I See." The melody was an ill fitting garment for the words, however noble the idea behind the effort. . . . But I do remember someone saying around that time that Sister might have been more successful had she tried to adapt the basic style and the various elements of Black music to the needs of our liturgical texts without forcing, as it were, a shotgun wedding of existing melodies with incompatible texts.⁵⁵

It is likely that Rivers would have found Sister Mary's argument for the use of spirituals in liturgical settings quite compatible with his own thinking. "The value of using spirituals in the service of a Church

---

[52] Wendelin J. Watson, review of *Lead Me, Guide Me: The African American Catholic Hymnal*, *The Journal of Black Sacred Music* 3, no. 1 (Spring 1989): 69.
[53] Watson, review of *Lead Me, Guide Me*, 69.
[54] Sister Esther Mary, N.C.T., "Spirituals in the Church," *The Southern Workman* 63 (1934): 308–314.
[55] Clarence Joseph Rivers, "Thank God We Ain't What We Was: The State of the Liturgy in the Black Catholic Community," *U.S. Catholic Historian* 5, no. 1 (1986): 84.

ministering to Colored people," she asserted, "seems to me to be threefold—the spirituals are a natural means of religious expression of the Negro people, they possess a beauty not dependent upon training and voice, [and] they offer a wealth of truly fine religious meanings."[56] Rivers recognized the contribution that the spirituals might make to what he called "effective worship"—that is, an instance of "humanly felt, perceived spiritual renewal/metanoia/uplift/healing." He grasped their essential simplicity, their "magnitude."[57]

Conclusion: The Enduring Role of Spirituals

The Institute for Black Catholic Studies (IBCS) continues as a foremost site of Black Catholic intellectual and cultural research and liturgical experimentation. The spirituals hold a treasured and commanding place in the institute. Not only are the spirituals sung frequently at daily morning prayer and daily Eucharist, they figure prominently in the annual ceremony of the Commemoration of Ancestors. Moreover, the spirituals are the topic of a course taught regularly at the institute, and along with the slave narratives (oral histories generated from interviews with former slaves and their descendants through the Federal Writers Project in the late 1930s), constitute primary source material for courses on Black spirituality, Black approaches to scripture, and African American religious experience. In July 1993, New York-based folk artist Reginald Wilson, director of Reginald Wilson's Fist and Heel Performance Group, was invited to conduct a special seminar at the institute on the ringshout, the holy dance that often accompanied the singing of spirituals during the period of enslavement. After a lecture and breathing and body exercises, Wilson led a group of IBCS participants in a most prayerful engagement with this centuries-old holy dance.

Singing the spirituals as my grandmother did, as we do at the institute, as so many Black Catholics have done and continue to do, is a way of reaching inward to what liturgist and composer Grayson

---

[56] Sister Esther Mary, "Spirituals in the Church," 309–310.
[57] Clarence Joseph Rivers, *The Spirit in Worship* (Cincinnati: Stimuli, 1978), 198, 199.

Brown identified as that *something* that is already within us but to which we may need a reintroduction.[58] Another way to say this is that we are trying to come home to ourselves. That homecoming may be the recognition of a cultural or cognitive orientation; it may be an admission of a hunger for polyrhythm, asymmetry, improvisation, and the drum; or it may be surrender to a yearning for release, for vision. No matter: the spirituals and *Lead Me, Guide Me* are important vehicles for African American Catholics in our journey.

---

[58] Grayson Warren Brown, "Music in the Black Tradition," in *This Far by Faith: American Black Worship and Its African Roots* (Washington, DC: National Office for Black Catholics and the Liturgical Conference, 1977), 93.

Sister Thea Bowman: Liturgical Justice through Black Sacred Song

KIM R. HARRIS*

What does it mean to be black and Catholic? It means that I come to my church fully functioning. That doesn't frighten you, does it? I come to my church fully functioning. I bring myself, my black self, all that I am, all that I have, all that I hope to become, I bring my whole history, my traditions, my experience, my culture, my African-American song and dance and gesture and movement and teaching and preaching and healing and responsibility as gifts to the church.[1]

—Sister Thea Bowman, F.S.P.A.,
to the United States Catholic Bishops, June 17, 1989,
Seton Hall University, South Orange, New Jersey

Sister Thea Bowman, a member of the Franciscan Sisters of Perpetual Adoration of La Crosse, Wisconsin (FSPA), famously spoke before the United States bishops as part of a two-hour study session during their semi-annual meeting in 1989, less than a year before her death due to cancer.[2] Reflecting on one of the central themes of that meeting, evangelization among Catholic "minorities," she chided, challenged, perhaps frightened, and certainly encouraged the bishops to seriously consider what it meant to be Black and Catholic, in the United States historically and during the late twentieth century. Among her points, Bowman advocated, as a matter of racial justice, for the comprehension and liturgical

---

* A version of this essay was first published in *U.S. Catholic Historian* 35, no. 1 (Winter 2017): 99–124.

[1] Celine Cepress, F.S.P.A., ed., *Sister Thea Bowman: Shooting Star* (Winona, MN: St. Mary's Press, 1993), 29–37, quote at 32.

[2] Sister Thea's cause for sainthood is progressing. She was declared a "Servant of God" on June 1, 2018. See "Sister Thea Bowman: Cause for Canonization," https://www.sistertheabowman.com/timeline/.

acceptance of the many expressions of Black spirituality by the leaders and people of the wider Church community.[3] The promotion and liturgical use of one form of this expression, spirituals, a historic and foundational form of Black sacred song, constituted a substantial portion of her efforts during the last twenty-five years of her life.[4] The results of her work in this area still reverberate among Black Catholics, the wider Catholic community and ecumenically, through Bowman's speeches, writings, recordings, in the liturgical use of the Black Catholic hymnal, *Lead Me, Guide Me* (1987), and through the contemporary compositions of Black Catholic composers and arrangers.

In Bowman's speech to the bishops, she chose not to address an evolving controversy that fractured the Black Catholic community. Only two weeks before the meeting, Washington, D.C., priest, Father George A. Stallings Jr., broke away from the Church and organized the Imani Temple as an independent church for Black Catholics.[5] Stallings had argued for the full liturgical expression of Black culture in a separate rite within Catholicism, but chose to leave the Church.[6] Stallings' departure divided Black Catholics. "Which side are you on?" soon became a pressing question and an existential choice.[7]

To open her presentation to the bishops, Bowman sang a spiritual and began to unpack its meaning in a brief reflection on the song:

"Sometimes I feel like a motherless child/ A long way from home...." Can you hear me church, will you help me church? I'm a pilgrim in the journey looking for home, and Jesus told me the church is my home, and Jesus told me that heaven is my home and I have here no

---

[3] Charlene Smith and John Feister, *Thea's Song: The Life of Thea Bowman* (Maryknoll, NY: Orbis Press, 2009), 260–261.

[4] Smith and Feister, *Thea's Song*, xv–xvi.

[5] Ronald L. Sharps, "Black Catholics in the United States: A Historical Chronology," *U.S. Catholic Historian* 12, no. 1 (Winter 1994): 139–140.

[6] Mary McGann, *Let It Shine: The Emergence of African American Catholic Worship* (New York: Fordham University Press, 2008), 16.

[7] Smith and Feister, *Thea's Song*, 268.

lasting city. Cardinals, archbishops, bishops: My brothers or church, please help me to get home.[8]

In both African American speech and traditional song, words such as "home" and "heaven" contain a surplus of meaning, referring to not only shelter, hospitality, and redemption, but also metaphorical and physical freedom. Historically, during the time of African American enslavement in the United States, freedom seekers and their allies on the Underground Railroad additionally utilized "home" and "heaven" as sung and spoken code words for territory beyond the reach of slavery.[9] As Bowman explained to the bishops, there was no "home" for Black Catholics in a church that devalued Black leaders, community, and consultation. Further, there was diminished Black Catholic participation in the teaching, preaching, witnessing, worshiping, reconciling, and justice-making work of the Church when Blacks were detached from their own history and heritage. To her critique of European-American Church leaders, she added an admonition to her own racial/cultural community:

> Some Black people don't approve of Black religious expression in Catholic liturgy. They've been told that it's not properly Catholic. They've been told that it's not appropriately serious or dignified or solemn or controlled, that the European way is necessarily the better way.[10]

The steps toward justice Sister Thea laid out included greater Black Catholic self-knowledge and self-acceptance, welcoming the gifts of Blackness within the wider Church, and working cooperatively with people of all heritages ministering in African American communities. Historic Black sacred song undergirded the foundation of the *home* she sought to build in the Church.

---

[8] "To Be Black and Catholic," *Origins* (July 6, 1989): 114–118, in Cepress, *Sister Thea Bowman*, 29.
[9] Charles L. Blockson, "Glossary of Secret Code Words and Phrases," unpublished, 1988. Used by permission of the author.
[10] "To Be Black and Catholic," *Origins* (July 6, 1989): 114–118, in Cepress, *Sister Thea Bowman*, 35.

As reactions and responses to Stallings' plans increased, Sister Thea covered her disappointment with public silence on the issue.[11] In reflection of her upbringing in Southern African American culture, Bowman decided not to "air out" this deep tension within the Black Catholic community. Personally, she chose to work for racial and liturgical justice from within the Church and in concert with the Black Catholic community.[12]

Early Life and Religious Conversion

Bowman participated in her own journey toward finding answers to the questions with which she challenged the bishops. Thea Bowman (née Bertha Elizabeth) was born in Yazoo City, Mississippi, on December 29, 1937. Though her parents lived in Canton, Bowman's mother, Mary Esther Coleman Bowman, stayed with a family friend in Yazoo City to await the birth of her child. Canton, Mississippi, located in the racially segregated South, offered no hospital for Blacks, or even an African American doctor in the area, other than Bertha's father, Theon Edward Bowman.[13] It was the fact that white doctors and hospitals routinely and lawfully denied medical care to Blacks that inspired Dr. Bowman to establish his practice in Canton.[14]

As the only child of a doctor and a teacher, Bertha grew up in relatively comfortable, middle-class circumstances. Black neighbors considered her family "rich." Her mother, Mary Bowman, did not work outside the home, unlike most Black women in the area.[15] Mary

---

[11] Stallings automatically incurred excommunication when he established an independent congregation in February 1990. After inviting Stallings to address their conference in 1989, the Joint Conference of Black Clergy, Sisters and Seminarians proposed to study the feasibility of establishing an African American Roman Catholic Rite at the 1992 National Black Catholic Congress. Sister Thea did not live to participate in this Congress. See Sharps, "Black Catholics in the United States," 139–141.

[12] Father Joseph A. Brown, S.J., phone conversation with the author, December 15, 2016.

[13] Smith and Feister, *Thea's Song*, 18.

[14] Maurice Nutt, ed., *Thea Bowman: In My Own Words* (Liguori, MO: Liguori Publications, 2009), vii.

[15] Paul Murray, interview with Flonzie Brown Wright, Germantown, Ohio, June 23, 2010.

encouraged and expected Bertha to be a sophisticated, "sweet young lady." Bertha, however, tended toward bold energy and a questioning spirit. Bertha listened to the elders teaching and singing spirituals. She joined in as they passed on stories, traditions, and lessons about Adam and Eve, Cain and Abel, Noah, Moses, David, and Jesus, informing not only her Black identity, but also her religious education.[16] Writing to introduce her book and recording of spirituals, Bowman recounted her early immersion in the music and its effect on her later ministry:

> I did not realize I was receiving a religious education—that I was being taught prayer, salvation history, morals and values, faith, hope, love and joy. . . . I did not know that I was being taught modes of prayer that would increasingly enrich my personal prayer, community prayer, liturgical prayer; modes of prayer that I have been privileged to share with my brothers, sisters, and children of diverse races and culture, economic backgrounds, and religions.[17]

In sharp contrast to the "environment of love and celebration" with which her Black family and community surrounded Bertha, she, like other African Americans in segregated Mississippi, endured legalized and custom-enforced discrimination, cruelty, racism, and daily indignities large and small. In a defining moment, repeated between legions of Black parents and children facing segregation, Bertha's mother "had a fit" when her thirsty child helped herself to a drink from a "Whites only" water fountain.[18] Young Bertha's experience also included hearing from her bedroom window, the police question, then shoot, an unarmed young Black man. That young man, Bertha's acquaintance from childhood, ran past her home and fell to the ground in a yard next door. Bertha heard the woman living in that home remark, "We've got to soak up the blood so the children won't be scared."[19]

---

[16] Nutt, *Thea Bowman*, viii.
[17] Thea Bowman, *Sister Thea: Songs of My People, A Compilation of Favorite Spirituals* (Boston: St. Paul Books and Media, 1989), 3.
[18] Smith and Feister, *Thea's Song*, 27.
[19] Margaret Walker and Thea Bowman, "God Touched My Life," in Smith and Feister, *Thea's Song*, 28–29.

Into this deeply segregated community, the Franciscan Sisters of Perpetual Adoration from La Crosse, Wisconsin, arrived in Canton in 1948 to start a school for Black children attached to the Holy Child Jesus Mission for African Americans. Black community members, meeting with the Missionary Servants of the Most Holy Trinity, the priests who staffed the new Catholic congregation, determined education for Black students to be their top priority.[20] The Missionary Servants, in turn, recruited the FSPA sisters to establish the school.

Flonzie Brown Wright, a schoolmate and Bowman's lifelong friend, remembers the strange sight of White women in long dresses and close fitting head coverings knocking on the doors of Black homes where children could be found playing in the yard. The sisters approached each family about sending their children to the new school. She also recalls the contrast between the segregated Black public school and the better educational opportunity the sisters offered at the Holy Child Jesus School. Wright's school experience up to that point featured outdated, torn books, and overcrowded conditions in a run-down building.[21] Bowman's parents noted with dismay that their energetic, inquisitive daughter, after five years in public school, did not read up to the requirements of her grade level. Both Wright's and Bowman's parents along with other Black parents, many whom struggled to pay the cost of tuition, enrolled their children in the new Catholic school. Wright remembers the girls loving the school, singing in the little church and school choir and being attracted to the sisters by their kindness, their teaching ability, and their generosity with ice cream cones and fresh baked cookies.[22]

Catholic education not only increased Bowman's academic achievement, but also influenced her spirituality. The students attended Mass each week. Wright recounts that young Bertha exhibited great interest in everything about the FSPA sisters and their Catholic religious tradition:

---

[20] Smith and Feister, *Thea's Song*, 31.
[21] Smith and Feister, *Thea's Song*, 34–36.
[22] Murray, interview with Flonzie Wright, 5.

Little by little she really began the conversion to Catholicism. She really wanted to be a Sister. She was intrigued with the culture. She was intrigued with their compassion. She was intrigued with how they would come to the homes and help families cook or how they would pick up kids whose noses were running and wipe the noses and all of that. Thea was really enamored with their culture.[23]

As a young person Bowman "tried" various churches: Episcopal, Baptist, Adventist, and African Methodist Episcopal, among others. After enrolling in the new school, the example of the FSPA sisters and the growing Black Catholic community inspired her. The Catholics Bowman observed loved and cared for each other as well as for those in urgent need due to racial segregation and poverty.[24] Bertha Bowman, of her own volition, joined the Catholic Church at age ten, receiving baptism and first Communion in June 1947 at Holy Child Jesus Mission.

It was principally Bowman's attraction to the works of compassion she saw among the sisters that drew her to begin the journey toward becoming an FSPA sister. Over the strong objections and deep disappointment of her parents, fifteen-year-old Bertha traveled to the FSPA motherhouse in La Crosse, Wisconsin. Far from her family and her cultural heritage, Bowman became the only African American aspirant and eventually the only Black woman in this European-American religious order.[25]

Bertha Bowman faced many adjustments in her new surroundings: snow; unfamiliar food; the La Crosse, Wisconsin, community composed largely of Caucasian, German, Irish, Catholic, Lutheran, Swedish, and Nordic identities; sleeping in a dormitory with the other aspirants; the formal prayer style of the religious community; the speech patterns of her new northern sisters; and the strict uniformity. Similar to the experiences of other Black women entering White religious communities, Bertha experienced racism and prejudice among the sisters, even as she made friends with

---

[23] Murray, interview with Flonzie Wright, 5.
[24] Nutt, *Thea Bowman*, ix.
[25] Murray, interview with Flonzie Wright, 2–3.

those whom she would share a deep relationship for the remainder of her life.[26]

The beginning of Bertha's new life with the FSPA sisters included the continuation of her formal education. Once in Wisconsin, she entered St. Rose High School as a junior. Sister Lina Putz, one of her FSPA teachers, reported Bertha's academic success, via mail, to her parents.[27] She was a gifted writer; national organizations that published essays and poems by high school writers recognized Bertha's work.[28]

A long illness interrupted both Bertha's high school education and postulancy with the sisters. While recovering at the River Pines Sanatorium for Tuberculosis in Stevens Point, Wisconsin, Bertha took a correspondence course from the University of Wisconsin in English composition. Bertha eventually received her high school diploma while still recovering at the sanatorium. After a year of ill health, Bertha returned to the FSPA motherhouse in La Crosse and entered the novitiate in August 1956, a year behind her original class. Bertha requested and received the name Thea, in honor of St. Thea, a fourth-century martyr, and of her father, Dr. Theon Bowman.[29]

During Bertha's time in the sanatorium, highly publicized and racially motivated events in Mississippi and Alabama incited African Americans and their allies to organize and take action for freedom: the murder of unarmed Black teenager Emmett Till in Money, Mississippi; the refusal of Rosa Parks to give up her seat on the Cleveland Street bus in Montgomery, Alabama; and the ensuing Montgomery Bus Boycott. It is possible that Bertha read about these events while in the sanatorium. The sounds of the Montgomery Bus Boycott mass meetings included the singing of hymns and spirituals to comfort and inspire the people. Did Bertha sing along with the activists what she heard on television? "This little light of mine, I'm gonna let it shine!"

---

[26] Smith and Feister, *Thea's Song*, 55–56.
[27] Smith and Feister, *Thea's Song*, 45.
[28] National Essay Association, National High School Poetry Association, *Scholastic Magazine*, in Smith and Feister, *Thea's Song*, 49.
[29] Smith and Feister, *Thea's Song*, xv.

By the time the Montgomery Bus Boycott ended in December 1956, Bertha was Sister Mary Thea and in her first year of novitiate formation. With the other new sisters, she immersed herself in spiritual practices and training in the history, legacy, and culture of her religious order. Reading from the secular press or listening to the radio was forbidden. When Sister Thea felt lonely for her culture and music, she sang spirituals softly to herself or aloud when possible.[30]

The second year of novitiate formation included full-time study at Viterbo College in La Crosse, operated by the FSPA sisters. Sister Thea majored in English and minored in drama. Her music activities in the community included singing in the St. Rose choir as well as in the more selective St. Rose schola, which sang Gregorian chant and music in Latin for the liturgies. On August 12, 1958, Sister Thea and nineteen other novice sisters made their first profession of vows.[31]

Thea continued full-time study for an additional year at Viterbo to make up for the courses she had missed while in the sanatorium (1958–1959). Her religious community, recognizing her talent for teaching, was grooming her to be an educator. During this year she also took voice lessons, studied music, and continued singing with the convent and church choirs. Her first teaching assignment in the fall of 1959 interrupted her formal education, a common occurrence in the late 1950s and early 1960s when young sisters were sent into classrooms before they completed their bachelor's degrees to meet the challenge of larger, "baby boom" Catholic school populations.[32]

The FSPA council assigned Sister Thea to teach fifth and sixth grades at Blessed Sacrament Elementary School in La Crosse, Wisconsin. The school population was almost exclusively European-American. The Catholic parish to which the school belonged served La Crosse's upper-middle class: educators, doctors, business owners, and lawyers. A few parents demanded a meeting with the school principal when they learned that their children were assigned to a Black teacher. The principal, Sister Clarice Kleinfeinz,

---

[30] Smith and Feister, *Thea's Song*, 72.
[31] Smith and Feister, *Thea's Song*, 74.
[32] Smith and Feister, *Thea's Song*, 72, 75–76.

arranged a meeting to introduce the parents to Sister Thea. The young sister's professionalism and personality allayed their fears. Over the next two years, Sister Thea's students grew to respect and love their teacher. She shared a small part of her cultural heritage with her music class, teaching them the spiritual, "Couldn't Hear Nobody Pray." They clamored for more. Regrettably, their music book contained only three Negro spirituals. Sister Thea taught all three, noting the students' enthusiasm. During this time, her excitement for teaching also grew.

Bowman's Return to Canton, Mississippi, in the Midst of Discord

In 1961 Bowman happily returned to her family, her cultural roots, and the Holy Child Jesus community as an FSPA sister and an elementary school teacher, instructing students in English and music.[33] But the deprivation and danger facing Black citizens in Canton tempered her joy. Her homecoming coincided with the last months of the Civil Rights Freedom Rides. Though she did not participate as a Freedom Rider when activists came through the area, Bowman's daily life included remaining vigilant as she traveled by car with the other sisters. Members of the local White community objected to a Black sister living or riding with White sisters, so Bowman ducked down in the car as they rode past Whites, especially police officers.[34]

As Sister Thea told author Margaret Walker in a 1992 interview, in addition to teaching, giving medical care, fundraising, and duties consistent with living in a religious community, the sisters' activities included "working hard" for voter registration in Canton's Black community. In 1962 and the first half of 1963, Bowman's activities also included traveling nearly 1,000 miles each way by train on designated weekends from Canton to La Crosse in preparation for her final profession as a sister. Given her unique social location among the sisters and the La Crosse community, Bowman was invited to speak at

---

[33] Nutt, *Thea Bowman*, 13.
[34] Thea Bowman to Margaret Walker Alexander, in Smith and Feister, *Thea's Song*, 90.

Viterbo College about the Civil Rights movement then growing in intensity. Bowman called for diminishment of prejudice against Negroes from the White community and recounted the prejudice against the sisters she worked to overcome after they arrived in Canton. Bowman dismissed accusations that Martin Luther King Jr., held Communist Party sympathies. At the same time, she expressed concern that the demonstrations King led not go "too far."[35]

Church bombings, the killing of children in Birmingham, Alabama, shots fired at the Freedom House (a Civil Rights headquarters and "dorm" in Canton), and the bombing of that same Freedom House punctuated Bowman's return to Canton as a fully professed sister in 1963. Bowman began teaching high school students at the Holy Child Jesus School in the midst of dangerous and turbulent events. Given the violence and discrimination in close proximately, it is no wonder that Bowman's students lacked enthusiasm for history, science, English, and math. Meeting student attitudes with her own creativity, Bowman added lessons to the curriculum she later described as essential for African American students. Bowman taught the students to sing spirituals, what she called a ". . . living repository of the thoughts, feelings and will of Black Spirituality." This music, through the voices of the elders and the enslaved and free communities that created it, carried messages of lament, resistance, faith, hope, love, and freedom. As Bowman repeatedly exclaimed, "Black music lifts up the lives we lived and live."[36]

The lives of the Holy Child Jesus students, teachers, and ministers continued to be affected by segregation and threats of racial violence in the mid-1960s. Canton was at that time 70% African American and an important locus for Civil Rights work. The Congress of Racial Equality (CORE) took the lead in Canton. The NAACP, considered a more moderate organization than CORE, also maintained an office there.[37]

---

[35] Smith and Feister, *Thea's Song*, 90–92.
[36] Presentation to the 1982 National Black Sisters' Conference, printed in "Spirituality: The Soul of My People," in Cepress, *Sister Thea Bowman*, 45.
[37] Paul Murray, e-mail to author, August 10, 2016.

All African Americans in Canton knew the dangerous climate facing local and visiting Civil Rights workers. On June 23, 1966, sheriff's deputies and Mississippi State Police beat and tear-gassed 1,000 Civil Rights marchers in Canton. Their march had its beginning eighteen days earlier. When James Meredith, known for integrating the University of Mississippi in 1962, began a solo march from Memphis, Tennessee, to Jackson, Mississippi, to challenge the fear under which African Americans lived daily, he hoped to encourage Mississippi's 400,000 eligible Blacks to register to vote.

On the second day of his solitary march, Aubrey Norvell shot Meredith three times with a sixteen-gauge automatic shotgun. Meredith survived and other Civil Rights leaders, including Dr. Martin Luther King, Jr., Floyd McKissick, and Stokely Carmichael continued the march. In Canton, the activists attempted to set up tents on the grounds of the Black public elementary school. The tear gas attack that followed forced marchers to run for refuge to Holy Child Jesus Mission. There the FSPA sisters, with the consent of the pastor, Father Luke Mikschl of the Missionary Servants of the Most Holy Trinity, housed, fed, and cared for 800 marchers, some of whom were seriously injured. The Holy Child Jesus Mission complex featured a large gymnasium, school, convent, rectory, and a modern church building. In the morning after the attack on the marchers, Father Mikschl received a call at 4:00 a.m. informing him that the Ku Klux Klan had bombed St. Joachim's Catholic School for African Americans in nearby Carthage, Mississippi. The priests, marchers, and sisters in Canton passed the next few hours in extreme fear and heightened vigilance.[38]

In the midst of these traumatic events, Bowman drew on the historic, truth-telling, justice seeking, and healing music of her people. She formed a singing group of her Holy Child Jesus students and recorded a fundraising album for the support of the school: *The Voice of Negro America* by the Holy Child Singers. The album was dedicated to "the promotion of brotherhood and universal

---

[38] Kim R. Harris, "Welcome Table, A Mass of Spirituals" (Ph.D. dissertation, Union Theological Seminary, 2013), 13.

peace."[39] The messages in the songs named injustice, called for peace, and affirmed a God who holds the world in his hands, while choosing the side of freedom and equality for all people.[40]

On two tracks between the thirteen spirituals on the LP, Bowman recorded strong appeals for pride in Black identity, for understanding and respect by Whites, for racial reconciliation, and for her people to remain strong. Sister Thea exhorted her listeners,

> Listen! Hear us! While the world is full of hate, strife, vengeance, we sing songs of love, laughter, worship, wisdom, justice, and peace because we are free. Though our forefathers bent to bear the heat of the sun, the strike of the lash, the chain of slavery, we are free. No man can enslave us. We are too strong, too unafraid. America needs our strength, our voices to drown out her sorrows, the clatter of war. . . . Listen! Hear us! We are the voice of Negro America.[41]

Liturgical Change in the Church

Through the second half of the 1950s into the 1960s, Sister Thea Bowman's utilization of her musical-cultural heritage grew and evolved from a means of personal sustenance in a foreign culture, to an addition to the musical education of her young White students, an inspiration and a fundraising tool for her Black high school students, and a means for promoting justice for her people in Canton, Mississippi, and beyond. During these years, experimentation by musicians, liturgists, and pastoral ministers led to the composition and promulgation of new liturgical music and documents which guided the place of music in Catholic worship. Eventually the singing of traditional, vernacular, culturally-cued music, such as spirituals, during the liturgy was accepted.

---

[39] *The Voice of Negro America*, LP record produced by Holy Child Jesus School (Canton, MS: 1967).

[40] The recorded spirituals include "Go Down Moses," "Down By The Riverside," "He's Got The Whole World," and "Year of Jubilo," among others. See https://www.discogs.com/Holy-Child-Singers-The-Voice-Of-Negro-America/%20release/5893977.

[41] *The Voice of Negro America*.

Father Joseph A. Brown, S.J., described the liturgical renewal and subsequent changes, focused through the documents of the Second Vatican Council (1962–1965), as more significant for Black Catholics in particular and for Catholic Christians in general than any other single event of Christian renewal in the twentieth century.[42] In addition to the Second Vatican Council, theologian M. Shawn Copeland added the Civil Rights movement and the Black Arts movement as a trio of nearly inseparable events influencing Black Catholic liturgical-musical development.[43] The Civil Rights movement inspired Black Catholics toward agitating for both social and ecclesial change. The movement gave Black Catholics the impetus to challenge "the persistent racism that denied them full participation and leadership in their Church."[44] The spirit and mandates of the Vatican II documents, particularly the document on the liturgy, *Sacrosanctum Concilium*, enabled Black Catholics to participate more fully in the liturgy while encouraging the wedding of elements of Black culture to the Catholic liturgy.[45] The Black Arts movement inspired artists to connect aesthetics and ethics to the whole experience of Black life, including their religious experiences.[46] Without the convergence of these events, Black Catholics like Sister Thea Bowman might have continued participating in their church without the benefit or recognition of the particular genius of their cultural heritage.[47]

In 1947, the year that Bertha Bowman joined the Catholic Church, Pope Pius XII affirmed the use of Latin as the language of liturgy in the encyclical *Mediator Dei*. Many saw this insistence on Latin as a blow to the burgeoning liturgical movements for greater congregational engagement and cultural inclusion in the Eucharistic

---

[42] Joseph A. Brown, S.J., *To Stand on the Rock: Meditations on Black Catholic Identity* (Maryknoll, NY: Orbis Books, 1998), 175.

[43] M. Shawn Copeland, "*The African American Catholic Hymnal* and the African American Spiritual," *U.S. Catholic Historian* 19, no. 2 (Spring 2001): 66–82.

[44] McGann, *Let It Shine*, 6.

[45] J-Glenn Murray, "The Liturgy of the Roman Rite and African American Worship," in *Lead Me, Guide Me: The Black Catholic Hymnal* (Chicago: GIA Publications, 1987).

[46] Copeland, "*African American Catholic Hymnal*," 68.

[47] McGann, *Let It Shine*, 6.

liturgy.⁴⁸ Thus, the Catholic worship that young Bertha first encountered was a new and foreign experience. Bowman's friend, Flonzie Wright, remembers the Latin and the ritual of the Mass as "strange and different," more than "good or bad."⁴⁹ Church regulations at this time banned women from liturgical singing, promoted Gregorian chant, and limited the use of most musical instruments except the organ. At this time, the Protestant churches of Bowman and Wright's experience featured gospel music sung by men and women and played on a variety of instruments.⁵⁰

On Christmas 1955, prior to the Second Vatican Council, and while Bertha recuperated in Stevens Point, Wisconsin, Catholic communities worldwide received encouragement from the encyclical *Musicae sacrae disciplina* to form liturgical choirs of men and women, utilize other instruments other than the pipe organ, and to invite the congregation to participate in the liturgy through singing. In this encyclical, Pope Pius XII and Church liturgical leadership cautiously approved the singing of popular vernacular hymns of individual national and racial groups:

> [T]hey must be in full conformity with the doctrine of the Catholic faith. They must also express and explain that doctrine accurately. Likewise they must use plain language and simple melody and must be free from violent and vain excess of words. Despite the fact that they are short and easy, they should manifest a religious dignity and seriousness. When they are fashioned in this way these sacred canticles, born as they are from the most profound depths of the people's soul, deeply move the emotions and spirit and stir up pious sentiments.⁵¹

It is highly unlikely that the FSPA convent choir or schola would have chosen to sing music from Sister Thea's tradition, but around the

---

⁴⁸ James F. White, *Roman Catholic Worship: Trent to Today* (New York: Paulist Press, 1995), 81.
⁴⁹ Murray, interview with Flonzie Wright, 4.
⁵⁰ Murray, interview with Flonzie Wright, 3.
⁵¹ *Musicae Sacrae*, Encyclical of Pope Pius XII on Sacred Music, 1955, http://www.vatican.va/holy_father/pius_xii/encyclicals/documents/hf_p-xii_enc_25121955_musicae-sacrae_en.html, no. 63.

country Black Catholic communities slowly began introducing the newly allowed liturgical-cultural innovations. They chose the spirituals Sister Thea loved as a first source for liturgical music. These historic songs of faith and freedom provided Black Catholics with a cultural and musical "touchstone," harkening back to the beginnings of African American religious experience on American soil.[52]

In Washington, D.C., for example, the music director at historic St. Augustine's parish, George A. "Gus" Jackson, added spirituals to the Negro history week liturgies. The song choices included "My Lord What A Morning."[53] After the implementation of *Musicae sacrae*, a spiritual could "officially" occupy the place of a hymn during the Eucharistic liturgy. The more hospitable atmosphere among official church liturgists, leaders, and musicians for the culturally related innovations also bore significant fruit on the African continent; fruit that very quickly fed and inspired White and Black Catholic communities in the U.S.

Beginning in 1957 Father Guido Haazen, Andre Lukusa, Joachim Ngoi, and forty-seven Congolese men and boys collaboratively linked traditional African melodies to the Latin text of the Mass. All the melodies for the common parts of the Mass originated from the indigenous traditions of the Luba people and the collective improvisation of the group. The choir first performed *Missa Luba* at St. Bavo, a Catholic mission in the town of Kamina in the Belgian Congo. Percussion instruments made up the only accompaniment. The Congolese choir went on an extended European tour, including stops in Holland and Belgium.[54]

Father Boniface Luykx, a Belgian Norbertine monk, brought an early recording of *Missa Luba* to Black Catholic liturgical pioneer

---

[52] McGann, *Let It Shine*, 11.

[53] Morris J. MacGregor, *Emergence of a Black Catholic Community: St. Augustine's in Washington* (Washington, DC: Catholic University of America Press, 1999), 503.

[54] Guido Haazen, interview by Marc Ashley Foster, translated by Peter Schütte, e-mail, August 28, 2003, in Mark Ashley Foster, "*Missa Luba*: A New Edition and Conductor's Analysis" (Ph.D. dissertation, University of North Carolina at Greensboro, 2005), 10–11, 17.

Father Clarence Rivers in Cincinnati, Ohio. Ordained in 1956 and then the only Black priest in the diocese, Rivers shared *Missa Luba* with the sisters who conducted the grade school in his parish of St. Joseph in Cincinnati's West End. Sisters Ephrem, Christopher (Mary O'Brien), Andre Burkhardt—all White—and African American Sister Francesca Thompson of the Sisters of St. Francis of Oldenburg, Indiana, in turn taught the new Mass setting to the children.[55]

When Msgr. Clement J. Busemeyer, the pastor of St. Joseph, heard the enthusiastic singing of the students, he rushed to see Rivers. He wondered aloud if something could be done to invigorate the congregational singing at parish Eucharistic liturgies. The children sang *Missa Luba* for the pastor's twenty-fifth ordination jubilee liturgy.[56] Rivers and others began to spread the word about *Missa Luba* and the vitality this Mass setting brought to liturgies. Msgr. Thomas Hadden, the retired vicar of African-Ancestry Ministry in the Diocese of Raleigh, North Carolina, reported that in his area, *Missa Luba* "spread like wildfire. . . . African Americans in the parishes he visited loved this Mass and sang it all the time." Black and White Catholic individuals and communities in other areas of the United States heard and appreciated *Missa Luba*, especially when a commercial recording became available in 1963. The first electronically engraved choral score followed in 1969.[57]

Inspired by his parish's success with *Missa Luba* and challenged by Father Luykx to compose from his own cultural-musical traditions, Rivers began to write music for liturgies.[58] He employed elements of spirituals, gospel, jazz, and his own creativity in his occasional musical pieces. Rivers' composition efforts were even more remarkable given the racial and ecclesial climate of the era and the timing of his pioneering work.

---

[55] Clarence Joseph Rivers, "Freeing the Spirit: Very Personal Reflections on One Man's Search for the Spirit in Worship," *U.S. Catholic Historian* 19, no. 2 (Spring 2001): 103.
[56] Rivers, "Freeing the Spirit," 98–99.
[57] Douglas Shadle, "Black Catholicism and Music in Durham, North Carolina: Praxis in a New Key" (M.A. thesis, University of North Carolina at Chapel Hill, 2006), 37–38, at https://cdr.lib.unc.edu/.
[58] Rivers, "Freeing the Spirit," 99.

As the first Black diocesan priest in Cincinnati, Rivers lived, ministered, and composed under scrutiny in a racist diocesan climate. He lamented the fact that Cincinnati Archbishop Karl J. Alter forbade a concert of spirituals at St. Peter in Chains Cathedral since Alter considered spirituals "secular" music.[59] Inspired by *Missa Luba*, Rivers arranged for drummed accompaniments to his liturgical compositions. When newspaper articles reported "drumming" in St. Joseph's Church, a letter came from Alter's office demanding only "sacred instruments" be used.[60]

Rivers' work and experimentation began before the implementation of the liturgical changes envisioned by Vatican II's *Sacrosanctum Concilium*. In the late 1950s, Rivers, like other liturgical reformers, already championed the "full, conscious, and active participation" of the faithful in the liturgy of the Church.[61] Fortuitously, his pastor, whom Rivers described as "exteriorly gruff and Teutonic," supported the attempts, cautiously anticipating an aspect of liturgical renewal that Vatican II would later promote.[62]

By the time Sister Thea returned to Canton to teach at the Holy Child Jesus School in fall of 1961, there were new and evolving liturgical ideas and tools at her disposal. Elementary school classmate Flonzie Brown Wright remembers the FSPA sisters introducing a popular spiritual when she and Bertha were students. "They taught us many songs. I think the first time I heard *Kumbaya* was from the Sisters."[63] Wright does not mention if *Kumbaya* was used liturgically, yet during Sister Thea's tenure as a teacher, spirituals became a part of the liturgy. By 1964–1965 Father Clarence Rivers' *American*

---

[59] Sharps, "Black Catholics in the United States," 133.
[60] Rivers, "Freeing the Spirit," 101.
[61] In 1956 at Assisi, Italy, Americans joined to petition Pius XII for the use of the vernacular in the Mass of the Roman Rite. See Rivers, "Freeing the Spirit," 101. At an earlier conference in Lugano, Switzerland (1953), and again at Assisi, Catholic missionaries, such as Johannes Hofinger, petitioned not only for the use of the vernacular, but also for greater simplicity in the rites, as an aid to liturgical accessibility for their congregations. See John W. O'Malley, *What Happened at Vatican II* (Cambridge, MA: Belknap Press of Harvard University Press, 2008), 101.
[62] Constitution on the Sacred Liturgy *Sacrosanctum Concilium*, no. 14.
[63] Murray, interview with Flonzie Wright, 5.

Mass Program was widely available for liturgical use. Given Bowman's leadership of the Holy Child Jesus Singers, one can easily imagine her utilizing these resources to enliven the liturgy and increase the people's participation in the Mass.

Expanding Spiritual, Cultural, and Ecclesial Awareness

Sister Thea Bowman completed a bachelor's degree in English at Viterbo College in July 1965. She returned to teach in Canton in the fall and then began graduate studies in English at the Catholic University of America, Washington, D.C., in the summer of 1966. The chance to study full-time, year-round beginning in the fall of 1968 along with her move on-campus was a life-changing opportunity for Sister Thea.[64] After thirteen years as a minority within the FSPA, she finally had the chance to be in continuous contact with an established Black Catholic community in Washington.[65]

The summer of 1968 was a socially, politically and ecclesiastically turbulent time nationally and for the burgeoning national Black Catholic movement. After the assassination of Dr. Martin Luther King Jr. on April 4, 1968, the people of Washington's Black communities erupted with shock, grief, anger, and rebellion. Violent unrest in the city lasted for four days, with fires and looting destroying White and Black businesses. Militant Black leaders called for continued rebellion while others pleaded for peace and reconciliation. Federal troops guarded federal buildings and eventually occupied Black neighborhoods.[66]

Sister Thea came to live in a city still traumatized by the events of April 1968. She also began to participate in the national Black Catholic community at the beginning of the contemporary Black Catholic movement.[67] Two weeks after the assassination of Dr. Martin Luther

---

[64] Nutt, *Thea Bowman*, x.
[65] Smith and Feister, *Thea's Song*, 99–100.
[66] Bryan N. Massingale, *Racial Justice and the Catholic Church* (Maryknoll, NY: Orbis Books, 2010), 57.
[67] Jamie T. Phelps, O.P., ed., *Black and Catholic: The Challenge and Gift of Black Folk* (Milwaukee, WI: Marquette University Press, 1997), 32.

King, Jr. approximately half of the nation's 150 Black priests met to discuss their challenges and concerns as the Black Catholic Clergy Caucus. Sister Martin DePorres (now Patricia Muriel) Grey, Religious Sister of Mercy, and Brother Joseph M. Davis, Society of Mary (Marianist) joined the meeting as observers.[68] The Black priests' group declared, in a widely publicized manifesto, that "the Catholic Church in the United States, primarily a White racist institution, has addressed itself primarily to White society and is definitely part of that society."[69] The manifesto concluded with a stark admonition: "Unless the Church, by an immediate, effective and total reversing of its present practices, rejects and denounces *all* forms of racism within its ranks and institutions and in the society of which she is a part, she will become unacceptable in the Black community."[70]

The meeting inspired Sister Martin DePorres to gather Black sisters in a group, inviting them to meet at Carlow College in Pittsburgh, Pennsylvania, in August. Sister Thea Bowman attended that meeting of 150 Black religious sisters from seventy-nine congregations, which resulted in the formation of the National Black Sisters' Conference. She led the group in song, an image the National Catholic News Wire flashed across the country. As Sister Antona Ebo reflected, it was with this meeting that Sister Thea "took wings and flew away." Her work moved from the personal and local to the national stage.[71]

Education and Formation Through Black Sacred Song

The newly-formed National Black Sisters' Conference resolved to "work unceasingly for the liberation of Black people."[72] They

---

[68] Joseph Davis, S.M., and Cyprian Rowe, F.M.S., "The Development of the National Office for Black Catholics," *U.S. Catholic Historian* 7, nos. 2–3 (Spring/Summer 1988): 269.

[69] Cyprian Davis, O.S.B., *History of Black Catholics in the United States* (New York: Crossroads, 1990), 258.

[70] Quoted in Massingale, *Racial Justice*, 58.

[71] John Feister, telephone interview with Antona Ebo, F.S.M., St. Louis, December 17, 2007, in Smith and Feister, *Thea's Song*, 103–104; quote at 104.

[72] "History," National Black Sisters' Conference, https://www.nbsc68.com/history.

committed to deepening their own self-development, encouraging Black community action, and agitating for civil and ecclesial institutional reform to root out the discrimination, powerlessness, and poverty affecting the Black community.[73] These themes guided Sister Thea Bowman for the rest of her life, particularly in her advocacy for and utilization of historic Black sacred song in Catholic liturgy.

While studying English literature and linguistics, Sister Thea sang spirituals for chapel liturgies and shared music informally with students through "hootenannies."[74] At this time she researched the musical, historical, and linguistic treasures of her African American heritage. This shaped the ways in which she taught, sang, and proclaimed the Word for scholarly and popular audiences.[75] English faculty member Professor Joseph Sendry remembers a lecture by Sister Thea in which she sang music from her Black tradition and then gave a complete rhetorical analysis of the gestures, intonation, lyrics, and their performance. Sister Thea eventually taught the first Black Studies course at the Catholic University of America, exploring works of African American literature.[76]

After completing her doctorate and returning to Viterbo College as a professor in 1972, Bowman continued to incorporate music into her teaching, as well as her academic, religious, and popular presentations. During her time at Viterbo, Bowman formed the Hallelujah Singers, a touring choir composed of students and friends. This choir showcased the "old songs that generations of Black Americans used to praise God, to comfort their brothers and to ease the pain of life's trying situations."[77]

---

[73] Phelps, *Black and Catholic*, 33; Amy Koehlinger, *The New Nuns: Racial Justice and Religious Reform in the 1960s* (Cambridge, MA: Harvard University Press, 2007), 12.
[74] Smith and Feister, *Thea's Song*, 101–102.
[75] Nutt, *Thea Bowman*, x.
[76] John Feister, interview with Joseph Sendry at Catholic University of America, Washington, D.C., November 6, 2007, in Smith and Feister, *Thea's Song*, 101.
[77] "Symphony Marks 'Sweetheart Night,'" *La Crosse* (WI) *Tribune*, February 2, 1972, in Smith and Feister, *Thea's Song*, 136.

In 1978 Sister Thea returned home to Canton to care for her aging parents. Taking advantage of her return to Mississippi, Bishop Joseph Brunini of the Diocese of Jackson, Mississippi, appointed Bowman to develop and eventually direct the diocesan Office of Intercultural Affairs. In this work Sister Thea promoted racial justice by assailing institutionalized racism in the local and national Church and promoting cultural pride, awareness, and sensitivity.[78] In addition to offering lectures and workshops, Bowman helped found the Black Catholic Theological Symposium, a national Catholic interdisciplinary theological society (1978). She also was an early faculty member for the Institute for Black Catholic Studies at Xavier University in New Orleans (beginning in 1982).[79] Sister Thea helped to shape its mission: "to provide an intellectual, spiritual, pastoral and cultural immersion into the Black Catholic experience."[80] Each summer through 1988 she taught courses in liturgy, preaching, and spirituality to religious and clergy who ministered in the Black community.[81]

Liturgical Justice-Making Beginning with Black Sacred Song

Sister Thea's use of Black sacred music extended to concerts and presentations. Remembering how she struggled to teach her first high school classes at Holy Child Jesus, Bowman expanded her use of Black music as a medium of spiritual, ethical, and liturgical formation. As she explained to the National Black Sisters' Conference in 1982, "Its symbols, images, rhythms and expressed values take Blacks *home*: Back to mamas and daddies, grandparents, godparents, aunts, uncles, neighbors and friends who taught us to 'hold on.'..."[82]

She continued to expound that through its melodies, lyrics, shouts, hollers, groans, moans, and "superasegmental phonemes (i.e., "yes," "Lord," "un huh," "well, well, well," and "Amen"), Black music

---

[78] Nutt, *Thea Bowman*, xi.
[79] Smith and Feister, *Thea's Song*, 167.
[80] Nutt, *Thea Bowman*, xi.
[81] Smith and Feister, *Thea's Song*, 167.
[82] Presentation at the 1982 National Black Sisters' Conference, printed in "Spirituality: The Soul of My People," in Cepress, *Sister Thea Bowman*, 45.

expressed the Black experience. The music engaged the "whole person," she believed, as the lyrics lifted up a God-awareness ("God is my father, my mother, my sister, my brother, my rock, my sword, my shield, etc."), a self-awareness ("We are sinners, we are redeemed, we may be rejected by others, but we are children of God, etc."), and an other-awareness ("Let us break bread together; Let us drink wine together; Let us praise God together on our knees, etc.").[83]

Bowman also reminded African American congregations and their ministers that Black music both calls and disposes the community to collective responsibility. The music, she posited, names communal beliefs and needs, calling for a sharing of talents and gifts. The Black sacred song she championed was a "valuable resource both for catechesis and for knowing those to be catechized."[84] The music helped to both form the Black Catholic community and inform those who sought to be in relationship with them in ministry. Thus, during the years that Sister Thea traveled the nation educating about Black sacred song, she encouraged and demonstrated the liturgical use of these songs.

For Sister Thea, the conscious inclusion of this music when communities gathered for prayer, and particularly for Eucharistic celebrations, was a matter of justice: the creation, maintenance, and extension of right relationships within the Church. Bowman envisioned the embodiment of this justice-making (liturgical and otherwise) among people of different races and cultures in the Church, as extended hospitality, conscious inclusion, continuing mutuality, and prayerful reconciliation.

In the 1980s Sister Thea, along with Black Catholic scholars, liturgists, and composers, continued to respond to the increased openness to their cultural gifts offered by *Sacrosanctum Concilium*'s implementation and the documents concerning liturgical music that followed.[85] While insisting that genres of music, such as spirituals

---

[83] Cepress, *Sister Thea Bowman*, 45–48.
[84] Cepress, *Sister Thea Bowman*, 45.
[85] Documents included the U.S. Catholic bishops' *Music in Catholic Worship* (1972) and *Liturgical Music Today* (1982).

and gospel, were appropriate to liturgical worship, Black Catholic liturgical pioneers such as Father Clarence Rivers were also adamant that White and Black Catholic leaders resist the temptation to stereotype Black congregants' musical or cultural preferences. Gregorian chant or a hymn derived from European classical sacred repertoire might suit a congregation's particular liturgical need. Rivers contended, as did the Black American bishops, that the African American community was not monolithic.[86]

Sister Thea insisted on a holistic view of the Black Catholic community. She acknowledged many influences on the spirituality of Black Catholics and their African American peers: for example, modes of prayer and music from African traditions, experiences from the time of slavery, life in rural and urban settings, socioeconomic levels, Black forbears in diverse Christian denominations (including Catholicism), and elements reflecting high-church, low-church, grass-roots, down-home, and unchurched gatherings.[87] Her emphasis on the diversity of preferences within the collective reality of Black Catholic spirituality anticipated and influenced the descriptions and admonitions of Black Catholic bishops concerning liturgy in the 1984 document *"What We Have Seen and Heard": A Pastoral Letter on Evangelization from the Black Bishops of the United States*. Therein, they articulated in broad terms what it meant to be "authentically Black and truly Catholic":

> The cultural idiom of American Black people has never been uniform but has varied according to region and ethos. . . . For this reason, an authentic Black Catholic liturgy need never be confined to a narrowly based concept of what is truly Black. There is a splendid opportunity for the vast richness of African American culture to be expressed in our liturgy.[88]

---

[86] Clarence Rivers, *Soulful Worship* (Washington, DC: National Office for Black Catholics, 1974), 21.

[87] Thea Bowman, "Spirituality: The Soul of the People," in *Tell It Like It Is: A Black Catholic Perspective on Christian Education* (Oakland, CA: National Black Sisters' Conference [NBSC], 1983), 84–85, in Nutt, *Thea Bowman*, 38.

[88] Joseph L. Howze, et al., *What We Have Seen and Heard": A Pastoral Letter on Evangelization from the Black Bishops of the United States* (Washington, DC: United States Catholic Conference, 1984), 4, 31.

Sister Thea reveled in the diverse sights and sounds of Black Catholic spirituality expressed in liturgy. She described a liturgically inclusive Black Catholic liturgy in *Extension Magazine*:

> What black culture looks and sounds like is exemplified in more and more churches where Blacks are sharing their gifts. One such parish is Holy Ghost in Opelousas, Louisiana, where visitors come from across the country to see what it means to be Black and Catholic....
>
> Holy Ghost has seven choirs with members of all ages. Some of the songs come from slave days: "Go Down Moses," "Wade in the Water," "Swing Low, Sweet Chariot." The music also includes traditional hymns and compositions by parishioners. The service is alive, yet contemplative; participatory and spontaneous, yet in accordance with liturgical norms.[89]

For Bowman, justice-making hospitality for Black Catholic cultural-liturgical gifts began "at home" through parish events, retreats, workshops, and local collaboration between her people and their close allies in ministry. Living out in her ministry the hopes and invitations of the Black bishops in *"What We Have Seen and Heard,"* Sister Thea and other Black Catholic leaders envisioned that they could be evangelizers to their own community as well as sharers of the gifts of Blackness to the whole Church.[90]

Through her work with the Diocese of Jackson's Office of Intercultural Affairs, Sister Thea collaborated with Bishop Joseph Brunini and his auxiliary bishop, William Houck, to convene a diocesan Organization of Black Catholics (1980). Guided by the goals for ministry to Black Catholics established by the U.S. Bishops' Conference, the new organization identified the needs of Black Catholics and the wider African American community in the diocese. They also shared resources for the mutual support of parishes and formed an advisory body. Sister Thea and the group's planning committee

---

[89] Thea Bowman, "Let the Church Say 'Amen!'" in *Extension* (March–April 1987): 10–11, in Cepress, *Sister Thea Bowman*, 70.

[90] Howze, et al., *"What We Have Seen and Heard,"* 3.

organized their liturgies for their meetings as well as liturgical workshops in the diocese.[91]

Due in part to Bowman's influence and expertise, the Institute for Black Catholic Studies at Xavier University in New Orleans became a national center for Black Catholic liturgical experimentation, as well as cultural, intellectual, and theological research. Black historic sacred song was highlighted in rituals and coursework from the time of its foundation and remained in the foreground of the educational and spiritual experience at the Institute. Students read the narratives formerly enslaved Blacks had written and dictated, which described the role of music in giving voice to faith and freedom. To this day an annual ceremony, punctuated by spirituals, commemorates enslaved and free ancestors. The community frequently sang spirituals as part of prayer and Eucharistic liturgies.[92]

The Institute for Black Catholic Studies began to form and send out culturally trained ministers, musicians, liturgists, historians, and scholars to serve in communities around the nation. Black Catholic parishes remained separated from their White counterparts by custom, location of parishes in segregated neighborhoods, or because of their desire to create a parish entirely based on African American spiritual and cultural gifts. All, however, lacked a basic liturgical tool: hymnals created to serve their specific needs. Bowman understood and experienced this lack as Black Catholics struggled to fill their liturgical-musical needs. There existed no hymnal that accommodated the needs of a majority of Black Catholic parishes. In their piecemeal efforts to create effective liturgies, the pews in Black Catholic churches were a mess! Congregations alternated the use of Black Protestant hymnals with Catholic missalettes, adapted Black music from memory, and often created folders of mimeographed or photocopied music.[93]

---

[91] Smith and Feister, *Thea's Song*, 166.
[92] Copeland, *"The African American Catholic Hymnal,"* 81.
[93] Cheryl Devall, "Hymnal To Let Black Catholics Find The Words," *Chicago Tribune*, November 7, 1986.

In 1978 and again in 1981, Black Catholic leaders considered proposals for the creation of a hymnal to serve the needs of their community.[94] In April 1983 the National Black Catholic Clergy Caucus authorized a hymnal project, soliciting ideas from composers, musicians, liturgists, scholars, leaders, and "ordinary people" representing diverse Black Catholic experiences. Sister Thea was supportive and actively involved in this process.[95] Sixty-three spirituals (among a diversity of culturally-cued, "traditional," and contemporary Catholic and musical choices) were included in the hymnal titled *Lead Me, Guide Me*.[96]

One of Sister Thea's key roles, adding to the catechetical value of the widely anticipated hymnal, was a scholarly, yet accessible, preface titled, "The Gift of African American Sacred Song." In it, she first gave a brief overview of the origins and development of African American sacred song. She highlighted the traditional functions of the worshiping assembly and the music itself. As she told audiences, Black sacred song comes from the people and expresses their individual and communal experiences, oppressions, hopes, dreams, values, and visions.

Sister Thea described the role of the song leader in *Lead Me, Guide Me*: "The leader (some would say soloist) leads the community in worship. The leader revives and inspires. The singer lifts the church, the people, to a higher level of understanding, feeling, motivation and participation."[97] Bowman explained to her readers that Black worshipers had in their heritage and cultural traditions a capacity for full, conscious, and active participation, as encouraged by *Sacrosanctum Concilium*.[98] She declared, "People participate. They sing, pray, clap, sway, raise their hands. Eye contact, voiced response, the silent testimony of tears, a smile of relief or contemplation or ecstasy says, 'This is my story; this is my song.'"[99]

---

[94] Copeland, "*African American Catholic Hymnal*," 67.
[95] Thea Bowman, "The Gift of African American Sacred Song" in *Lead Me, Guide Me*; Smith and Feister, *Thea's Song*, 205.
[96] Copeland, "*African American Catholic Hymnal*," 69.
[97] James Weldon Johnson and J. Rosamond Johnson, *The Books of American Negro Spirituals* (Cambridge, MA: Da Capo Press, 1989), 21–22.
[98] Constitution on the Sacred Liturgy, *Sacrosanctum Concilium*, no. 14.
[99] Bowman, "The Gift of African American Sacred Song."

Bowman's preface prepared the congregants to read the article that followed: "The Liturgy of the Roman Rite and African American Worship" by J-Glenn Murray, S.J. Murray briefly brought together the traditions of African American music and worship with explanations and references to the rubrics and guiding documents of the Roman Rite.[100] The balance between the two articles reflected the guiding principles of Black Catholic liturgy articulated in *"What We Have Seen and Heard."* Sister Thea described the nature of "authentically Black" sacred song while Murray described ways in which African American worship, especially music, could be "truly catholic."

Part of Bowman's enduring legacy is that Black Catholic scholars, leaders, and "ordinary" congregants alike have continued to appreciate her article. They refer to it in presentations and articles or simply take the time to pray and reflect on her ideas while waiting for a worship service to begin. When parishes replaced the hymnal with the second edition of *Lead Me, Guide Me*, congregants lamented that Bowman's article was not reprinted.[101] Sister Thea was pleased with the hymnal's impact. In the first four years, 100,000 copies sold. The collection, compilation, and catechetical work of the hymnal committee influenced later hymnals produced to meet the needs of African American Christian worshipers.[102]

Liturgical Justice-Making Beyond Black Sacred Song

As a culturally and classically trained musician, Sister Thea understood that music is sound ordered in time. As Paul Westermeyer, professor of church music at Luther Seminary in St. Paul, Minnesota, described, music is about relationships; "... dissonance, and consonance, tension and release, sound and silence, fast and slow, loud and quiet, simple and multiple lines, harmony and

---

[100] Murray, "Liturgy of the Roman Rite" in *Lead Me, Guide Me*.
[101] Comments made to author at the Black Catholic Theological Symposium in response to a presentation on "Welcome Table: A Mass of Spirituals," St. Thomas University, Miami, Florida, October 12, 2012.
[102] See *Lift Every Voice and Sing II: An African-American Hymnal* (New York: Church Publishing, 1993) and *African-American Heritage Hymnal* (Chicago: GIA Publications, 2001).

polyphony." Westermeyer connected the right relationship needed to lift music to the form of art, especially in liturgy, to the correct relationships of justice and peace.[103]

For Sister Thea, liturgical justice included not only Black Catholics delving into their cultural treasures to enliven worship, but also Catholics of different races choosing to worship together in ways that welcomed the gifts of all. As she enthusiastically shared songs from the abundance of African American cultural treasures, she presupposed a mutual sharing of gifts.[104] As she said to the bishops in her historic 1989 address, "See, you all talk about what you have to do if you want to be a multicultural church: Sometimes I do things your way; sometimes you do things mine. . . ."[105] Bowman expected this cultural sharing to extend to intercultural relationship and reconciliation before, during, and after the liturgical event. In her view, this process, though centered in the liturgy, began with a planning process that involved all of the participants and extended to social interactions and programming in which all would have a voice in creating the agenda and fulfilling the mission. As Sister Thea stated in a video presentation about her life:

> I don't think it starts in church. I think it starts outside of church. When we love one another, when we become friends. Then we can walk hand in hand into the house of the Lord. And celebrate, but to me to pray together when our hearts are not one, when we are not at least trying to bridge the gaps is sacrilege.[106]

Conclusion

In 1984 Sister Thea's life took several difficult turns. Both of her parents died and her first diagnosis of breast cancer occurred that year. Encouraged by her community, students, and friends, Sister

---

[103] Paul Westermeyer, *Let Justice Sing: Hymnody and Justice* (Collegeville, MN: Liturgical Press, 1998), 81; quote at 89–90.
[104] Nutt, *Thea Bowman*, xi.
[105] "To Be Black and Catholic," *Origins* (July 6, 1989): 114–118, in Cepress, *Sister Thea Bowman*, 35.
[106] *Sister Thea: Her Own Story* (Belleville, IL: Oblate Media and Communications, 1991), videocassette.

Thea famously vowed to "live till I die" and kept up her rigorous itinerary of engagements as much as her health permitted.[107]

To extend the reach and ensure the continuation of her message, Sister Thea recorded songs specifically for catechesis and formation, compiling them as *Sister Thea: Songs of My People*.[108] The following year, she published a songbook containing transcriptions of the music, prayers, and commentary based on the original audio recording. In the published text, she offered meditations to be used when praying with the spirituals.[109] With the help of five musicians, including Leon Roberts, liturgical composer and musical director of historic St. Augustine's Church, Washington, D.C., she sang and directed the recording sessions, despite her rapidly declining health. Musicians and producers in the studio were amazed and inspired by her determination.[110]

Bowman's liturgical legacy continues in the *Lead Me, Guide Me* hymnal's second edition, which includes a wide spectrum of culturally-cued music, though the inclusion of spirituals for which she advocated composes a smaller percentage of the music than in the first edition. Spirituals continue to be utilized by Black Catholics in liturgy, though their popularity is waning in favor of popular gospel and praise and worship music favored by their Black Christian neighbors. Sister Thea, while valuing spirituals, chose primarily gospel music and hymns for her twenty-fifth anniversary as a professed sister, showing an appreciation for contemporary trends in music.[111] As a musician, song leader, scholar, educator, and cultural advocate, Sister Thea's promotion of Black sacred song retained a primary concern for justice and for the wellbeing of the Black Catholic community. For her and many others, sacred song inspired by the African American experience helped Black Catholics to fully function in their cultural authenticity, to find, or even create, a true *home* in the Catholic Church.

---

[107] Sister Thea underwent isolated treatments for cancer while continuing a rigorous travel and speaking schedule until 1988. Sister Thea Bowman died on March 30, 1990, at age fifty-two. See Smith and Feister, *Thea's Song*, xv–xvi; Nutt, *Thea Bowman*, xii.
[108] (Boston: Krystal Records 1988), audiocassette.
[109] *Sister Thea, Songs of My People*, 6–7.
[110] Smith and Feister, *Thea's Song*, 241.
[111] Smith and Feister, *Thea's Song*, 174.

Writing Black Catholic Lives: Black Catholic Biographies and Autobiographies

CECILIA A. MOORE*

Introduction: Stories Worth Telling

ALTHOUGH BLACKS COMPRISE only 3% of the Catholic population in the United States, there is an important and growing body of autobiographical and biographical works whose authors or subjects are both black and Catholic. Black Catholics writing their own stories and others writing about them offer important insights into the intersection of race and religion, providing particular perspectives on what it has meant to be black and Catholic. The authors and subjects of black Catholic autobiographies and biographies are from different backgrounds, regions, and generations. Some are priests and religious; others are lay Catholics. Among them are six African Americans currently being considered for canonization, while others demonstrated great difficulty with the official moral, social, and political positions of the institutional church. This essay examines a sample of black Catholic autobiographies and biographies from the mid-twentieth century to today, offering insight into black Catholic experience, identity, and self-consciousness.

Any examination of autobiographies and biographies must proceed with certain cautions. Autobiographies can highlight eras and experiences to the neglect of others. Sometimes aspects of a writer's life are purposely omitted or not fully developed. Details can be compressed or manipulated to protect or disguise. This can

---

* An earlier version of this work appeared in *U.S. Catholic Historian* 29, no. 3 (Summer 2011): 43–58.

elicit the need for additional research. Biographies can be driven by strong intellectual and ideological bents as writers distort lives to fit the arguments they wish to make. The failure to place a biographical study in its proper historical and racial contexts presents another potential pitfall. Despite these possible difficulties, the autobiographies and biographies that detail black Catholic lives are often portals to greater understanding of not just individual lives but also the communities from which they came and which they influenced.

Most of the autobiographies and biographies considered here possess an explicitly Catholic viewpoint or worldview. They were written because their subjects are Catholic, or more specifically, black and Catholic. They focus on how they lived their lives as black Catholics and how they related to the Church. Many of the biographies were published by Catholic presses for a Catholic readership. With the exception of a few notable and historically significant persons, the majority are not about especially well-known figures. This distinguishing feature of black Catholic biography prompts the question: What is it about these mostly ordinary lives that prompts further examination? The answer is that their stories need to be told. They witness to the diversity of experience while contributing to the wider understanding of race, religion, and culture in U.S. history.

Black Catholic Lives: Notable Persons

Among the best-selling autobiographies and biographies of black Catholics are those of well-known and famous African Americans, who also happened to be Catholic. They include writers, composers, musicians, actors, politicians, and lawyers. Their contributions to society and culture are highlighted in their biographies, yet a careful reading reveals a strong Catholic influence on their lives. For example, *Soul on Soul: The Music and Life of Mary Lou Williams*, by jazz historian Tammy L. Kernodle, is the seminal biography of jazz pianist and composer Mary Lou Williams (1910–1981). Though known for her secular career, she was on the cutting edge of inculturating Catholic worship with jazz idioms beginning in the late 1950s. Kernodle looks intensively at Williams' conversion to

Catholicism in the 1950s and shows how her faith changed the trajectory of her musical career.[1]

Kathryn Talalay treats the Catholicism of piano prodigy Philippa Duke Schuyler (1931–1967) in *Composition in Black and White: The Life of Philippa Schuyler*. According to Talalay, Schuyler was attracted to Catholicism from the time she attended the convent school of Manhattanville College as a young girl. Schuyler converted to Catholicism in 1958 at Harlem's St. Charles Borromeo Church. A self-identified "Catholic intellectual," she authored *Jungle Saints*, a book about the Catholic missionaries in Africa whose work she observed and admired on her travels around the continent.[2]

Billie Holiday (1915–1959), in her autobiography *Lady Sings the Blues*, discusses her life as a Catholic and the haven she found with the Sisters of the Good Shepherd in Baltimore when she was a teenager.[3] Collectively, these early biographical works open new lines of questioning, including: How did Catholicism influence or inform the art, ideas, and politics of influential and famous black Catholics? How did their religious faith and their relationships to the Church impact them?

Black Catholic Lives: Converts

Among the earliest autobiographies of black Catholics are those of converts. Elizabeth Laura Adams (1909–1982), a young black Catholic Californian, published her autobiography with Catholic publisher Sheed and Ward in 1942.[4] According to literary scholar

---

[1] Tammy L. Kernodle, *Soul on Soul: The Life and Music of Mary Lou Williams* (Boston: Northeastern University Press, 2004).
[2] Kathryn Talalay, *Composition in Black and White: The Life of Philippa Schuyler* (New York: Oxford University Press, 1995), 214.
[3] Billie Holiday, *Lady Sings the Blues* (Garden City, NY: Doubleday, 1956). Two academic studies of Billie Holiday offer insights about the role of Catholicism in shaping Holiday as an artist: Farah Jasmine Griffin, *If You Can't Be Free, Be A Mystery: In Search of Billie Holiday* (New York: Ballantine Books, 2002); and Tracy Fessenden, *Religion Around Billie Holiday* (University Park: Pennsylvania State University Press, 2018).
[4] Elizabeth Laura Adams, *Dark Symphony* (New York: Sheed and Ward, 1942).

Clara Kaplan, *Dark Symphony* was a huge success for the time, selling ten thousand copies between 1942 and 1946 and ultimately over fifteen thousand in total.[5] Periodicals, including *America*, *Ave Maria*, *Catholic World*, *Interracial Review*, and *Sign*, reviewed *Dark Symphony* and encouraged those wanting to understand the role of the Catholic Church in interracial justice to read it. In addition to reviewing the book, *Interracial Review* also published a "portrait" of Adams as an up-and-coming Catholic voice. *Dark Symphony* was touted as one of the three books on blacks and the Catholic Church that one needed to read, along with *The Race Question and the Catholic Church* by John LaFarge, S.J., and *Colored Catholics in the United States* by John T. Gillard, S.S.J.[6] Placing a young black Catholic laywoman on par with white priests who were regarded as leaders and authorities on racial justice signified a small victory on the part of Catholic interracialism. In addition to *Dark Symphony*, which focused on her conversion to Catholicism, Adams wrote about her experiences of being a black Catholic in essays, stories, and poems published in the late 1930s and early 1940s in Catholic journals, most notably *The Torch*.

A decade later, Sheed and Ward published another young black Catholic woman's autobiography, which also featured her finding a spiritual home in the Catholic Church. Helen Caldwell Day (Riley) (1926–2013) titled her 1951 autobiography *Color, Ebony*.[7] Unlike Adams, whose autobiography gained immediate attention in the Catholic world, only one Catholic journal, *Ave Maria*, reviewed *Color, Ebony*. Helen Caldwell Day was pulled toward Catholicism, in part, through the social justice work of Dorothy Day and the Catholic Worker movement. Two years after publishing *Color, Ebony*, Caldwell Day wrote about her new life as a Catholic and as an organizer of a Catholic Worker house in Memphis, Tennessee. Her book, *Not Without Tears*, unlike *Color, Ebony*, was reviewed by at least nine Catholic journals as well as the secular

---

[5] Carla Kaplan, ed., *Dark Symphony and Other Works* (New York: G. K. Hall, 1997), xvii.
[6] Kaplan, *Dark Symphony*, xvii.
[7] Helen Caldwell Day, *Color, Ebony* (New York: Sheed and Ward, 1951). Helen Caldwell Day married Jesse Riley after her literary career commenced, so one may see her referenced as Helen Caldwell Day or Helen Caldwell Day Riley.

press.⁸ The *Library Journal*'s review summarized the work, "This is the story of the founding of Blessed Martin House in Memphis, Tennessee, an interracial Catholic home which grew out of an interracial discussion group in Memphis. The author, a Negro and a convert to Catholicism, tells in simple and sincere language of the events in her own life and those of others which led to the founding of this home."⁹ Caldwell Day published a third book, *All the Way to Heaven*, on the topic of the Catholic Union of the Sick in America, an organization for those with incurable illnesses.¹⁰ Believing that the suffering and prayers of the terminally ill had redemptive power, she sought to make the work of the union better known. The Catholic press reviewed the book, as did a couple of secular publications. R. P. Breaden of the *Library Journal* found it "well-written in spite of the nature of the subject."¹¹

Ellen Tarry (1906–2008), a children's book writer and essayist, published the third major black Catholic autobiography of this period in 1955. Tarry titled her autobiography *The Third Door: The Autobiography of an American Negro Woman*.¹² In the foreword, Tarry explained the choice to write about her life: "This story is part of the story of a young, growing America, and told so that future generations may know the price we have paid for tomorrow. It is the hope of the author that this book will sow happiness in place of discord, hope in place of despair, and faith in our American future."¹³ By the time Tarry wrote *The Third Door*, she was already known in the Catholic world through her many essays on the

---
⁸ Helen Caldwell Day, *Not Without Tears* (New York: Sheed and Ward, 1954).
⁹ Leo R. Etzkern, review of *Not Without Tears*, by Helen Caldwell Day, *Library Journal* (December 1, 1954): 2321–2322.
¹⁰ Helen Caldwell Day, *All the Way to Heaven* (New York: Sheed and Ward, 1956).
¹¹ R. P. Breaden, review of *All the Way to Heaven*, by Helen Caldwell Day, *Library Journal* (October 1, 1956): 2255.
¹² Ellen Tarry, *The Third Door: The Autobiography of an American Negro Woman* (New York: David McKay, 1955). Interestingly, the David McKay Company was a well-known publisher of American comics, though it also published world literature, textbooks, and children's books. Since Ellen Tarry was a children's book author, she may have chosen McKay as the publisher since she had worked on previous projects with them. But *The Third Door* was certainly not a children's book.
¹³ Tarry, *The Third Door*, vii.

challenges blacks faced in the Catholic Church and on how the Catholic Church in the U.S. could better assist the development of the black community and cooperate with blacks to press for racial justice. Tarry approached telling her story with a sense of spiritual responsibility. She believed that her experiences of racism and of God's grace demanded that she share her story with others. Tarry said, "He has led me across angry waters and guided my feet through hostile lands. For me and for my people, He has thrown open doors long closed by hate blinded men. And in His infinite mercy, He has shown me the long narrow road that leads every pilgrim home."[14]

Though also a convert, Tarry was older than both Adams and Day and also had been a Catholic longer than either of them when she published her autobiography. While the post-conversion zeal of Adams and Day is quite palpable in their autobiographies, Tarry presents a more mature and critical relationship with the Catholic Church. In *The Third Door*, Tarry focused on the personal, professional, political, and spiritual challenges she faced as a Catholic and how she hoped to be part of a positive racial transformation of church and society. Reviewers of *The Third Door* included Catholic journals such as *America, Ave Maria, Catholic Business Editorial Review, Catholic World, Commonweal, Integrity, Interracial Review,* and *Sign*. In *Catholic World*, J. M. Gillis contended that Tarry was able to contain her anger about American racism because of her "feeling for literary art and her religion." This made it possible for her to write constructively and optimistically about race relations in America. For these reasons, Gillis recommended it as a work that "deserves wide reading."[15]

Dark Symphony; Color, Ebony; and *The Third Door* placed conversion to Catholicism at the center of their authors' lives. Conversion to Catholicism defined them and their personal and public commitments. Adams, Day, and Tarry presented their own cases for choosing Catholicism, described their relationships with their fellow

---

[14] Tarry, *The Third Door*, vii.
[15] J. M. Gillis, review of *The Third Door: The Autobiography of an American Negro Woman*, by Ellen Tarry, *Catholic World* (May 1955): 154.

Catholics and the Church, and expressed their hopes for the future relationship of their race to their religion. These autobiographies contributed to the Catholic Church's extraordinary evangelization among African American communities, adding the voices of Black Catholics to efforts to spread the faith.[16]

Black Catholic Lives: Clergy and Religious

In addition to these conversion narratives, another kind of black Catholic biography made its debut in the 1950s. Father Albert S. Foley, S.J. (1912–1990), a sociologist by training, began researching and writing about black people and their relationships with the Catholic Church in his dissertation, "The Catholic Church and the Washington Negro." After receiving his doctorate from the University of North Carolina at Chapel Hill in 1950, Foley sought to publish the dissertation with Chapel Hill's press, only to have it thwarted by some priests of the Archdiocese of Washington who were angry that Foley "had recorded some of the methods used by pro-segregation clergy to suppress Catholic Negroes' efforts to secure equal access to the parish churches and sacraments."[17] These priests won, and Foley never published this work. However, this did not deter him from continuing his effort to understand and teach about the relationship of the Catholic Church to African Americans.

His research led him to the topic of the history of black priests in the United States, which resulted in two major works: *Bishop Healy: Beloved Outcaste* (1954) and *God's Men of Color: The Colored Catholic Priests of the United States, 1854–1954* (1955). He called these books the fruits of his "adventures and misadventures in the research and writing of these Black Catholic history stories."[18]

Foley published *Bishop Healy: Beloved Outcaste* with a major American publishing house, Farrar, Straus and Young, upon "the

---

[16] Cecilia A. Moore, "African American Catholic Conversion," *Sacred Rock: Journal of the Institute for Black Catholic Studies* (Summer 1999): 1–6.
[17] Albert S. Foley, S.J., "Adventures in Black Catholic History: Research and Writing," *U.S. Catholic Historian* 5, no. 1 (1986): 105.
[18] Foley, "Adventures in Black Catholic History," 103.

strong recommendation of Cardinal Spellman of New York."[19] *Bishop Healy* brought to light the story of the Healy family, the Georgia-born sons and daughters of Michael Healy, an Irish immigrant and plantation owner, and Eliza, the African American woman whom Healy purchased when she was sixteen years old for the sum of $600.[20] Three sons of this union became priests, and two daughters entered religious life. The Healy family members' ability to serve in religious vocations was based on their facility, more or less, to pass for white. Foley focused on the life of Bishop James Augustine Healy, bishop of Portland, Maine. The work received, in Foley's assessment, critical acclaim: "It made the Catholic best seller list for six months after its publication on April 14, 1954. It was reviewed in the *New York Times* book review section. At that time this amounted to a sort of secular canonization of striving young authors."[21] The popularity of *Bishop Healy* led to discussions with Hollywood agents over making the book into a movie, but this was unsuccessful.

The next year, Father Foley published *God's Men of Color: The Colored Catholic Priests of the United States, 1854–1954.*[22] Though it did not have *Bishop Healy*'s mass appeal, it presented the lives of over seventy black Catholic priests ordained in and for the United States between the mid-nineteenth and mid-twentieth centuries. The publication of *God's Men of Color* was not without controversy. According to Foley, some superiors of religious orders that served African American communities and had black priests in their ranks opposed the work. In particular, Foley named members of the Society of the Divine Word as "concerned that the book would hurt its apostolate among blacks."[23] Foley agreed to leave out anything

---

[19] Albert S. Foley, S.J., *Bishop Healy: Beloved Outcaste: The Story of a Great Priest Whose Life Has Become a Legend* (New York: Farrar, Straus and Young, 1954). See Foley, "Adventures in Black Catholic History," 115. Even with Spellman's recommendation, Foley had to raise $2,000 to put toward the book's publication.

[20] Barbara Miles, *Catholic New Hampshire* (Charleston, SC: Arcadia, 2020), 12. *Catholic New Hampshire* contains a daguerreotype of Eliza, the mother of the Healy children.

[21] Foley, "Adventures in Black Catholic History," 115.

[22] Albert S. Foley, S.J., *God's Men of Color: The Colored Catholic Priests of the United States, 1854–1954* (New York: Farrar, Straus, 1955).

[23] Foley, "Adventures in Black Catholic History," 116.

in the history of the Society of the Divine Word that they thought might harm their evangelization efforts. With this, the book proceeded to press.[24] *God's Men of Color* sold only about four thousand copies, while *Bishop Healy* went into seven printings.[25] What the former lacked in terms of public appeal and sales, it gained in being an invaluable and inspiring resource for black Catholics, many of whom had never seen a black priest, much less known the stories of black priests, past or present. In the 1980s, Sister Caroline Hemesath, O.S.F., followed up on Foley's work by writing biographical sketches of the black bishops of the United States in *Our Black Shepherds: Biographies of the Ten Black Bishops in the United States*.[26] Foley's last black Catholic priest biography was about Father Patrick Healy, S.J., one of Bishop James Augustine Healy's younger brothers. Foley titled that book *Dream of an Outcaste: Patrick Healy, S.J.*[27]

More recently, in 2002, James M. O'Toole returned to the subject of the Healy family with his publication of *Passing for White: Race, Religion, and the Healy Family, 1820-1920*.[28] Though well-researched and written in an engaging manner, it offered some problematic interpretations that resulted from the speculative filling in of historical gaps. O'Toole argues the Healy family's Catholicism assisted them in making themselves white Americans who "escaped the prison house of race."[29] In reviewing the book for the *Journal of Southern History*, Diane Batts Morrow drew attention to the interpretation, pointing out that O'Toole "posits an agency and purposive choice unavailable to a group of children eighteen months to seven years old, whose father had permanently removed them from their only exposure to black people and had ensconced them in an

---

[24] Foley, "Adventures in Black Catholic History," 116.
[25] Foley, "Adventures in Black Catholic History," 118.
[26] Caroline Hemesath, O.S.F., *Our Black Shepherds: Biographies of the Ten Black Bishops in the United States* (Baltimore: Josephite Pastoral Center, 1987).
[27] Albert S. Foley, S.J., *Dream of an Outcaste: Patrick F. Healy, S.J.: The Story of the Slave-Born Georgian Who Became the Second Founder of America's Great Catholic University, Georgetown* (Tuscaloosa, AL: Portals Press, 1976).
[28] James M. O'Toole, *Passing for White: Race, Religion, and the Healy Family, 1820-1920* (Amherst, MA: University of Massachusetts Press, 2002).
[29] O'Toole, *Passing for White*, 228.

exclusively white milieu."[30] Morrow also challenged the claim that Catholicism allowed the Healys to become white, reminding readers that Catholicism is a universal religion, not practiced by whites alone, and that the Healys had black Catholic contemporaries who made a way for themselves as blacks in the Catholic Church. In particular, she referenced the Oblate Sisters of Providence in Baltimore and the Sisters of the Holy Family in New Orleans, orders of black women religious that achieved success in the nineteenth century. Finally, Morrow stated the danger of O'Toole's "unsubstantiated speculation" that Eliza Healy's death "was surely a blow to her husband, who had devoted his life to this unusual woman" and that he died of a "broken heart" a mere three months after she died. Morrow writes, "Such blatant romanticization ignores the relentless power dynamic and potential abuse inherent in owner/slave concubinage."[31] Morrow's critique is important because it clearly identifies some of the interpretive problems that biographies can present.

Sister Caroline Hemesath published in 1974 the first study of the life of Venerable Father Augustus Tolton, the first recognized black American priest. Her book, *From Slave to Priest*, was intended for a juvenile audience.[32] It attempted to inspire young people, particularly young blacks, to pursue lives of gentleness, devotion, determination, and courage—the virtues of Father Tolton that she emphasized in her study. Hemesath dramatically presented the life of Father Tolton and his family from the time of their escape from slavery in Missouri and the start of their new lives in Quincy, Illinois, during the Civil War to his long quest to become a priest to the highlights and low periods that characterized his ministry until his untimely death at the age of forty-three. Hemesath used archival sources and conducted interviews with people who knew Father Tolton for the biography. More recently, Sabrina A. Penn, a great-great

---

[30] Diane Batts Morrow, review of *Passing for White: Race, Religion, and the Healy Family, 1820–1920*, by James M. O'Toole, *Journal of Southern History* 70, no. 1 (February 2004): 137.

[31] Morrow, review of *Passing for White*, 138.

[32] Caroline Hemesath, O.S.F., *From Slave to Priest: A Biography of the Reverend Augustine Tolton (1854–1897), The First Black Priest in the United States* (Chicago: Franciscan Herald Press, 1974).

niece of Father Tolton, self-published a biography of him that shed new light on the wider circle of his family and the legacy of his ministry in Chicago. Penn's biography, *A Place for My Children: Father Augustus Tolton, America's First Known Black Priest and His Ancestry*, follows essentially the same chronology of Hemesath's biography and uses many of the same sources.[33] What makes it distinct is the focus on Father Tolton as a son, brother, and uncle and information on the Tolton family after the priest's death in 1897. Penn writes, "I wrote this book to inform all Americans about the history, purpose, and life of the first Black Catholic priest in the United States of America and to help his relatives to know their family history."[34]

Black Catholic priests and religious began writing autobiographies by the early 1970s. The best known is *Black Priest/White Church: Catholics and Racism* by Father Lawrence Lucas (1933–2020). At the time of its publication by Random House in 1970, Lucas was the Archdiocese of New York's only black pastor. Father Lucas, who grew up in Harlem, wrote, "I am not a convert to Catholicism. I am what many choose to refer to as a 'born' Catholic. I am so by virtue of the baptism I received at the hands of a white Catholic priest thirty-seven years ago, but since then ratified of my own free choice."[35] Nearly all of his education was "in the Catholic system," paving the way for his ordination to the priesthood in 1959.

When Lucas wrote *Black Priest/White Church*, he was angry at the Church for its history of racial discrimination. However, as someone who freely "ratified" his Catholicism, Lucas asserted, "Today, also by my own free choice, I am in my eleventh year of the priesthood."[36] Lucas was a founding member of the Black Catholic Clergy Caucus, which convened for the first time in Detroit a few weeks after the assassination of Martin Luther King Jr. This 1968 gathering was the first time black priests met consciously as a

---

[33] Sabrina A. Penn, *A Place for My Children: Father Augustus Tolton, America's First Known Black Priest and His Ancestry* (Chicago: PennInk, 2007).
[34] Penn, *A Place for My Children*, vii.
[35] Lawrence E. Lucas, *Black Priest/White Church: Catholics and Racism* (New York: Random House, 1970), 5.
[36] Lucas, *Black Priest/White Church*, 5.

black and Catholic body. Together they declared the Catholic Church in the United States "a white racist institution." Explaining the nature of his anger in *Black Priest/White Church*, Lucas reasserted, "The reason why being black and a Catholic priest causes me anger and disappointment is that the Catholic Church in this country is a white racist institution; it looks white; it thinks white; it acts white."[37] Lucas wrote *Black Priest/White Church* in part to explain how he could be both angry at and committed to the Catholic Church. When he was asked, "Why is Father Lucas so bitter?" he explained that what others interpreted as bitterness was a blend of anger, disappointment, and hope.[38] Therefore, to be a black Catholic priest, according to Lucas, was to be angry and disappointed, yet also hopeful. His book presented a black and Catholic experience without reservation. Though his story was particular to him, other black priests recognized in his account their own struggles.

A more recent work resonates with Lucas' writing. Readers of Bryan Massingale's *Racial Justice and the Catholic Church* are certain to note the important role of autobiography in Massingale's study. He draws on his own experiences of racism growing up black and Catholic in Milwaukee, his efforts to follow his vocation to the priesthood, and his present work as a moral theologian and professor. The book serves to contextualize, analyze, and theologize about the role racism has played in the Catholic Church throughout the twentieth century and into the twenty-first century.[39] Though more than forty years separate the works of Lucas and Massingale, it is striking how they use their life stories to advocate for reform, compelling Catholics to come to terms with racism and to create a new experience of church that welcomes all people.

Four years after *Black Priest/White Church*, Sister Mary Gabriella Guidry (1914–2003), a Sister of the Holy Family, published, *The Southern Negro Nun: An Autobiography*. The two books represent

---

[37] Lucas, *Black Priest/White Church*, 6.
[38] Lucas, *Black Priest/White Church*, 3.
[39] Bryan N. Massingale, *Racial Justice and the Catholic Church* (Maryknoll, NY: Orbis Books, 2010).

radically different experiences of Catholicism and religious life. Unlike black priests who began to gain support for their vocations in the twentieth century, black sisters, particularly those in black religious communities, had over one hundred years of struggle and achievement from which to draw strength and inspiration. Black sisters had been ministering since 1828, when Mother Mary Elizabeth Lange and Father James Joubert, S.S., founded the Oblate Sisters of Providence in Baltimore, Maryland. By 1842, another order of black sisters, the Sisters of the Holy Family, had emerged in New Orleans, led by Mother Henriette Delille, and in 1916 a third community for black sisters, the Franciscan Handmaids of the Most Pure Heart of Mary, was founded in Savannah, Georgia, by Mother Theodore Williams and Father Ignatius Lissner, S.M.A.

By the time Sister Mary Gabriella wrote about her life, she could place herself in a long line of black women religious making a spiritual and educational difference in the lives of black people, particularly Catholics. While Father Lucas' primary objective in *Black Priest/White Church* was to use his own personal history to expose and address racism in the Catholic Church, Sister Mary Gabriella set out to celebrate the lives of black women religious and to highlight the historic contributions of black sisters through conveying her story. She explained, "This autobiography was written to show how grace works in the soul, and to give a clear understanding of the fact that God chooses us—we do not choose him."[40] She aimed to show the world "that there is a religious congregation of black sisters in the South who have done and are still doing a tremendous job in the field of education and human relations."[41]

Father Albert J. McKnight, C.S.Sp., (1927–2016), published his autobiography, *Whistling in the Wind*, in 1994. Its purpose and perspective is a cross between *Black Priest/White Church* and *The Southern Negro Nun*. Like Sister Mary Gabriella, Father McKnight attempted to place his life as a black priest in the historical record of his order, the Congregation of the Holy Spirit, a community with few

---

[40] Sister Mary Gabriella Guidry, *The Southern Negro Nun: An Autobiography* (New York: Exposition Press, 1974), Preface.
[41] Guidry, *The Southern Negro Nun*, Preface.

African American vocations.[42] Like Lucas, McKnight addressed racism in the Church, the complicity of some African Americans in racism, and racism's impact on his life and his ministry. McKnight wrote, "I am a priest. I hope to die a priest of the Roman Catholic Church or the proposed African American Catholic rite in union with Rome if I live that long."[43] His reference to the proposed African American Catholic rite is significant because McKnight wrote his autobiography not long after Father George Stallings, a priest of the Archdiocese of Washington, went into schism and founded the Imani Temple. The question of whether black Catholics could and should pursue a separate rite in the Catholic Church was an important conversation from the late 1980s through the 1990s. Although most black Catholics were not willing to leave the Roman Catholic Church, many were interested in pursuing an African American Catholic rite that would allow them to imbue the Mass with a black aesthetic and spirituality.[44]

Father McKnight was the primary founder and organizer of the Southern Cooperative Development Fund (SCDF), through which McKnight taught low-income Southern families to work together in cooperatives and helped them establish a system of credit unions. He also created what he called "a church without walls" in the form of the movement Black Unity and Spiritual Togetherness, more commonly referred to as BUST.[45] McKnight wrote, "BUST is an idea whose time has come. Each person and each ethnic group must determine their own destiny—fulfill it or betray it. The Black community is in a state of crisis because seventy years ago, during the 1920s, it failed to determine its destiny, and therefore, betrayed it. Today, the Black community is suffering from seventy years of accumulated problems with wrong solutions."[46] A serious health scare in

---

[42] Today, there are many African members of the Congregation of the Holy Spirit serving in the United States.

[43] Albert J. McKnight, C.S.Sp., *Whistling in the Wind: The Autobiography of The Reverend A. J. McKnight, C.S.Sp.* (Opelousas, LA: Southern Development Foundation, 1994), 13.

[44] Marjorie Heyer, "Prelates to Study Need for African American Rite," *Washington Post*, July 26, 1989.

[45] McKnight, *Whistling in the Wind*, 166.

[46] McKnight, *Whistling in the Wind*, 166.

1992 prompted Father McKnight to write *Whistling in the Wind*. Committed to the idea of black self-determination, he was motivated to tell the story of his life as a priest, community organizer, and social justice advocate.[47]

Black Catholic Lives: Saints-in-the-Making

In addition to the autobiographies of religious men and women, numerous biographical works have highlighted the lives of black Catholics being considered for sainthood. Currently, the canonization causes of six Americans of African descent have been introduced: Venerable Pierre Toussaint; Venerable Mother Henriette Delille, S.S.F.; Venerable Father Augustus Tolton; Servant of God Mother Mary Lange, O.S.P.; Servant of God Julia Greeley; and Servant of God Sister Thea Bowman, F.S.P.A. While some studies of these men and women pre-dated their causes for canonization, additional biographies were produced as they grew in notoriety.

Among the many biographies of Pierre Toussaint (1766–1853), a Haitian Catholic and former slave, immigrant, and philanthropist, is *Pierre Toussaint: A Citizen of Old New York* by Arthur Sheehan and Elizabeth Odell Sheehan; *Pierre Toussaint: Apostle of Old New York* by Ellen Tarry; and *Pierre Toussaint: A Biography* by Arthur Jones.[48] In 1992, Maria M. Lannon wrote a biography of Mother Mary Lange (1784–1882) titled *Response to Love: The Story of Mother Mary Elizabeth Lange, O.S.P.*[49] Among the biographies of Mother Henriette

---

[47] The memoir *Hallelujah Song! Memoir of a Black Catholic Priest from the Jim Crow South* by William L. Norvel, S.S.J., and Paulette Norvel Lewis (CreateSpace Independent Publishing Platform, 2016) and *Pickin' Cotton On the Way to Church: The Life and Work of Father Boniface Hardin, O.S.B.*, by Nancy Van Note Chism (Indianapolis: Indiana Historical Society Press, 2019) are two recent biographical works about the extraordinary lives of black priests from the middle of the twentieth century through the first part of the twenty-first century.

[48] Arthur Sheehan and Elizabeth Odell Sheehan, *Pierre Toussaint: A Citizen of Old New York* (New York: Candle Press, 1953); Ellen Tarry, *Pierre Toussaint: Apostle of Old New York* (Boston: Pauline Books and Media, 1998); Arthur Jones, *Pierre Toussaint: A Biography* (New York: Doubleday, 2003).

[49] Maria M. Lannon, *Response to Love: The Story of Mother Mary Elizabeth Lange, O.S.P.* (Washington, DC: Josephite Pastoral Center, 1992).

Delille (1813–1862) are *Henriette Delille: Servant of Slaves and Witness to the Poor* by Cyprian Davis, O.S.B., and *Henriette Delille* by Virginia Meacham Gould and Charles Nolan.⁵⁰ *In the Secret Service of the Sacred Heart: The Life and Virtues of Julia Greeley* by Blaine Burkey, O.F.M., Cap., is a compilation of stories and events in the life of Julia Greeley (1833–1918), the only black Catholic laywoman who is a candidate for canonization.⁵¹

Even before her death, Sister Thea Bowman, F.S.P.A. (1937–1990), was the best-known and admired African American religious sister. A wide spectrum of Catholics nationally and internationally found inspiration in the courage and faith with which she faced terminal cancer as well as in her passionate affirmation of the inherent beauty and dignity present in all cultures, especially African American culture. Her cause for canonization opened in November 2018. A major biography of Sister Thea, titled *Thea's Song*, was written by two of her associates: Sister Charlene Smith, F.S.P.A., a member of her congregation, and John Feister, one of the last journalists to interview her before her death in 1990. Smith and Feister drew from Sister Thea's personal papers, the archives of her religious community, and extensive interviews with those who knew her.⁵² Since the introduction of Sister Thea's cause, *Thea Bowman: Faithful and Free* by Maurice J. Nutt, C.Ss.R., and *Sister Thea Bowman: Do You Hear Me, Church?* by Peggy Sklar, a book for youth, have been published.⁵³

---

⁵⁰ Cyprian Davis, O.S.B., *Henriette Delille: Servant of Slaves and Witness to the Poor* (New Orleans: Archives of the Archdiocese of New Orleans, 2004); Virginia Meacham Gould and Charles E. Nolan, *Henriette Delille: "Servant of Slaves"* (New Orleans: Sisters of the Holy Family, 1998).

⁵¹ Blaine Burkey, O.F.M., Cap., *In the Secret Service of the Sacred Heart: Remembering the Life and Virtues of Denver's Angel of Charity Julia Greeley* (Denver: Julia Greeley Guild, 2012).

⁵² Charlene Smith and John Feister, *Thea's Song: The Life of Thea Bowman* (Maryknoll, NY: Orbis Books, 2009). Smith and Feister won a Christopher Award in 2011 in the category of books for adults. The Christopher Awards honor writers, producers, directors, authors, and illustrators whose work "affirms the highest values of the human spirit."

⁵³ Maurice J. Nutt, C.Ss.R., *Thea Bowman: Faithful and Free* (Collegeville, MN: Liturgical Press, 2019); Peggy Sklar, *Sister Thea Bowman: Do You Hear Me, Church?* (New York: Paulist Press, 2020).

Two biographies of Father Tolton appeared before his cause was opened in 2011, but since that time, several new works have been published, including Bishop Joseph Perry's *Father Augustus Tolton: A Brief Biography of a Faithful Priest and Former Slave* and a youth-oriented book in graphic novel format, *Fr. Augustus Tolton: The First Recognized Black Catholic Priest in America*, by two sisters, Corrina and Maria Laughlin.[54] These biographies focus on the virtues of their subjects, the ways these women and men responded to God's call, and how they dealt with life's challenges, disappointments, and tragedies by relying on their faith.

Black Catholic Lives: Laity

The lives of black Catholics continue to be written. The story of A. P. Tureaud (1899–1972), a civil rights attorney and devoted Catholic layman who worked very closely with Thurgood Marshall on a series of NAACP cases that ultimately led to the 1954 *Brown v. Board of Education* Supreme Court decision, is an example. Familiar mostly to legal and civil rights scholars, his life is becoming more widely known. In *A More Noble Cause*, Rachel L. Emanuel and Alexander P. Tureaud Jr. have introduced a truly fascinating and historically significant figure. The authors present a "personal biography," providing insight into how Tureaud's relationships and religious commitments led him to advance civil rights.[55]

Lay Catholics, many of whom seemingly lived ordinary lives, are increasingly authoring autobiographies. Recent titles include *A Light Will Rise in Darkness: Growing Up Black and Catholic in New Orleans* by Jo Anne Tardy; *Why I Left the Church, Why I Came Back and Why I Just*

---

[54] Harold Burke-Sivers, *Father Augustus Tolton: The Slave Who Became the First African American Priest* (Irondale, AL: EWTN Publishing, 2018); Joyce Duriga, *Augustus Tolton: The Church Is the True Liberator* (Collegeville, MN: Liturgical Press, 2018); Joseph N. Perry, *Father Augustus Tolton: A Brief Biography of a Faithful Priest and Former Slave* (Chicago: Father Tolton Guild, 2016); and Corrina Laughlin and Maria Laughlin, *Fr. Augustus Tolton: The First Recognized Black Catholic Priest in America* (Chicago: Liturgy Training Publications, 2015).

[55] Rachel L. Emanuel and Alexander P. Tureaud Jr., *A More Noble Cause: A. P. Tureaud and the Struggle for Civil Rights in Louisiana* (Baton Rouge: Louisiana State University Press, 2011).

Might Leave Again by Jean K. Douglas; and *Trouble Don't Last Always* by Deacon Shelby M. Friend. Tardy, born in the Algiers neighborhood of New Orleans, experienced both a warm and idyllic childhood and the tensions of growing up black and Catholic. Published a year after Hurricane Katrina hit New Orleans, her book is full of colorful and engaging stories, such as the importance of church and family celebrations and darker stories about color consciousness and religious people not always living up to the gospel's demands.[56]

Using a pseudonym, Jean K. Douglas begins her memoir with an African proverb. According to the proverb, though the lion is the king of the jungle, the hunter will always win until the lion tells his own story.[57] Determined to be a storytelling "lion," Douglas sets out in *Why I Left the Church, Why I Came Back, and Why I Just Might Leave Again: Memories of Growing Up African American and Catholic* to talk about her life in and out of the Catholic Church from her perspective as an African American laywoman. From the time she was a young girl in Catholic schools in Detroit until now as a college professor involved in her local parish in the Southeast, Douglas "the hunter" has contended with racism.

Telling her story in four parts, Douglas contextualizes her memories from the past and her experiences of the present using theological and spiritual sources, news stories, and the works of black Catholic scholars. Her storytelling is fluid. Douglas floats from her childhood to her college and graduate school years to her contemporary experience as a black Catholic to tell of profound racism in the Catholic Church braided with Catholics' profound graciousness. From the outset, Douglas is clear that the same church that has rejected her and caused her great pain has also been the church that saved her family when their father abandoned them and their mother, who suffered from schizophrenia, worked to keep the family together. Douglas writes, "I'll never forget how the sisters rescued us. Throughout the remainder of the school year, they gave

---

[56] Jo Anne Tardy, *A Light Will Rise in Darkness: Growing Up Black and Catholic in New Orleans* (Skokie, IL: Acta Publications, 2006), 57.

[57] Jean K. Douglas, *Why I Left the Church, Why I Came Back, and Why I Just Might Leave Again* (Astor, FL: Fortuity Press, 2006), 11.

us little things—jars of homemade preserves and cookies, shoes, clothing, crayons. They may have saved our lives."[58]

Catholics did "save" Douglas, her siblings, and her mother, but they also made them feel unworthy, inferior, and unwanted, hence the title of her memoir. One of the most searing instances of racism that marked the Douglas children's relationship to the Church began before any of them were born. The marriage of their parents in 1957 was a mixed marriage, religiously and racially. Of her parents, their marriage, and the Church, Douglas writes,

> Beatrice had always been an obedient Catholic, a regular church-goer. She attended Catholic schools all her life, even helped the nuns clean the church after hours. Roger wasn't Catholic, although he agreed to raise their children in the Church. He said he'd consider converting. But Beatrice's pastor refused to marry them. She and Roger asked again and again, but Father Charles absolutely refused. Why? Because Beatrice is Black, and Roger is White.[59]

From the beginning, Douglas' family received the message that they were not accepted in the Church. In weaving her memories with her contemporary experience as an African American Catholic, Douglas identified the many ways that Catholicism diminished her family and other black Catholics. As an adult, her gratitude to the Church and her experience of rejection by it remain with her and leave her contemplating exiting the Catholic Church for good.

In *Trouble Don't Last Always*, Shelby Friend tells the story of growing up poor but well-loved in 1950s and 1960s Tennessee. His early adulthood was marked by many troubles, most of his own making, but some were the price for being poor and black. When he decided to turn his life around, he sought a spiritual home, believing that to be a good husband and father, he needed to connect with

---

[58] Douglas, *Why I Left the Church*, 111.
[59] Douglas, *Why I Left the Church*, 18. Douglas explains that this same priest eventually convalidated her parents' marriage after they had been married for three years. However, this did not undo the emotional damage. When Douglas' father left the family, her mother believed she was being punished for going against the priest and marrying a white man. She never stopped believing this.

God. His wife—a "cradle Catholic"—suggested that he consider coming to her church. Friend's first visit to St. Henry Catholic Church in Cleveland, Ohio, was underwhelming. While he considered the church "very interesting," it was also "stuffy and unfriendly."[60] The music was "traditional European, nothing close to soulful," and the people seemed "so serious." The lack of emotion troubled him, but he was intrigued by "the solitude, the ritual, and the flow of the Mass. The intercessions, the praying for the living *and* the dead, the sharing of one cup, the ideas of a universal church where people of different cultures and diverse ethnic backgrounds gathered to worship and give thanks and praise to God were impressive and exciting."[61]

Because he had many questions and theological reservations about the faith, it took Friend three years to decide whether to commit to Catholicism. He wondered, "How could a simple piece of bread and a cup of wine become the body and blood of Christ?" After three years of religious education, he finally decided to enter the Catholic Church. Soon he was a Eucharistic minister and an "official cook and bottle washer for the Church."[62] Not long after becoming a Catholic, his pastor and fellow parish members encouraged him to pursue the permanent diaconate. He wondered if he, a former "hell-raiser," was smart enough, strong enough, humble enough, and worthy to answer this call.[63] On May 24, 1994, fifty members of Friend's family (all non-Catholics) took a bus from Greenville, Tennessee, to Cleveland, Ohio, to witness what he described as "a miracle": his ordination as a deacon in the Catholic Church. He related, "The St. Henry's Church community, which I had once considered stuck-up and unfriendly, housed all fifty of my family and friends in their homes."[64]

What seems to connect these various black Catholic lives and experiences is the indelible mark Catholicism made on their characters,

---

[60] Shelby M. Friend, *Trouble Don't Last Always* (Bloomington, IN: AuthorHouse, 2007), 86.
[61] Friend, *Trouble Don't Last Always*, 87.
[62] Friend, *Trouble Don't Last Always*, 89.
[63] Friend, *Trouble Don't Last Always*, 90.
[64] Friend, *Trouble Don't Last Always*, 96.

motivations, and commitments. The autobiography of Charles B. Rangel, who served in the U.S. House of Representatives from 1971 to 2017, demonstrates this well. In *And I Haven't Had a Bad Day Since*, Rangel offered a reflection on his relationship with the Church, appreciating his Catholic upbringing, but writing, "I'm afraid I no longer believe in Catholic or even Christian theology and dogma the way I once did. Traveling all over the world as I have, and being exposed to so many different faiths, all I want to be able to do when I get to heaven is to have a little time with St. Peter to explain who I am."[65] Rangel also discussed his "not love-hate but love-difficulty relationship" with New York Cardinal John O'Connor. O'Connor, though troubled by Rangel's support for abortion rights, admired Rangel for assisting the poor.[66] The two men attempted to collaborate on social issues, but they never quite connected in the way that either wished. O'Connor thought Rangel needed to better understand the faith, and Rangel thought O'Connor needed to more boldly advocate for the poor and disadvantaged. Rangel criticized the Church for not striving for "a morality above and beyond their faith and their dogma."[67]

Despite his criticisms, Rangel also acknowledged what the Catholic Church gave him: "My mom didn't have much to give me in life, but if there is one thing she valued ... it was membership in that St. Aloysius Catholic Church at the western end of my world. She insisted on passing it on to me, and from about the eighth grade I not only attended but served as an altar boy there."[68] According to Rangel, growing up amid the worst neighborhood in Harlem with "hoodlum-minded boys" and going to a Catholic church near a better neighborhood prepared him for a successful political career. According to Rangel, "Learning to explain to my Catholic kids why my hoodlum friends were always picking on them, and answering when the hoodlums asked 'Why are you hanging around those uppity so-and-so's in the first place,' probably prepared me for

---

[65] Charles B. Rangel and Leon Wynter, *And I Haven't Had a Bad Day Since: From the Streets of Harlem to the Halls of Congress* (New York: St. Martin's, 2007), 250.
[66] Rangel and Wynter, *And I Haven't Had a Bad Day Since*, 250.
[67] Rangel and Wynter, *And I Haven't Had a Bad Day Since*, 252.
[68] Rangel and Wynter, *And I Haven't Had a Bad Day Since*, 28.

bridging factions in the army, the Harlem Democratic clubhouses, the state legislature, and ultimately the Congress."[69]

Rangel expressed deep gratitude for his law school education at St. John's University in New York City. Receiving the Catholic Scholarship for Negroes, Rangel was granted "three years tuition, books and a stipend—a full ride."[70] Rangel's time at St. John's was transformative. He dove into his studies and social life. He was involved in law school elections and organized the black students into a coalition with Italian students, "who in those days were not treated as well as the Irish." He also brought Jews and other minorities together. St. John's gave Rangel the chance to learn about the lives of New Yorkers who were unlike him, and these lessons informed his life in politics. Much of his life, as he relates in his autobiography, was directly connected to Catholicism.

Conclusion: Freedom through Writing

Black Catholic autobiographies are marked by a sense of freedom. The black Catholic women and men who record their own life stories do so with aplomb. The good, the bad, and the seemingly mundane come to life in their writing. It is as if these authors realize that opportunities to speak, write, and be heard as black Catholics must not be taken for granted, and they must seize the moment. Their autobiographical writings are candid, sincere, personal, and enlightening. Through reading the lives of individual black Catholics, one may gain insights into their experiences in various time periods, regions, and cultures, and also a sense of black Catholic values. These writings make it possible to see how Catholicism has shaped the lives of black men and women and how in turn they have helped to shape the Catholic and African American communities of which they have been a part.

---

[69] Rangel and Wynter, *And I Haven't Had a Bad Day Since*, 29.
[70] Rangel and Wynter, *And I Haven't Had a Bad Day Since*, 102.

Freeing the Spirit: Very Personal Reflections on One Man's Search for the Spirit in Worship

CLARENCE JOSEPH RIVERS*

Prologue

Brothers and Sisters in Christ: Although some sayings may be hard for us to hear and bear, we have been told to be open to the liberating truth. And the truth is that worship in most of our churches, most of the time, is dull and uninspiring. Whereas the worshiping congregation should be a dramatic dance life, instead it is all too often like the dry bones in the vision of Ezekiel, a static, stagnant sprawl of lifeless limbs, a tableau of death. We seem to be there merely physically, not really hearing anything that moves us, not saying anything that moves others. Our faith would seem to make us exuberant proclaimers of the Joy of Life. But we appear deaf and dumb, unmoved and unmoving. We do not seem to be God's chosen people, rather God's frozen people. And to the extent that we appear deaf and dumb and dead and lifeless, to that extent we are not witnesses for everlasting life, but witnesses for never-ending death.

Cold Worship: Our Starting Point

OUR FOREPARENTS, when allowed to attend the worship services of those who enslaved them, *found the worship incomplete.* They would remain in the churchyard afterwards and would form a circle and dance until they felt possessed by the Spirit of God. Many generations later, my maternal grandmother, Eugenia Houser Echols, used to say how much she admired the charitable works of the Catholic Church, when finally there was a Catholic presence in the

---

* This is an excerpt of an essay first published in *U.S. Catholic Historian* 19, no. 2 (Spring 2001): 95–143.

Black community of Selma. She told over and over again how this Catholic nun rolled back layers and layers of skirt, like an onion, and got down on her bare knees to scrub the splintered floor of this sick and aged colored woman. My grandmother had never before witnessed a White person serving, in a menial capacity, the needs of a colored person. She was impressed, and even in the retelling of the story her voice took on all the emotion, all the surprise and her own joy-filled enthusiasm that she had first felt when witnessing this Sister of St. Joseph performing corporal works of mercy. Eugenia was always on fire during the telling of this marvelous narrative and would always, reaching for the strongest notes in her speaking voice, exclaim and proclaim: "If there ever was a Christian, he was a CATHOLIC!!!" Moreover, she enjoyed the humane blend of ritual movement, color, and pageantry, the dignified drape of vesture, and the provocative and evocative smell of incense in Catholic worship. But when someone asked her why she was not a Catholic, she answered, almost-not-quite shivering, "Their worship is much too cold." There was the slightest hint of regret in her voice.

For her and most Blacks (and, I believe, "for most people"), Catholic worship lacks the warmth and fire of the "HOLY GHOST." It is not inspiring. Our worship did not leave my grandmother spiritually fulfilled; it left her spiritually unfed. It did not move her beyond admiration of the vesture and the rites of the Church to the ardent fervor of spiritual growth and continuing conversion. It would be a mistake to think that the spiritual vitality sought by my grandmother was a cultural phenomenon inherited uniquely out of her African/African American background. Eugenia Houser Echols' needs were also the needs of Europeans, because they are human needs....

The Beginning of a Professional Liturgist

As a newly ordained minister (1956) and associate pastor to Msgr. Clement J. Busemeyer at St. Joseph's Parish in the West End of Cincinnati, I expected this exteriorly gruff, teutonic pastor to be unconcerned about the *quality* of worship; his Masses took from twenty to thirty minutes, the "sacred words" slovenly raced over in the widespread custom of the day. However, he was very much concerned that worship was not reaching and touching the people in the pews. One day he said to me, "People are coming to church only because they're afraid of *catching hell*, if they don't!" He then pointedly asked, "Can you do something about this?" His clumsy question is much more vivid in memory than my crazy response, which, I believe, was an unequivocal, though naive, "Yes, I think I can! I can do something about THIS!"

My response, in the clear light of looking back, was not as ambitious as the words would seem to indicate. In presiding at Mass, usually the main parish Mass, I would intensify my efforts to read the Latin texts so as to convey their meaning. There was no illusion that the people would understand the Latin, but they must see that I, for the most part, did understand and was more or less raptured by my understanding. There was a certain validity in presuming that they could be moved by experiencing that I was moved. However, they must understand their own responses, and they must convey the meaning in the English hymns, psalms, and songs, to themselves and to one another. That was not to ask a great deal for the moment, and it laid a basis for further development.

Beginning to Compose

Father Busemeyer had also indicated that he saw a place for Black music in the Catholic Church. He lamented the fact that the archbishop had not allowed a concert of Negro spirituals at the (not yet restored) cathedral. My own interpretation of this was that there should be a place for all Black religious culture in worship. Around the same time Father Boniface Luykx, a Belgian Norbertine monk, on his way going to or coming from his annual courses in liturgy taught at Notre Dame, began to stop off in Cincinnati. On one occasion he challenged Father Giles Harry Pater, a very dear friend of mine, and me to start composing music for the liturgy out of our own backgrounds. There was nothing wrong with challenging Harry; he was a trained, educated musician. But there was a danger in challenging me: I did not know enough to know that I could not compose. Or closer to the truth, I really believed that musical compositions, especially with words, must be as natural as speaking a language even before becoming literate in that language. So I accepted the challenge.

I knew that a Sister of the Blessed Sacrament had set the text of the *Latin Ordinary of the Mass* to the tune of several Negro spirituals. The *Kyrie* was set to the tune of "Nobody Knows the Trouble I See." Though Sister's vision of introducing the power and pathos of African American music into worship was nothing less than commendable, I remember Father Charles Rehling suggesting that the results might have been more effective had she used the "elements" of the spirituals, instead of forcing whole, unchanged and undiluted melodies onto the Latin text, where they did not fit. Her efforts and Charles' comments were the only technical, critical preparation I had before rushing in past the nontreading angels.

One Sunday afternoon I was returning from Virginia Beach where I had delivered a speech on race relations. I was not yet used to flying, and, I must say, Piedmont Airlines' little prop jet did not inspire confidence. We were flying over the Appalachian Mountains during a thunderstorm. I needed to do something to take my mind off Piedmont's little prop jet and the thunderstorm. I took out my (before-its-time) English-language breviary and started to read the Sunday Office. I was struck with the words of St. John: "God is love; and he who abides in love abides in God; and God in him." I started applying a melody and a musical rhythm to the piece, mostly in my head, and possibly humming very softly to myself and occasionally scrawling lines and dots as pegs to my memory. I repeated the melody incessantly in my head. When I got back to St. Joseph's, I taught the melody to the Sisters of St. Francis (from Oldenburg, Indiana) who taught in our school, who in turn taught the whole of the primary school to sing the refrain. Meanwhile, I had to compose verses and teach them to Phil Schoch and Joe Muldrow, our instantly created cantors. With one stroke, almost unconsciously, a change in American church music had begun.

But the way had already been prepared. Father Luykx had brought me a tape of the *Missa Luba*, which the sisters had taught to the primary school.[1] One day, Msgr. Busemeyer had heard the children's

---

[1] Editor's note: The *Missa Luba*, developed at a mission in the Congo in the late 1950s, was a musical setting linking traditional African melodies to the Latin text of the Mass.

lusty, robust singing of the Luba Mass as he strolled through the school. He returned to the rectory almost breathless with enthusiasm. He said that he had never heard the *Kyrie* and the *Sanctus* and other parts of the Mass Ordinary sung with such enthusiasm. Therefore, he asked, weren't we obliged to let the children sing this at Mass? Not entirely guileless I responded, "I guess so Father!" Msgr. Busemeyer insisted that the children sing the Luba Mass for his twenty-fifth ordination jubilee. The barn door had been left open! In due time, in rushed the spirituals, gospel, jazz, my occasional compositions, and all the rest. As I remarked earlier, a Cincinnati archbishop had forbidden a concert of Negro spirituals at the cathedral on the implausible and shaky grounds that they were "secular" songs, but by this time the patently implausible grounds were much too shaky to stand up under the potentially weighty charge of racism. Certainly, not even an archbishop would have risked his authority being tainted with the opprobrium of being politically incorrect.

However, music, from any source, whatever its vitality, could not and cannot carry the full weight of effective worship. In line with our pastoral mandate to improve worship and to encourage congregational vitality and responsiveness, I worked hard at improving my sermons. With hindsight, I know that my sermon efforts were not very moving, but in the homiletic desert of the times they were frequently "interesting" by reason of content and perspective. If in spite of strenuous effort I came up with nothing that was even interesting, I simply did not preach. I did not preach in spite of congregational encouragement to do so *anyhow*. The congregations figured, I think, that I was being modest and would have always had "something" of interest to say, but I knew that their confidence was misplaced. Moreover, I continued to feel the "urge" to make worship focused and coherent. Without the latter the total liturgy would not have its most intense impact and effect in spite of the fact that one or more parts might be individually effective.

My Co-workers

Very few people get anything done without the intimate collaboration of others. My co-workers were the Sisters of Saint Francis from Oldenburg, Indiana. They always had the schoolchildren well prepared to participate in the main Sunday liturgy, and, when necessary, they prodded and disturbed my own inertia, reminding me: "You promised us a new communion hymn." It was not only the schoolchildren who had to be taught, however; the full congregation itself had to be taught to sing in a manner that was alive rather than dead and deadening. The entire congregation had to become collaborators and concelebrants, and so, only half-vested, I came before the parish assembly before the main liturgy on Sunday morning. No matter how long it took, I reasoned that the Mass could not proceed until the primary witness of the faith, the worshiping assembly, was ready to express that faith. I tried to teach them to sing and respond with a vitality that betokened a living faith. I "threatened," cajoled, made fun of their bad singing habits, and encouraged them to repeat their best attempts. Not everybody could have gotten away with this outrage that I was perpetrating, but they loved me, and I knew that and took advantage of my place in their hearts. Moreover, and perhaps more profoundly, the congregation enjoyed succeeding. Gratefully, they started to give of themselves in a manner that was fitting, at least for the moment.

Nothing Succeeds Like Success

Keep in mind that this was happening before the Second Vatican Council's exhortations on congregational participation. So in spite of the fact that we did nothing to specifically advertise our parish liturgies, the church started to have a few visiting strangers each Sunday, and that was encouraging. There were a few of our own parishioners, however, who could not stand the strain of active participation and took refuge in the pastor's twenty to thirty minute "quiet" Mass.

Msgr. Busemeyer wanted us to make the main liturgy spiritually alive. ("Spiritually alive" is redundant). But for complex reasons, he continued the "quiet" Mass. Among other things, the pastor wanted a comparison, and those who were aware and capable of judging saw that the quiet Mass was not alive with silent prayer. Rather the quiet of this Mass was like that in the valley of Ezekiel's dry bones before the miracle. The sisters and I were not given to academic worship analysis. We never really discussed to any great extent, if at all, the things that made our Sunday worship moderately effective. We knew we were effective by an occasional comparison to the liturgies that we witnessed elsewhere. (Remember, there was not a great deal going on elsewhere until sometime after the council). Sometimes, it was the comment of an occasional visitor that helped label and categorize some of our efforts: "Your parish Mass seems to flow so smoothly." At the time, I felt the need to stitch together the sequential parts of the liturgy with a few discreet words taken from Scripture, songs, or simply poetic language taken from other literature. I did not realize it immediately, but I was feeling the need to keep worship from being static by giving it movement. Ultimately, I realized that all drama, including the drama of worship, needed movement from beginning to middle to end. The loose strings from various studies or from comments of professors started to be woven into a coherent pattern. Given a few years and a great deal of experience, I was beginning to understand how to plan a liturgy. It slowly dawned on me that a well-structured (aesthetically structured) worship was the same as a vitally effective, spiritually moving worship. Even this slow learner caught on eventually. St. Joseph's parish was moving with moderate speed toward an effective worship and a more comprehensive idea of inculturation, i.e., synthesizing and integrating African American culture and Catholic worship. This was a matter more sophisticated and complex than adding a few Black-flavored hymns/songs onto an otherwise unyielding Roman rite.

Our schoolchildren at St. Joseph's were invited to other parishes, but this was getting us unwanted attention. When word finally reached the newspapers that there was "drumming" in St. Joseph's Church on Ezzard Charles Drive, a letter came from the archbishop's office demanding that we use only "sacred instruments." But as I said before, the barn door was open! Some weeks after the receipt of that letter, Bishop Paul Leibold, who had written the "no secular instruments" letter at the mandate of Archbishop Karl Alter, was coming to St. Joseph's to administer the sacrament of Confirmation. Msgr. Busemeyer declared three evenings of preparation: (1) to explore the meaning of confirmation; (2) to practice the ceremonies; and (3) to prepare and invigorate the congregational participation—especially the music. Imagine pastors telling their congregations they have to turn out for all four evenings, three immediately prior to the evening of Confirmation and the evening of Confirmation itself. In those days, however, when Msgr. Busemeyer spoke, everyone (almost) listened and obeyed, for they respected and loved him because he was good to his people.

In our music preparations we were mainly using Gelineau psalm settings.[2] We did not have an organist, so the schoolchildren borrowed my set of Ugandan drums. I said it was only for temporary use in rehearsing. In the back of my mind, however, I knew we had to have some instrument to help the congregation keep its ensemble. So I went to Purcell High School, where I taught, borrowed the timpani set, and snuck it up into the choir loft. When the procession stepped into church, I unleashed the energy of the schoolchildren on the timpani; the congregation sang with all their hearts. Msgr. Busemeyer was seen patrolling the side aisles with a smile on his face that out-toothed the Cheshire Cat.

Bishop Leibold, when asked by an "unwise" young sister how he liked the music, very wisely avoided the subject (i.e., the mandate forbidding "non-sacred" instruments) and responded: "I'm for giving these people all the singing they can get." The local clergy were gathered there, as was the commendable custom *in diebus illis*—in comradeship and martinis. When I walked into the pastor's living room to join this clerical assembly, someone yelled across the room, "Hey Rivers, were these drums 'liturgical'?" (He meant "rubrical.") However, before I had a chance to respond, Msgr. Busemeyer intervened: "You know, five years ago you wouldn't have heard THAT." He too, like the bishop, avoided the subject. Moreover, Msgr. Busemeyer had the full understanding that I had, without his permission, put his "prestige" on the line by violating a direct order written to him by the bishop. If we had not succeeded, I might have gotten a tongue lashing. If one is going to violate orders for pastoral reasons, one had better succeed in the endeavor, making incarnate aesthetic and pastoral insight and thereby outweighing the "theory or abstraction" of legislated principle. I had gambled on that, and nothing more was ever said about THAT.

---

[2] Editor's note: A reference to the work of French composer and Jesuit priest Joseph Gelineau (1920–2008).

This foolish assistant pastor, with the dedicated collaboration of "unwise" Oldenburg Franciscan Sisters, had rushed in where angels feared to tread and had not been rebuked, nor reprimanded, nor scolded. Why? Because we had done it well. Armed only with naiveté, a little skill (in handling, teaching, and leading people), and a strong desire to make worship vital, we had gained (or always had) the allegiance of the congregation who sang their hearts out, and we found the results satisfying. The sisters and I had few abstract ideals to lead us. We were simply in love with incarnate, authentic, and vital worship. Even so we could only do what the pastor allowed us to do. Gratefully, he wanted what we wanted, so he allowed us what, in those days, was a great deal of freedom in handling parish worship. The result: we did much of what Vatican II would eventually encourage....

Not By Music Alone

There should be one clarification about our use of music in worship. In my experience the kind of music was not as important as its effective delivery. I worked with the congregation before main liturgies, and they responded well. Backed up by the schoolchildren and prepared by the nuns, the congregation was able to sing and otherwise participate very actively in our communal worship. The distinction between the High Mass and the Low Mass began to fade before the decrees of Vatican II were ever promulgated. As I have previously touched on, I had always thought that our sermons should be worked on, written out, and written as poetically as possible. Above all I thought I had to have something worth saying, something that touched people. Otherwise I did not preach. I also thought that the liturgy ought to have integrity and be a staged religious play, with its parts stitched together with embroidering threads of scripture text or song phrases—so that parts of the worship flowed naturally from one to another. I had not fully thought this out; I was simply acting from the instincts that made me very uncomfortable when presiding at worship when worship did not have the appropriate qualities that inspired the people. Without these qualities, I felt that worship was not only inappropriate, it was not really worship. Not being entirely a slow learner, moving at the speed of an opening flower petal, it dawned on me, as a fully articulated concept, that well-sung music was not sufficient for effective, authentic worship....

It goes without saying that I felt a need to perform, to proclaim, to announce, and to pray as if I meant the texts that I was saying or singing. That is to say, I never felt comfortable unless I was habitually familiar with the texts of the missal (not yet divided into sacramentary, lectionary, and Gospel books), understood them, and delivered them with the appropriate understanding evident in my voice through pronunciation, enunciation, inflection, various pitches, pauses, and, sometimes, repetition....

Freeing the Spirit

During the early 1960s invitations started to come in for our workshops in music and worship. I urged the sponsors of these workshops to allow seven to ten days for programming, which consisted of evening lectures on worship. Two hours each evening were devoted to learning the music, which was then used in a climactic concert and/or a Sunday morning Eucharist.

The intensive music rehearsals were not merely for the sake of the music. These rehearsal sessions were used to get across certain points about worship and performance in worship. For example, when the participants were tired and seemed not to have the energy to enter fully into the program of the evening, I used the occasion to disabuse them of the notion that in public worship we ought to communicate our personal feelings. I called that belief "the idolatry of sincerity," pointing out that on Easter Sunday the parish priest did not have the right to communicate his "hangover"; rather he must transcend his personal feeling in order to convey the hope and the joy of the Resurrection.

Another favorite "idol" was that liturgy ought to be "spontaneous," and that too much practice would make the performer in worship too stiff. Wrong again, I countered; too little practice makes one stiff and awkward. After years of grueling practice, a gymnast appears to do his/her routine effortlessly. Effortlessly, after years of practice!?! They would get the point! Then, I would say, you do not have to believe, but I want you to sing as if you did. All such ideas were handled casually and with as much wit and humor as I could summon.

If there were a lecture or concert scheduled, the lecture (basically a humorous monologue) was meant to break down their inhibitions, to allow the assembly to participate more freely, and to close up all of the little dark pigeonholes where people were wont to hide from active and vital participation in worship. Again, the musical portion of the evening was not an end in itself; it was a way of involving the entire assembly rather than letting them be onlookers and voyeurs in this love song that we sing to God, i.e., the liturgy.

In many cases the sponsors asked for just a weekend program. In this situation, I felt obliged to pack more talk and conversation into the all-day Saturday program than I would have liked to do, but I felt obliged to let pastors and people know about all the elements of a liturgy. I felt it would have been, at the very least, unfaithful on my part to leave people with the impression that music was the alpha and omega of worship. On the other hand, I did and do believe that the whole of the liturgy should be, in the deepest sense of the word, musical/poetic/dramatic. However, this would involve infinitely more than singing a few good songs at Mass....

Drama School at the Catholic University of America

I was convinced that worship and theater were more closely allied than most people wanted to admit. For my own personal and professional development, I wanted the experience of learning the art of acting under competent direction. Teaching at Purcell High School, I had the chance, along with Brother Ray McQuade, S.M., to revive the school drama guild, the Queen's Men. I chose to direct a play from Shakespeare each year, while Brother chose a contemporary work. This afforded me the opportunity of working in undiluted drama and getting a feel for and a sense of fundamental theater artistry.

After seven or so years of teaching I asked Archbishop Karl J. Alter if I might study drama. He wanted me to attend Yale, "a school with a name," but I was interested in getting stage experience. I was under the illusion that stage experience was more readily and more frequently available at Catholic University of America (CUA). When the first play came around, with Helen Hayes as the star, I signed up for the tryouts. Professor Leo Brady called me aside and told me that clerics were not allowed on stage. I explained to him that getting on stage was my only reason for being at CUA, and that I had made it clear to the department head, Gilbert V. Hartke, O.P., to my faculty advisor, Donald Waters, and to everyone else who would listen that my whole purpose, my only purpose, was to get on stage and be directed as an actor. I explained that no one had said anything about a policy that discriminated against clerics. If I had been warned, I argued, when I first applied to enter the graduate program, I could have withdrawn, and I could have been off to Yale with my bishop's blessing. However, no one had given the slightest hint that onstage experience was not available to me at CUA. All my pleading and reasoning got me nowhere.

Later in the year, in a course on literary criticism, I wrote a paper on morality and aesthetics for that same Leo Brady (of *Brother Orchid* fame). Professor Brady gave me an "Excellent," and he praised my paper for a "fine and vigorous style of writing." He then opened the door to all of my pent-up anger: "This is the first thing that you seemed to have your heart in!" He had not seen vigorous writing yet. I laid it all out in longhand on legal-sized tablet paper. I reviewed my reasons for being at CUA, and the reason my heart had found no home there. Further, I went on to say that a visitor to the campus, a priest of the Washington diocese, had asked me, "Is it true that you were not allowed on stage because you were Black?" I also mentioned that a fellow graduate student, Robert Murch, and I had visited a former CUA student. After introducing us, Robert said to the other young man, "Clarence has the same trouble that you had at the school." Now the man was Black, but he was not a cleric. It dawned on me that this was the very man that Father Hartke had bragged about as being one of the finest actors to pass through the school. Obviously, the man had been kept off stage because of his color!

I took these several pages, steeped in my anger, and had them reproduced for distribution not only to Leo Brady but also to my own bishop, the entire faculty and staff of the drama department, and a few other people that I wanted to inform. It was not until I was literally on my way home from CUA that I found out the tear that the knife of my epistle had caused in the fabric of the Drama Department.... I bring this up in abbreviated form to say that it was the only fully deliberate obstacle placed in my way as I prepared myself to become a professional liturgist.... There was a great deal of good, however, that came from being at CUA. Although it was not *the* center of the American Church, it was, nonetheless, certainly *a* center for the American Church, simply because its student body and faculty/staff were drawn from every part of the country.... Had I not been in Washington I would never have come into contact with the official and unofficial leadership of the Liturgical Conference, nor would I have been privileged to sit on its board. I might never have been invited to share my "new" music with the American Church at the meeting of the Liturgical Conference in St. Louis at Kiel Auditorium in August of 1964. The Conference convened some twenty thousand strong for the first Mass in English.

The First Mass in English

As I remember it, I was only on the program to lead one communion hymn. The song was "God Is Love" (the very first I ever composed). The music so energized the crowd, however, that I was called back, again and again, to share more of the music with the assembly. And, lucky us, the Purcell High School Mafia (the Queen's Men, bedecked in red and scarlet blazers emblazoned with Shakespeare's coat of arms with the addition of the *fleur de lis*) was there to sell thousands of our album, *An American Mass Program*. It was not a Mass, I had insisted to Omer Westendorf, who was publishing the first "hard copies" of the music, with accompaniments by Maestro Henry Papale. (Later Henry did many arrangements of various pieces for me). Omer liked to make or could not help making long titles: *Father Rivers Leads His Congregation in an American Mass Program*. The most I could do was get the first half of the title subordinated into small letters. Even Omer had been a bit squeamish about publishing the printed text until the money started rolling in and the "rave" reviews came in from the secular and religious presses.

At the conference in St. Louis, I was made into an instant celebrity. All I did was smile and shake hands and try to answer all sorts of questions that I was ill-equipped to handle. I retreated to my hotel room at night, unable to remove the frozen smile from my face and relax my aching right hand. I had learned all too quickly the price of being a celebrity, and it was not a price that I was willing to pay. The next year, I was so anxious to get away from people at the Chicago meeting of the Liturgical Conference that I exchanged my identity badge festooned with pretty ribbons for Donald Clark's plain one with only his name thereon. Shamelessly I walked the halls of the Chicago Hilton passing myself off as Donald, an almost skinny and rather tall seminarian looking nothing like me. I never dreamed that I would crave anonymity; I surprised myself....

Change Is Called For

It had been apparent for some time that I was spreading myself too thin: teaching literature at Purcell High School; directing the Queen's Men theatre group; part-time duty in a parish (after seven years at St. Joseph's, a record for assistant pastors, I was transferred to the Church of the Assumption, in Walnut Hills); accepting invitations to do music and worship workshops on university campuses and in a few parishes; and giving lectures on race relations. Consequently, I asked Archbishop Alter to free me from regular assignments so I could concentrate on worship. He did not really understand what that meant. To help him decide, he sent (through the help of Bishop Edward McCarthy) my proposal to several liturgists, including Godfrey Diekmann, O.S.B., of Saint John's Abbey. The responses came back so positive, even enthusiastic, that the archbishop could no longer simply say "no," so we compromised. I was given my pick of liturgy schools in the United States or Europe. I first reminded him that the head of General Motors did not have to be a mechanic, but I chose to go to Paris to the Centre Pastorale de Liturgie, in the Institut Catholique.

Pere Gy, the director of the Pastoral Center, and other faculty members insisted that *"La mode ici c'est scientifque et historique!"* Everybody assumed that, beyond the class lectures, I would be pursuing a study of music, or at least a study about music. It was suggested that I contact Pere Gelineau. Father Gelineau and even the members of the faculty treated me as a peer because of my work in the United States developing a new music for worship, but I knew my limitations. I did not know anything about music from the academic perspective. I thought I might try working with a French Dominican sociologist, but he did not see any relationship between liturgy and social life.

There was a deeper problem, however: *La mode scientifique et historique*. I wanted to take another approach. Father Gy listened patiently to my exposition on liturgy and aesthetics—solving the problem of ineffective worship by examining the worship for its aesthetic effectiveness. He understood, but what I wanted was not what the school offered or should offer. We agreed to disagree. In order to get the most out of the courses without frustrating myself, I simply audited the courses so that I had a clear idea of what I could expect from an academic liturgist—or more precisely from a liturgiologist. I gave up on the idea of getting a doctorate there. It would not have proven useful, in light of my own goal. I needed to assure myself that the goal of effective worship was not just an elusive phantom, but I did receive something invaluable from the professors of the Institut Catholique. . . . I learned how isolated the Atlantic Ocean can leave the Americas, and how smug and uninformed it can leave some Europeans. At a meeting of *Universa Laus* at Pamplona, Spain, the Spaniards laughed—to the point of disrespect—at the non-lisping, non-guttural Spanish of Sergio Mendez Arceo, the bishop of Cuernavaca. This at a time when English speakers on both sides of the Atlantic had become reasonably tolerant of one another's strange handling of the language.

At that same meeting *An American Mass Program* was played; it was the only North American music that the movers and shakers in France and Germany knew of. In the summer of 1967 there was little else, and the only North American representatives there (excluding the bishop of Cuernavaca) were the newly elected Abbot Primate of the Benedictines, Rembert Weakland, O.S.B., myself, and Stephen Somerville, priest of Toronto. *Universa Laus* was born in opposition to another international group that would have kept us singing mostly nineteenth-century music in Latin. Needless to say, that could not have succeeded in this country even without *Universa Laus*.

Returning to the Life of an Active Liturgist

I returned home from Europe mid-year of 1968. I wrote ahead informing Archbishop Alter of my plans to work full-time in the field of liturgy. Sometime before, Bishop Edward McCarthy (who had been my advocate, behind the curtains, as it were) had noted that I was no longer asking permission, but rather simply informing the archbishop of my plans. I pointed out that I did "inform" well in advance and always received a response approving of my course of action. The truth is that the Archdiocese of Cincinnati did not know how to—was afraid to—make use of me and my talents in the structure of the diocese and may have been glad to be relieved of the decision.

When I was still a seminarian, as my ordination approached, the priests played the game, I think sincerely, of wondering how I might take being rejected by White parishes, and whether or not I could stand it *if* I were placed in a White parish. It never occurred to them that I might do very well in a White parish. They did assign me to teach in a school that was 99.9% White; many were surprised that I did well there not only with the students but also with their parents. They dared not place me in a Black parish for fear of being accused of racism. I suppose the times and the prevailing "chancery" mentality did not allow them to ask me directly what I thought or desired. The seminary rector did ask me whether I wanted to be stationed in my home parish, and when I said "no," he spread it throughout the diocese that Clarence did not wish to be in a Black parish. Consequently, I was assigned to St. Joseph's, a White parish in a Black neighborhood, where the school was already significantly Black, and where the pastor, Msgr. Busemeyer, never refused any priest food and shelter, no matter who he was or what he had done.

At a later date, when my reputation was already established nationally and internationally, I turned down the advances of a Hollywood team, including an agent, a manager, and a publicist, who were in hot pursuit. Why? Because I wanted to be available in Cincinnati, if the call from the diocese should come. Of course, I wanted to work in the field of worship, but I would gladly have done it for the archdiocese. The call never came, however, and I have been seeing a psychiatrist ever since. It was the severest rejection I had ever experienced—however subtle.

Please don't misunderstand me. I am supremely glad, 98.9% of the time, that I was left free to develop myself as a professional liturgist and to concentrate on the worship needs of the African American community. I never sought a pastorate, because my experience had taught me that a pastor could not devote himself to worship. All parish priests have to compromise their pursuit of excellence in worship. That is not merely my opinion but also the opinion of those who understood and understand, and in some respects wish, that the possibilities might have been otherwise. What might have been a curse was for me, as a professional liturgist, a great grace and an undeserved blessing. . . .

The First National Workshop: The University of Detroit

As the summer of 1971 approached, Joseph Dulin, president of the National Black Lay Catholic Caucus, encouraged the Black Clergy Caucus and the Black Sisters Conference to meet with the Lay Caucus in Detroit. This gave me an idea: Why not have—under sponsorship of the National Office for Black Catholics (NOBC) and Brother Joseph Davis, S.M., executive director—a workshop in liturgy and music for Black Catholics before the Lay Caucus meeting? The workshop could then supply the music and worship for the meeting in Detroit. With the help of Sister Mary Ann Smith, who did outstanding administrative, organizational, and public relations leg work in Detroit, and with the cooperation of Garland Jaggers, from Cardinal Dearden's offices, the program turned out fine. Brother Davis sent Michael St. Julien from the staff of the NOBC to help. Mr. Redmond from the University of Detroit staff saw to it that we lacked nothing the university could offer.

I had made a special trip to Detroit to meet with Mr. Dulin and his board. I had asked specifically if what I was proposing, in light of Mr. Dulin's invitation, would be in line with what the Lay Caucus and their president had in mind. The answer was a positive "yes!" I returned to Cincinnati with the full cooperation of the NOBC and,

I thought, the approval of Mr. Dulin and his board. David Camele developed the national mailing pieces and posters for the event. The latter were to be sent to Sister Mary Ann Smith for distribution in Detroit.

Before we could go to press, however, the connection with the Lay Caucus, which had pleaded for a show of unity and solidarity, had proved to be no proof against the "Amos and Andy lodge meeting" politics of Mr. Dulin's Lay Caucus Board. We could not have the closing concert of the workshop open the caucus meeting, and, believe it or not, the reason given was that they were gathering to do serious business, not to be entertained! We changed the posters before they went to press. Then, by the time of the workshop's opening, we were no longer supplying the liturgies for the caucus, and a youth choir from Baltimore was supplying the music! I will not here go into the petty jealousies and myopic small-mindedness, which my mother classified as "n-----r s-----t." Strangely, none of this bothered me; perhaps, as my mother had characterized it, I simply did not want to play in the dirt lest I besoiled myself. More to the point, Sister Mary Ann Smith made it possible for us to carry on with the workshop as if nothing had happened. Cincinnati and Dayton, with the no-nonsense persistence of Mattie Davis and a little prodding from me in the Cincinnati area, allowed us to send two Greyhound buses full of participants from the Archdiocese of Cincinnati.

Participants came from Connecticut, New York, New Jersey, Ohio, Pennsylvania, Kentucky, Michigan, Illinois, Maryland, Oklahoma, and Minnesota. It was apparent that the way to reach widespread numbers of Black Catholics was to invite them to a central location. Unfortunately, these individuals could not take the workshop experiences home except in their own somewhat changed (converted?) persons. They were professional singers with careers and just plain teenagers that the late Mattie Davis (a woman of grand spiritual dimensions and great determination) rounded up from Dayton, Ohio.

The participants worked hard during the day and entertained themselves and each other in the evenings with dancing, arias from operas, pop music of the day, and their own compositions. Joyce

Jaxon, who was there, later became music supervisor for the Detroit school system. Marjorie Burrow was then a teenager who later became a leading influence in compiling and shaping *Lead Me, Guide Me,* the Black Catholic hymnal. The late Keith Davis, an unimaginable high school baritone, went on to Broadway.

In addition to my daily lectures and discussions on worship, there were daily music sessions. The faculty members for these sessions were chosen to teach a wide variety of musics: gospel, spirituals, renaissance, baroque, and my own "new" music. Edwin R. Hawkins (who brought his whole family with him: Walter, Trumaine, Daniel, and Lynette) taught his contemporary gospel sound fresh from the pop charts. McKinley Genwright taught spirituals, renaissance, and baroque pieces. William Foster McDaniel, music director for the Fantastiks, brought the feel of jazz in his piano accompaniment and fresh jazz improvisations. Along with these music professionals, I was there with my satchel of tricks.

The workshop climaxed with a two-and-a-half-hour concert before an enthusiastic, packed house. The purely musical results were spotty at best, but the spirit of the event was pure magic. We made a two-record album culled from the many pieces in the program. CBS producers Joe Clement and Bernie Seabrooks videotaped the whole concert, and made a half-hour documentary of the event. They had come to cover the meeting of the Catholic Lay Caucus but found it to be reminiscent of certain "lodge" meetings. In spite of my own immediate reactions and in defense of Mr. Dulin and the Lay Caucus, I must say that "all people find self-government a difficult process." Witness the more than two hundred-year history of the United States Congress! The Lay Caucus, so recently born, was just approaching the toddler stage.

Looking back at "Freeing the Spirit," the name I had given to all my workshops, the event in Detroit was, in one respect, a coming of age event for Stimuli (the incorporation under which I worked) and the NOBC. The work I had been doing in my own name was now, in this instance and for the first time, a work of the National Office for Black Catholics. Soon afterwards, I became, under the administration of Joe Davis, S.M., the first director of Culture and Worship, with due acknowledgement of the paving work done by Michael Mtumishi St. Julien. Up until this event, the focus of the NOBC was to educate the White clergy and religious who staffed most Black parishes....

Soulfull Worship

At some point near the beginning of our "official" working together, Joseph Davis asked if I would publish some of the liturgies that I had put together. I convinced him that this would be futile if one expected the *"esprit"* of the original liturgies to be lifted off the printed page. We made the effort, however, and reinforced the attempt with a prelude of several essays. The text of each service was accompanied by notes explaining why we did what we did. The result was the first of two volumes on worship, entitled *Soulfull Worship*. (The *full* of *Soulfull* is intentional; *soulful* has different over tones).

I had given up on the idea of acquiring a doctorate. The experiences of friends who had taken the traditional route to the Ph.D. convinced me, if I needed convincing, that I did not need useless suffering for the sake of additional letters behind my name. If the relatively benign process of the Pastoral Center in Paris was not suitable for my purposes, what would be? Meanwhile I went about my research into the worship of the traditional Black church—looking for the connection between the worship of traditional religions in West Africa and the worship of the Black church (regardless of denominational names). I knew that the music of the Black church was *sui generis* and had too much internal strength to be merely a derivative (not to mention a distortion) of European music. It was most likely that Black religion was not a derivative of colonial religion. Rather, Blacks looked at the scriptures with totally different eyes and heard different messages; their religion emphasized themes that the colonials were not about to preach to an enslaved population. Contemporary attitudes toward religion in the Black church, in some respects, are distinctly different from that in the White church. In the common parlance, "church" sometimes has a distinctly derogatory connotation (boring and dead come to mind) in the White community, but "to have church" in the Black community connotes excitement and "a good time."

I was writing and reflecting on these matters, thinking of the process already begun by some of borrowing indiscriminately certain externals from the Black church in order to breathe life into the worship of the Black Catholic community. How were we to do this without being caught in the trap of mere mimicry of Black church practices? The latter attempt has all of the pitfalls of "reconstructing initiation rites from the detailed notes of an 'observant' anthropologist." This did not mean that we should discard and dismiss observable practices from the traditional Black church; it is a caution against slavish mimicry....

The Doctorate: Union Graduate School

A friend persuaded me to contact Dr. Roy Fairfield, a professor at Antioch College and co-founder of the Union Graduate School (UGS), then headquartered in Yellow Springs, Ohio (now the Union Institute is headquartered in Cincinnati). Dr. Fairfield was quite persuasive. Had he tried to persuade directly, I would have been very wary, but he did not. In fact, he had no way of knowing that I might need persuading. He described the Union's "way" to the doctorate for "self-motivated learners" and similar eccentrics. I was, to say the least, impressed. It was what I needed in order to complete my work on the synthesis between African (African American) culture/religion and European American worship forms/styles. There was no place on this planet where the subject was approached, and it certainly was not taught. There was no expert on the subject that I could name. Only the Union would give me full rein to continue pursuing the subject on my own....

There was no one on the Union faculty who was familiar with my field of research/work, so I chose a long-time friend and collaborator, now professor of drama at Marian College in Indianapolis, Sister Francesca Thompson, O.S.F. (Oldenburg) as one of my chief faculty advisors. She had done her doctoral work in theatre at the University of Michigan and was told that she would never find enough material to research the Lafayette Players, the first Black theatre company in New York. Her mother and father were members of that troupe; her mother was a (perhaps *the*) major star of the company. It was hard work, but she proved the academic skeptics wrong and unearthed an old treasure that has yet to be fully viewed. Since the Aristotelian principles (with a grain of salt) of theatre were at the heart of my approach, I needed a drama expert, and Francesca Thompson, Ph.D., was my choice....

There was very little new writing that I had to do in this process, but I did need more experience of the worship in the traditional Black church. First, I concentrated on getting more of that experience by worshiping in those churches as a member of the congregation. Only after I had completed that did I turn to ordering my thoughts in writing for my PDE, i.e., Project Demonstrating Excellence, which in its final form was a book complementing *Soulfull Worship* entitled *The Spirit in Worship*. Rightly understood, both volumes had the same name. When I had finished writing, I submitted the book to the scrutiny of my committee and other concerned people. For financial and other reasons, my goal was to finish my work at the UGS in one year, understanding that twenty or more years had been spent getting to that point. The flexibility of the UGS process allowed for those considerations, though in most cases their concern in those days was to limit the maximum number of years (seven) in the process.

Long-time friends of mine and long-time patrons of Stimuli, Gerald David and Jeanne Etienne Rape, would not hear of a graduation that was less than public. They went about acquiring the facilities of Mount St. Mary's Seminary in Norwood: the faculty dining room for my academic committee to dine in before its final meeting upstairs; the chapel for the actual graduation ceremony; the Aula Magna (the great hall) for the reception; and, not the least, the caterers that ran the seminary dining facilities to supply the grand supper for my committee and thousands of hors d'oeuvres and drinks for the "public."

I entered the Union Graduate School on March 27, 1977, and I was graduated on March 27, 1978. As Jeanne and Jerry had determined, it was a public (anyone was welcome) ceremony with a nice-sized crowd (one hundred to two hundred persons), mainly people I knew personally or professionally. The procession included the Archbishop of Cincinnati, Joseph Louis Bernardin, draped in renaissance finery—a ferraiolo (the rose side of purple) over black cassock with a rose sash and buttons—as I had requested; many of the seminary faculty in their doctoral gowns with various hoods; my academic committee appropriately gowned; and myself in a new black mohair and wool blend suit. Under the direction of Ronald Dean Harbor, the organ with timpani, choir, and congregation greeted us with my favorite processional, "Old One Hundreth," as arranged by Ralph Vaughn Williams for the coronation of Elizabeth II. Oh, I do love pageantry! . . .

After they had dressed me in gown and hood, Archbishop Bernardin went on to present me with a stole to match the academic gown: light blue on dark blue outlined by an overlay of gold threads in a pattern of flowing waters. Marcus Prensky, a friend that I had met in Paris and a virtuoso on the guitar and the lute, brought his lute and serenaded the assembly with two renaissance pieces:

> Start the Music,
> Strike the Drums,
> Sound the song-full Strings.
> (Ps 81:3)

With African drumming and classical organ plus choir, the ceremony lofted to a close to the strains of "Black Thankfulness":

> Halleluia, Halleluia, Halleluia! Amen!
> Thank the Lord for the Holy Spirit,
> Who revives my soul again!

The ceremony had a blend of cultural elements! Side by side there was solemnity with humor, and all of it with grace and style. To say that I was pleased does not come near to what I actually felt. . . .

Black Catholic Scholarship, 1854–2020

RONALD LAMARR SHARPS

STUDIES OF BLACK CATHOLICISM have many sources: books, magazines, journals, newspapers, theses and dissertations, and unpublished letters, reports, and manuscripts. This bibliography of Black Catholic scholarship, while not exhaustive, offers a chronicle of books that relate the story of Black Catholics. It does not include works of fiction, but focuses on genres including biography, history, sociology, and theology.

Of the 300-plus entries, very few were published in the nineteenth century. The meager output of books related to Black Catholicism (mostly written by whites) continued through the early twentieth century. In the 1930s and '40s output increased, primarily due to the contributions of white religious and clergy. By the 1950s, Black Catholics began to author a substantial number of works, a trend that would accelerate through the 1960s and '70s. In the 1970s, more than thirty works were authored, and for the first time, Black contributions matched or exceeded the number of books by whites.

In the 1980s, thirty-three books were written, with nearly an equal number of them authored by lay and religious, Blacks and whites. However, from the 1990s forward, lay authors predominated. A larger production of books appeared in the 1990s, with more than half authored by Black writers. The level of production was sustained into the 2000s, with a marginal increase in the total of Black and lay contributions. (See table on next page.)

Works Published	1800–1899	1900–1909	1910–1919	1920–1929	1930–1939	1940–1949	1950–1959
Black Authored	1	1	2	0	1	1	7
Total	5	1	4	3	11	15	17

Works Published	1960–1969	1970–1979	1980–1989	1990–1999	2000–2009	2010–2020	Total
Black Authored	2	17	15	30	38	28	143
Total	19	33	33	57	65	68	331

The following bibliography is ordered chronologically by date of publication. Black authored or edited works are noted with an asterisk at the end of each entry.

Lee, Hannah Farnham Sawyer. *Memoir of Pierre Toussaint, Born a Slave in St. Domingo.* Boston: Crosby, Nichols, 1854.

Maes, Camillus Paul. *The Life of Rev. Charles Nerinckx: With a Chapter on the Early Catholic Missions of Kentucky.* Cincinnati: Robert Clarke, 1880.

Herbert, Elizabeth Lady, trans. *The Life of Blessed Martin de Porres.* New York: Catholic Publications Society, 1888.

Catholic Church Commission. *Mission Work among the Negroes and the Indians; What is Being Accomplished by Means of the Annual Collection Taken Up for Our Missions.* Baltimore: Catholic Missions Among the Colored People and the Indians, 1890–1899.

Rudd, Daniel Arthur. *Three Catholic Afro-American Congresses.* Cincinnati: *American Catholic Tribune*, 1893.*

McNorton, Augustine Joseph. *The Catholic Church: The Only Hope of the Negro.* Washington, DC: The Catholic Herald, 1905.*

Boston, Mary Petra, OSP. *Blossoms Gathered from the Lower Branches, or, A Little Work of an Oblate Sister.* St. Louis: Con. P. Curran Printing, 1914.*

Butsch, Joseph, SSJ. *Negro Catholics in the United States.* Reprint from Washington, DC: Association for the Study of Negro Life and History, 1917.

McGill, Anna Blanche. *The Sisters of Charity of Nazareth, Kentucky.* New York: Encyclopedia Press, 1917.

Rudd, Daniel Arthur, and Theophilus Bond. *From Slavery to Wealth, The Life of Scott Bond: The Rewards of Honesty, Industry, Economy and Perseverance.* Madison, AR: Journal Printing, 1917.*

Semple, Henry Churchill, ed. *The Ursulines in New Orleans and the Prompt Succor: A Record of Two Centuries, 1727–1925.* Dorchester, MA: P. J. Kenedy & Sons, 1925.

Vogel, Claude Lawrence, OFM Cap. *The Capuchins in French Louisiana (1722–1766).* Washington, DC: Catholic University of America, 1928.

Gillard, John Thomas, SSJ. *The Catholic Church and the American Negro.* Baltimore: St. Joseph's Society Press, 1929.

Sherwood, Grace Hausmann. *The Oblates' Hundred and One Years.* New York: Macmillan, 1931.

Guilday, Peter Keenan. *A History of the Councils of Baltimore (1791–1884).* New York: Macmillan, 1932.

Gillard, John Thomas, SSJ. *The Negro American: A Mission Investigation.* Cincinnati: Catholic Students' Mission Crusade, 1935.

Rouse, Michael Francis (Brother Bede, CFX). *A Study of the Development of Negro Education under Catholic Auspices in Maryland and the District of Columbia.* Baltimore: Johns Hopkins Press, 1935.

Diggs, Margaret Agneta. *Catholic Negro Education in the United States.* Washington, DC: Catholic University of America, 1936.

LaFarge, John, SJ. *Interracial Justice: A Study of the Catholic Doctrine of Race Relations.* New York: America Press, 1937.

Gillard, John Thomas, SSJ. *Christ, Color and Communism.* Baltimore: Josephite Press, 1937.

Gillard, John Thomas, SSJ. *The Negro Challenges Christianity, Communism, Catholicism.* Baltimore: Josephite Press, 1937.

Kearns, John Chrysostom, OP. *The Life of Blessed Martin de Porres: Saintly American Negro Patron of Social Justice.* New York: P. J. Kenedy & Sons, 1937.

Baudier, [Joseph] Roger. *The Catholic Church in Louisiana.* New Orleans: A. W. Hyatt Stationery Mfg., 1939.*

LaFarge, John, SJ. *A Catholic Interracial Program*. New York: America Press, 1939.

Murphy, John C. *An Analysis of the Attitudes of American Catholics Toward the Immigrant and the Negro, 1825–1925*. Washington, DC: Catholic University of America Press, 1940.

Georges, Norbert, OP. *Meet Brother Martin!: A Little Life of Blessed Martin de Porres*. New York: Blessed Martin Guild, 1940.

Gillard, John Thomas, SSJ. *Colored Catholics in the United States: An Investigation of Catholic Activity in Behalf of the Negroes in the United States and a Survey of the Present Condition of the Colored Missions*. Baltimore: Josephite Press, 1941.

Madigan, James J., SJ. *The Catholic Church and the Negro*. St. Louis: Queen's Work, 1941.

Preher, Leo Marie, OP. *The Social Implications in the Work of Blessed Martin de Porres*. Washington, DC: Catholic University of America Press, 1941.

Adams, Elizabeth Laura. *Dark Symphony*. New York: Sheed and Ward, 1942.*

LaFarge, John, SJ. *The Race Question and the Negro: A Study of the Doctrine on Interracial Justice* (extension and revision of *Interracial Justice*). New York: Longmans, Green, 1943.

Windeatt, Mary Fabyan. *Lad of Lima: The Story of Blessed Martin de Porres*. New York: Blessed Martin Guild, 1943.

Rice, Madeleine Hooke. *American Catholic Opinion in the Slavery Controversy*. New York: Columbia University Press, 1944.

Blied, Benjamin Joseph. *Catholics and the Civil War*. Milwaukee: 1945.

Scally, Mary Anthony, RSM. *Negro Catholic Writers, 1900–1943: A Bio-Bibliography*. Detroit: Walter Romig, 1945.

Harte, Thomas J., CSsR. *Catholic Organizations Promoting Negro-White Race Relations in the United States*. Washington, DC: Catholic University of America Press, 1947.

Corrigan, D. J., CSsR. *Message to Negroes*. Oconomowoc, WI: Liguorian Pamphlet Office, 1947.

Roche, Richard J., OMI. *Catholic Colleges and the Negro Student*. Washington, DC: Catholic University of America Press, 1948.

Reynolds, Edward D., SJ. *Jesuits for the Negro.* New York: America Press, 1949.

LaFarge, John, SJ. *No Postponement: U.S. Moral Leadership and the Problem of Racial Minorities.* New York: Longmans, Green, 1950.

Day [Riley], Helen Caldwell. *Color, Ebony.* New York: Sheed and Ward, 1952.*

Cantwell, Daniel M. *Catholics Speak on Race Relations.* Chicago: Fides Publishers Association, 1952.

Matthews, Dom Basil, OSB. *Crisis of the West Indian Family.* Kingston, Jamaica: University College of the West Indies, 1953.*

Doherty, Eddie. *Blessed Martin de Porres.* St. Paul: Educational Society, 1953.

Foley, Albert Sidney, SJ. *Bishop Healy, Beloved Outcaste: The Story of a Great Man Whose Life Has Become a Living Legend.* New York: Farrar, Straus, and Cudahy, 1954.

LaFarge, John, SJ. *The Manner Is Ordinary.* New York: Harcourt Brace, 1954.

Day [Riley], Helen Caldwell. *Not Without Tears.* New York: Sheed and Ward, 1954.*

Fichter, Joseph H., SJ. *Social Relations in the Urban Parish.* Chicago: University of Chicago Press, 1954.

Foley, SJ, Albert Sidney. *God's Men of Color: The Colored Catholic Priests of the United States, 1854–1954.* New York: Farrar, Straus, 1955.

Sheehan, Arthur T. and Elizabeth Odell Sheehan. *Pierre Toussaint: A Citizen of Old New York.* New York: P. J. Kenedy, 1955.

Tarry, Ellen. *The Third Door: The Autobiography of an American Negro Woman.* New York: David McKay, 1955.*

Day [Riley], Helen Caldwell. *All the Way to Heaven.* New York: Sheed and Ward, 1956.*

LaFarge, John, SJ. *The Catholic Viewpoint on Race Relations.* Garden City, NY: Hanover House, 1956.

Holiday, Billie, with William Duffy. *Lady Sings the Blues.* New York: Doubleday, 1956.*

Burton, Katherine. *Golden Door: The Life of Katharine Drexel*. New York: P. J. Kenedy and Sons, 1957.

Tarry, Ellen. *Katharine Drexel: Friend of the Neglected*. New York: Farrar, Straus and Cudahy, 1958.*

Delaney, Ralph B., SJ. *Born . . . Not of Blood . . . but of God: A Play About Martin de Porres, Child of God, Brother of Men*. New York: Blessed Martin Guild, 1960.

O'Neill, Joseph E., SJ. *A Catholic Case Against Segregation*. New York: Macmillan, 1961.

Berrigan, Philip. *The Catholic Church and the Negro*. St. Louis: Queen's Work, 1962.

Georges, Norbert, OP. *Meet Saint Martin de Porres, Patron of Social and Interracial Justice, a Living Model of the Encyclicals*. New York: Saint Martin Guild, 1962.

Tarry, Ellen. *Martin de Porres: Saint of the New World*. New York: Farrar, Straus, 1963.*

Haas, Capistran J., OFM. *History of Midwest Clergy Conference on Negro Welfare*. Cincinnati: Franciscan Press, 1963.

Merton, Thomas, OCSO. *The Black Revolution*. Atlanta: Southern Christian Leadership Conference, 1963.

Pillar, James J., OMI. *The Catholic Church in Mississippi, 1837–1865*. New Orleans: Hauser Press, 1964.

Merton, Thomas, OCSO. *Seeds of Destruction*. New York: Farrar, Straus, and Giroux, 1964.

Clark, Mary Twibill, RSCJ. *Discrimination Today: Guidelines for Civic Action*. New York: Hobbs, Dorman, 1966.

Osborne, William A. *Segregated Covenant: Race Relations and American Catholics*. New York: Herder & Herder, 1967.

Hunton, George K. *All of Which I Was, Part of Which I Was: The Autobiography of George K. Hunton, as told to Gary MacEoin*. New York: Doubleday, 1967.

Traxler, Mary Peter, SSND, ed. *Split-Level Lives: American Nuns Speak on Race*. Techny, IL: Divine Word Publishers, 1967.

National Conference of Catholic Bishops. *Statement on National Race Crisis*. Washington, DC: United States Catholic Conference, 1968.

Ellis, John Tracy. *The Catholic Church and the Negro.* Huntington, IN: Our Sunday Visitor, 1968.

Griffin, John Howard. *The Church and the Black Man.* Dayton, OH: Pflaum Press, 1969.

Rivers, Clarence Joseph. *Celebration.* New York: Herder & Herder, 1969.*

Walsh, Martin de Porres, OP. *The Ancient Black Christians.* San Francisco: Julian Richardson Associates, 1969.

Garcia-Rivera, Alejandro (Alex). *St. Martin de Porres: The "Little Stories" and the Semiotics of Culture.* Maryknoll, NY: Orbis Books, 1969.

Lucas, Lawrence E. *Black Priest/White Church: Catholics and Racism.* New York: Random House, 1970.*

Rivers, Clarence Joseph. *Reflections.* New York: Herder & Herder, 1970.*

McCants, Dorothea Olga, DC, ed. and trans. *They Came to Louisiana: Letters of a Catholic Mission, 1854–1882.* Baton Rouge: Louisiana State University Press, 1970.

Labbé, Dolores Egger. *Jim Crow Comes to Church: The Establishment of Segregated Catholic Parishes in South Louisiana.* New York: Arno Press, 1971.

Green, Nathaniel E. *The Silent Believers: Background Information on the Religious Experience of the American Black Catholic, with Emphasis on the Archdiocese of Louisville, Kentucky.* Louisville, KY: West End Council of Louisville, 1972.*

Thibodeaux, Mary Roger, SBS. *A Black Nun Looks at Black Power.* New York: Sheed and Ward, 1972.*

Lacy, Dan Mabry. *The White Use of Blacks in America.* New York: Atheneum, 1972.

Hemesath, Caroline, OSF. *From Slave to Priest: A Biography of the Rev. Augustine Tolton (1854–1897), First Afro-American Priest of the United States.* Chicago: Franciscan Herald Press, 1973.

Faherty, William Barnaby, SJ. *Dream by the River: Two Centuries of Saint Louis Catholicism, 1766–1967.* St. Louis: Piraeus Publishers, 1973.

Blassingame, John Wesley. *Black New Orleans, 1860–1880.* Chicago: University of Chicago Press, 1973.*

Guidry, Mary Gabriella, SSF. *The Southern Negro Nun: An Autobiography*. New York: Exposition Press, 1974.*

Rivers, Clarence Joseph. *Soulfull Worship*. Washington, DC: National Office for Black Catholics, 1974.*

Caravaglios, Maria Genoino. *The American Catholic Church and the Negro Problem in XVIII–XIX Centuries*. Charleston, SC: Maria Genoino Caravaglios, 1974.

Haskins, James. *The Creoles of Color of New Orleans*. New York: Crowell, 1975.*

Detiege, Audrey Marie, SSF. *Henriette Delille, Free Woman of Color: Foundress of the Sisters of the Holy Family*. New Orleans: Sisters of the Holy Family, 1976.*

Lannon, Maria Mercedes. *Mother Mary Elizabeth Lange: Life of Love and Service*. Washington, DC: Josephite Pastoral Center, 1976.

Lannon, Maria Mercedes. *Mary Dyson: Life of Love and Service*. Washington, DC: Josephite Pastoral Center, 1976.

Clements, George, ed. *Black Catholic Men of God*. Washington, DC: National Office for Black Catholics, 1976.*

Foley, Albert Sidney, SJ. *Dream of an Outcaste: Patrick F. Healy. The Story of a Slaveborn Georgian Who Became the Second Founder of America's Great Catholic University, Georgetown*. Tuscaloosa, AL: Portals Press, 1976.

Shuster, George, SSJ, and Robert M. Kearns, SSJ. *Statistical Profile of Black Catholics*. Washington, DC: Josephite Pastoral Center, 1976.

Rummel, Leo, OPraem. *History of the Catholic Church in Wisconsin*. Madison: Wisconsin State Council, Knights of Columbus, 1976.

Faherty, William Barnaby, SJ, and Madeline Barni Oliver. *The Religious Roots of Black Catholics of St. Louis*. St. Louis: St. Stanislaus Historic Museum, 1977.

Hovda, Robert W., ed. *This Far by Faith: American Black Worship and Its African Roots*. Washington, DC: National Office for Black Catholics and the Liturgical Conference, 1977.

St. Julien, Aline. *Colored Creole: Color, Conflict, and Confusion in New Orleans*. New Orleans: Ahidania-Habari, 1977.*

Johnson, Nessa Theresa Baskerville. *A Special Pilgrimage: A History of Black Catholics in Richmond*. Richmond, VA: Diocese of Richmond, 1978.*

Dolan, Jay Patrick. *Three Catholic Afro-American Congresses (Proceedings and Correspondence)*. New York: Arno Press, 1978.

Rivers, Clarence Joseph. *The Spirit in Worship*. Cincinnati: Stimuli, 1978.*

Simpson, George Eaton. *Black Religions in the New World*. New York: Columbia University Press, 1978.

Raboteau, Albert J. *Slave Religion: The "Invisible Institution" in the Antebellum South*. New York: Albert J. Raboteau, 1978.*

Williams, Clarence, CPPS. *The Black Catholic and the Urban Experience*. Detroit: Academy of the Afro-world Community, 1979.*

Williams, Clarence, CPPS. *The Black Man and the Catholic Church*. Detroit: Academy of the Afro-world Community, 1979.*

Williams, Clarence, CPPS. *Mission and Ministry of the Black Church*. Detroit: Academy of the Afro-world Community, 1979.*

Scally, Mary Anthony, RSM. *Medicine, Motherhood, and Mercy: The Story of a Black Doctor*. Washington, DC: Associated Publishers, 1979.

Braxton, Edward Kenneth. *The Wisdom Community*. Mahwah, NJ: Paulist Press, 1980.*

Giese, Vincent. *You Got It All: A Personal Account of a White Priest in a Chicago Ghetto*. Huntington, IN: Our Sunday Visitor, 1980.

Holtzclaw, Robert Fulton. *The Saints Go Marching In*. Shaker Heights, OH: Keeble Press, 1980.*

Posey, Thaddeus, OFM. *Theology: A Portrait in Black (Proceedings of the Black Catholic Theological Symposium)*. Denver: Capuchin Press for the National Black Catholic Clergy Caucus, 1980.*

Tarry, Ellen. *The Other Toussaint: A Modern Biography of Pierre Toussaint, a Post-Revolutionary Black*. Boston: St. Paul Editions, 1981.*

Maultsby, Portia Katrenia. *Afro-American Religious Music: A Study in Musical Diversity*. Springfield, OH: Hymn Society of America, 1981.*

Davis, Cyprian, OSB. *The Church: A Living Heritage*. Morristown, NJ: Silver Burdett, 1981.*

Lumas, Eva Marie, SSS. ed. *Tell It Like It Is: A Black Catholic Perspective on Christian Education*. Oakland, CA: National Black Sisters' Conference, 1982.*

Miller, Randall M., and Jon L. Wakelyn. *Catholics in the Old South: Essays on Church and Culture*. Macon, GA: Mercer University Press, 1983.

Freyberg, Elizabeth Hadley. *Black Catholics in the United States: An Annotated Bibliography of Works Located in the Indiana University, Bloomington Libraries*. Bloomington: Afro-American Arts Institute, Indiana University, 1983.*

McLaughlin, Arthur Leo. *The Black Friar: Champion of the Poor*. Nashville: Winston-Derek Publishers, 1983.

Scally, Mary Anthony, RSM. *Dr. Lena Edwards: People Lover*. Washington, DC: Association for the Study of Afro-American Life and History, 1983.

Houzeau, Jean-Charles. *My Passage at the New Orleans Tribune: A Memoir of the Civil War Era*. Edited by David C. Rankin and translated by Gerard F. Denault. Baton Rouge: Louisiana State University Press, 1984.

Healey, Joseph Graham, MM. *A Fifth Gospel: The Experience of Black Christian Values*. Maryknoll, NY: Orbis Books, 1984.

Smithson, Sandra O., SSSF *To Be the Bridge: A Commentary on Black/White Catholicism in America*. Nashville: Winston-Derek Publishers, 1984.*

Butler, Loretta Myrtle, and Eleanor Shelton. *History of Black Catholics in the Archdiocese of Washington, DC, 1634–1898: A Selected Bibliography of Works Located in Maryland and Washington, DC/Archives and Libraries*. Washington, DC: Archdiocese of Washington, 1984.*

Bowman, Thea, FSPA. *Families: Black and Catholic, Catholic and Black: Readings, Resources, and Family Activities*. Washington, DC: United States Catholic Conference, 1985.*

Koren, Henry J., CSSp. *The Serpent and the Dove: A History of the Congregation of the Holy Ghost in the United States, 1745-1984.* Pittsburgh: Spiritus Press, 1985.

Poole, Stafford, CM, and Douglass Slawson. *Church and Slave in Perry County, Missouri, 1818-1865.* Lewiston, NY: Edwin Mellen Press, 1986.

Lyke, James P., OFM, ed. *Lead Me, Guide Me: The African American Catholic Hymnal.* Chicago: G.I.A. Publications, 1987.*

Hemesath, Caroline, OSF. *Our Black Shepherds: Biographies of the Ten Black Bishops of the United States.* Washington, DC: Josephite Pastoral Center, 1987.

Falvan, Michael. *Faith and Culture: A Multicultural Catechetical Resource.* Washington, DC: U.S. Catholic Conference, 1987.

Baldwin, Lou. *A Call to Sanctity: The Formation and Life of Mother Katharine Drexel.* Philadelphia: Catholic Standard and Times, 1988.

Nickels, Marilyn Wenzke. *Black Catholic Protest and the Federated Colored Catholics, 1917-1933: Three Perspectives on Racial Justice.* New York: Garland, 1988.

Boles, John B., ed. *Masters and Slaves in the House of the Lord: Race and Religion in the American South, 1740-1870.* Lexington: University Press of Kentucky, 1988.

Smith, Glenn C., ed. *Evangelizing Blacks.* Washington, DC: Paulist National Catholic Evangelization Association, 1988.

Johnson, MayLee. *Coming Up on the Rough Side: A Black Catholic Story.* South Orange, NJ: Pillar, 1988.*

National Conference of Catholic Bishops. *In Spirit and Truth: Black Catholic Reflections on the Order of Mass.* Washington: U.S. Catholic Conference, 1988.

White, Joseph Michael, ed. *The American Catholic Religious Life: Selected Historical Essays.* New York: Garland, 1988.

Hastings, Adrian Christopher. *African Catholicism: Essays in Discovery.* Philadelphia: Trinity Press, 1989.

Davis, Cyprian, OSB. *Christ's Image: The Black Catholic Community Before the Civil War*. Notre Dame, IN: University of Notre Dame Press, 1989.*

Gordon, Greer G. *Heritage and Vision: A Study of the Church*. New York: Harcourt Religion, 1989.*

Vicchio, Stephen John. *Perspectives on the American Catholic Church, 1789–1989*. Westminster, MD: Christian Classics, 1989.

Wood, Forrest G. *The Arrogance of Faith: Christianity and Race in America from the Colonial Era to the Twentieth Century*. New York: Alfred A. Knopf, 1990.

Wilson, Jacqueline E., ed. *Our Roots and Gifts: Evangelization and Culture: An African American Catholic Perspective, Proceedings of the Rejoice! Seminar, Rome, Italy, November 1989*. Hyattsville, MD: Archdiocese of Washington, 1990.*

Davis, Cyprian, OSB. *The History of Black Catholics in the United States*. New York: Crossroad/Continuum, 1990.*

Ochs, Stephen J. *Desegregating the Altar: The Josephites and the Struggle for Black Priests, 1871–1960*. Baton Rouge: Louisiana State University Press, 1990.

Braxton, Edward Kenneth. *The Faith Community: One, Holy, Catholic, and Apostolic*. Notre Dame, IN: Ave Maria Press, 1990.*

National Conference of Catholic Bishops, Secretariat for Black Catholics. *Many Rains Ago: A Historical and Theological Reflection on the Role of the Episcopate in the Evangelization of African American Catholics*. Washington, DC: National Conference of Catholic Bishops, 1990.

National Conference of Catholic Bishops. *Plenty Good Room: The Spirit and Truth of African American Worship*. Washington, DC: United States Catholic Conference, 1990.

Johnson, John L. *The Black Biblical Heritage*. Nashville: Winston-Derek Publishers, 1991.*

Koontz, Christian, RSM, ed. *Thea Bowman: Handing on Her Legacy*. Kansas City, MO: Sheed and Ward, 1991.

Lannon, Maria Mercedes. *Response to Love: The Story of Mother Mary Elizabeth Lange; With Biographical Sketches of the Women Who*

Followed Her as Major Religious Superiors of the Oblate Sisters of Providence. Washington, DC: Josephite Pastoral Center, 1992.

Desmangles, Leslie G. *The Faces of the Gods: Vodou and Roman Catholicism in Haiti.* Chapel Hill: University of North Carolina Press, 1992.*

Mcdonogh, Gary Wray. *Black and Catholic in Savannah, Georgia.* Knoxville: University of Tennessee Press, 1993.

Cepress, Celestine, FSPA, ed. *Sister Thea Bowman, Shooting Star: Selected Writings and Speeches.* Winona, MN: St. Mary's Press, 1993.

Josephite Fathers. *The Josephites: A Century of Evangelization in the African American Community.* Baltimore: St. Joseph's Society of the Sacred Heart, 1993.

Hastings, Adrian Christopher. *The Church in Africa, 1450–1950.* Oxford, UK: Clarendon Press, 1994.

Zanca, Kenneth J., ed. *American Catholics and Slavery, 1789–1866: An Anthology of Primary Documents.* Lanham, MD: University Press of America, 1994.

McKnight, Albert J., CSSp. *Whistling in the Wind: The Autobiography of the Reverend A. J. McKnight.* Opelousas, LA: Southern Development Foundation, 1994.*

Raboteau, Albert J. *A Fire in the Bones: Reflections on African-American Religious History.* Boston: Beacon Press, 1995.*

Hayes, Diana L. *Hagar's Daughters: Womanist Ways of Being in the World.* Mahwah, NJ: Paulist Press, 1995.*

Egbulem, Nwaka Chris, OP. *Power of Afrocentric Celebrations: Inspirations from the Zarian Liturgy.* New York: Crossroad, 1995.*

Isichei, Elizabeth. *A History of Christianity in Africa.* London, UK: SPCK, 1995.*

McGarry, Cecil, SJ, ed. *What Happened at the African Synod?* Nairobi: Paulines, 1995.

Talalay, Kathryn Marguerite. *Composition in Black and White: The Life of Philippa Schuyler.* New York: Oxford University Press, 1995.

Hayes, Diana L. *Trouble Don't Last Always: Soul Prayers.* Collegeville, MN: Liturgical Press, 1995.*

Dayan, Joan (known also as Colin Dayan). *Haiti, History, and the Gods.* Berkeley: University of California Press, 1995.*

Oates, Mary Josephine, CSJ. *The Catholic Philanthropic Tradition in America.* Bloomington: Indiana University Press, 1995.

Blatnica, Dorothy Ann, VSC. *"At the Altar of Their God": African American Roman Catholics in Cleveland, 1923–1961.* New York: Garland, 1995.

Hayes, Diana L. *And Still We Rise: An Introduction to Black Liberation Theology.* Mahwah, NJ: Paulist Press, 1996.*

Burton, Richard, Andrew Billingsley, Cyprian Davis, OSB, Joseph P. Fitzpatrick, SJ, Bernard Glos, David Gibson, Eleace King, Che Fu Lee, and Raymond Herve Potvin. *Keep Your Hands on the Plow: African American Presence in the Catholic Church.* Washington, DC: United States Catholic Conference, 1996.*

Irvine, Jacqueline Jordan, and Michele Foster, eds. *Growing Up African American in Catholic Schools.* New York: Teachers College Press, 1996.*

McGreevy, John T. *Parish Boundaries: The Catholic Encounter with Race in the Twentieth Century Urban North.* Chicago: University of Chicago Press, 1996.

Weisenfeld, Judith, and Richard A. Newman. *This Far by Faith: Readings in African American Women's Religious Biography.* New York: Routledge, 1996.*

Butler, Loretta Myrtle. *Mosaic of Faith: Grace, Struggle, Commitment: African American Catholic Presence in Prince George's County, 1696–1996.* Washington, DC: Archdiocese of Washington, Office of Black Catholics, 1996.*

Southern, David W. *John LaFarge and the Limits of Catholic Interracialism, 1911–1963.* Baton Rouge: Louisiana State University Press, 1996.

Chineworth, Mary Alice, OSP, ed. *'Rise 'n' Shine: Catholic Education and the African American Community.* Washington, DC: National Catholic Educational Association, 1996.*

Phelps, Jamie T., OP, ed. *Black and Catholic: The Challenge and Gift of Black Folk; Contributions of African American Experience and Thought to Catholic Theology.* Milwaukee: Marquette University Press, 1997.*

Brown, Joseph A., SJ. *A Retreat with Thea Bowman and Bede Abram: Leaning on the Lord.* Cincinnati: St. Anthony Messenger Press, 1997.*

Williams, Clarence, CPPS, ed. *People of the Pyramids. The Dialogue Between the African American and the Hispanic/Latino Communities.* Detroit: Building Bridges in Black and Brown, 1997.*

National Conference of Catholic Bishops. *Reconciled Through Christ: On Reconciliation and Greater Collaboration between Hispanic American Catholics and African American Catholics.* Washington, DC: National Conference of Catholic Bishops, 1997.

Hanger, Kimberly S. *Bounded Lives, Bounded Places: Free Black Society in Colonial New Orleans, 1769–1803.* Durham, NC: Duke University Press, 1997.

Baker-Fletcher, Karen, and Garth Kasimu Baker-Fletcher. *My Sister, My Brother: Womanist and Xodus God-Talk.* Maryknoll, NY: Orbis Books, 1997.*

Hayes, Diana L., and Cyprian Davis, OSB, eds. *Taking Down Our Harps: Black Catholics in the United States.* Maryknoll, NY: Orbis Books, 1998.*

Brown, Joseph A., SJ. *To Stand on the Rock: Meditations on Black Catholic Identity.* Maryknoll, NY: Orbis Books, 1998.*

Davies, Susan E., and Paul Teresa Hennessee, SA, eds. *Ending Racism in the Church.* Cleveland: United Church Press, 1998.*

Lumbala, François Kabasele. *Celebrating Jesus Christ in Africa: Liturgy and Inculturation.* Maryknoll, NY: Orbis Books, 1998.*

Shorter, Aylward, MAfr. *Christianity and the African Imagination: After the Synod: Resources for Inculturation.* Nairobi: Paulines, 1998.

Mich, Marvin L. Krier. *Catholic Social Teaching and Movements.* Mystic, CT: Twenty-Third Publications, 1998.

Tarry, Ellen. *Pierre Toussaint: Apostle of Old New York.* Boston: Pauline Books and Media, 1998.*

Gould, Virginia Meacham, and Charles E. Nolan. *Henriette Delille: Servant of the Black Slaves.* New Orleans: Sisters of the Holy Family, 1998.

Murrell, Nathaniel Samuel, William David Spencer, and Adrian Anthony McFarlane, eds. *Chanting Down Babylon: The Rastafari Reader*. Philadelphia: Temple University Press, 1998.*

MacGregor, Morris J. *The Emergence of a Black Catholic Community: St. Augustine's in Washington*. Washington, DC: Catholic University of America Press, 1999.

Coburn, Carol K., and Martha Smith, CSJ. *Spirited Lives: How Nuns Shaped Catholic Culture and American Life, 1836–1920*. Chapel Hill: University of North Carolina Press, 1999.

National Black Catholic Congress. *A Study of Opinions of African American Catholics*. Baltimore: National Black Catholic Congress, 1999.*

Landers, Jane Gilmer. *Black Society in Spanish Florida*. Urbana: University of Illinois Press, 1999.

Jaggers, Garland. *FOG: An Analysis of Catholic Dogma*. Conneaut Lake, PA: First Page Publications, 1999.*

Din, Gilbert C. *Spaniards, Planters, and Slaves: The Spanish Regulation of Slavery in Louisiana, 1763–1803*. College Station: Texas A&M University Press, 1999.

Dahl, Linda. *Morning Glory: A Biography of Mary Lou Williams*. New York: Pantheon Books, 1999.

Hayes, Diana L. *Were You There? Stations of the Cross*. Maryknoll, NY: Orbis Books, 2000.*

Ochs, Stephen J. *A Black Patriot and a White Priest: Andre Cailloux and Claude Paschal Maistre in Civil War New Orleans*. Baton Rouge: Louisiana State University Press, 2000.

Sundkler, Bengt. *A History of the Church in Africa*. New York: Cambridge University Press, 2000.

Tarry, Ellen. *Saint Katharine Drexel: Friend of the Oppressed*. Boston: Pauline Books and Media, 2000.*

Butler, Loretta Myrtle, and Jacqueline E. Wilson. *O, Write My Name: African American Catholics in the Archdiocese of Washington, 1634–1990*. Hyattsville, MD: Archdiocese of Washington, Office of Black Catholics, 2000.*

Brandewie, Ernest. *In the Light of the Word: Divine Word Missionaries of North America.* Maryknoll, NY: Orbis Books, 2000.

Deggs, Mary Bernard, SSF. *No Cross, No Crown: Black Nuns in Nineteenth-Century New Orleans.* Edited by Virginia Meacham Gould and Charles E. Nolan. Bloomington: Indiana University Press, 2001.*

O'Malley, Vincent J., CM. *Saints of Africa.* Huntington, IN: Our Sunday Visitor, 2001.

United States Conference of Catholic Bishops. *Love Thy Neighbor as Thyself: US Catholic Bishops Speak Against Racism.* Washington, DC: US Conference of Catholic Bishops, 2001.

Murphy, Thomas J., SJ. *Jesuit Slaveholding in Maryland, 1717–1838.* New York: Routledge, 2001.

Morrow, Diane Batts. *Persons of Color and Religious at the Same Time: The Oblate Sisters of Providence, 1828–1860.* Chapel Hill: University of North Carolina, 2002.*

Raboteau, Albert J. *The Sorrowful Joy: A Spiritual Journey of an African American Man in Late Twentieth-Century America.* Eugene, OR: Wipf and Stock, 2002.*

Quinn, Frederick. *African Saints: Saints, Martyrs, and Holy People from the Continent of Africa.* New York: Crossroad, 2002.

O'Toole, James M. *Passing for White: Race, Religion, and the Healy Family, 1820–1920.* Boston: University of Massachusetts Press, 2002.

Ward, Mary A. *A Mission for Justice: The History of the First African American Catholic Church in Newark, New Jersey.* Knoxville: University of Tennessee Press, 2002.

Gordon, Greer G. *Symphonies of the Heart: Spiritual Harmony and the Quest for Holiness.* New York: Pauline Books and Media, 2002.*

McSheffery, Daniel. *Saint Katharine Drexel: Pioneer for Human Rights.* Totowa, NJ: Resurrection Press/Catholic Book Publishing, 2002.

Koester, Anne Y., ed. *Liturgy and Justice: To Worship God in Spirit and Truth.* Collegeville, MN: Liturgical Press, 2002.

Davis, Cyprian, OSB, and Jamie T. Phelps, OP. *"Stamped with the Image of God": African Americans as God's Image in Black*. Maryknoll, NY: Orbis Books, 2003.*

Kelly, William. *A Servant of Slaves: The Life of Henriette Delille*. New York: Crossroad, 2003.

Gordon, Greer G. *God's Grace and Human Sexuality*. Chicago: Thomas More Publishing, 2003.*

Butler, Loretta Myrtle. *Grace, Struggle, Commitment: Memoirs of an African American Woman*. Washington, DC: Loretta Myrtle Butler, 2003.*

Jones, Arthur. *Pierre Toussaint: A Biography*. New York: Doubleday, 2003.

Blaney, Retta. *Working on the Inside: The Spiritual Life through the Eyes of Actors*. Kansas City, MO: Sheed and Ward, 2003.

Davis, Cyprian, OSB. *Henriette Delille: Servant of Slaves and Witness to the Poor*. New Orleans: Sisters of the Holy Family, 2004.*

Angus, Jack D. *Black and Catholic in Omaha: A Case of Double Jeopardy, The First Fifty Years of St. Benedict the Moor Parish*. Lincoln, NE: iUniverse, 2004.

Kernodle, Tammy Lynn. *Soul on Soul: The Music and Life of Mary Lou Williams*. Boston: Northeastern University Press, 2004.*

McGann, Mary E., RSCJ. *A Precious Fountain: Music in the Worship of an African American Catholic Community*. Collegeville, MN: Liturgical Press, 2004.

Phan, Peter C., and Diana L. Hayes, eds. *Many Faces, One Church: Cultural Diversity and the American Catholic Experience*. Kansas City, MO: Sheed and Ward, 2004.*

van Deusen, Nancy E. *The Souls of Purgatory: The Spiritual Diary of a Seventeenth-Century Afro-Peruvian Mystic, Ursula de Jesús*. Albuquerque: University of New Mexico Press, 2004.

Bell, Caryn Cossé. *Revolution, Romanticism, and the Afro-Creole Protest Tradition in Louisiana, 1718–1868*. Baton Rouge: Louisiana State University Press, 2004.*

Gaspar, David Barry, and Darlene Clark Hine, eds. *Beyond Bondage: Free Women of Color in the Americas*. Chicago: University of Illinois Press, 2004.*

Cosby, Camille O., and Renee Poussaint, eds. *A Wealth of Wisdom: Legendary African American Elders Speak*. New York: Atria Books, 2004.*

Foskett, Ken. *Judging Thomas: The Life and Times of Clarence Thomas*. New York: HarperCollins, 2004.

Anderson, R. Bentley, SJ. *Black, White, and Catholic: New Orleans Interracialism, 1947–1956*. Nashville: Vanderbilt University Press, 2005.

Pinn, Anthony B. *The African American Religious Experience in America*. Boston: Greenwood, 2005.*

Marshall, Paul M., SM, Cecilia Annette Moore, and C. Vanessa White, eds. *Songs of Our Hearts, Meditations of Our Souls: Prayers for Black Catholics*. Cincinnati: St. Anthony Messenger Press, 2006.*

Collum, Danny Duncan. *Black and Catholic in the Jim Crow South: The Stuff That Makes Community*. Mahwah, NJ: Paulist Press, 2006.

Tardy, Jo Anne. *A Light Will Rise in Darkness: Growing Up Black and Catholic in New Orleans*. Skokie, IL: Acta Publications, 2006.*

Jones, Alex C. *No Price Too High: A Pentecostal Pastor Becomes Catholic (The Inspirational Story of Alex Jones as Told to Diane Hanson)*. San Francisco: Ignatius Press, 2006.*

Brown, Joseph A., SJ, with Fernand Cheri III, OFM. *Sweet, Sweet Spirit: Prayer Services from the Black Catholic Church*. Cincinnati: St. Anthony Messenger Press, 2006.*

Douglas, Jean K. *Why I Left the Church, Why I Came Back and Why I Just Might Leave Again*. Astor, FL: Fortuity Press, 2006.*

Okure, Aniedi, OP, and Dean R. Hoge. *International Priests in America: Challenges and Opportunities*. Collegeville, MN: Liturgical Press, 2006.*

McGrane, Janice, SSJ. *Saints to Lean On: Spiritual Companions for Illness and Disability*. Cincinnati: Franciscan Media, 2006.

Penn, Sabrina A. *A Place for My Children: Father Augustus Tolton, America's First Known Black Catholic Priest and His Ancestry*. Chicago: PennInk, 2007.*

Friend, Shelby M. *Trouble Don't Last Always*. Bloomington, IN: AuthorHouse, 2007.*

Rangel, Charles B., and Leon Wynter. *And I Haven't Had a Bad Day Since: From the Streets of Harlem to the Halls of Congress*. New York: Martin's Press, 2007.*

Nilson, Jon. *Hearing Past the Pain: Why White Catholic Theologians Need Black Theology*. Mahwah, NJ: Paulist Press, 2007.

Yockey, Roger. *I Never Stopped Believing: The Life of Walter Hubbard*. Bloomington, IN: Xlibris, 2007.

Harris-Slaughter, Shirley. *Our Lady of Victory: The Saga of an African-American Catholic Community*. Lincoln, NE: iUniverse, 2007.*

Koehlinger, Amy. *The New Nuns: Racial Justice and Religious Reform in the 1960s*. Cambridge, MA: Harvard University Press, 2007.

Hill, Brennan. *8 Freedom Heroes: Changing the World with Faith*. Cincinnati: Franciscan Media, 2007.

Baker-Fletcher, Karen. *Dancing with God: The Trinity from a Womanist Perspective*. St. Louis: Chalice Press, 2007.*

Thomas, Clarence. *My Grandfather's Son: A Memoir*. New York: HarperCollins, 2007.*

McGann, Mary E., RSCJ, Eva Marie Lumas, SSS, and Ronald (Rawn) D. Harbor. *Let It Shine: The Emergence of African American Catholic Worship*. New York: Fordham University Press, 2008.*

Brown, Camille Lewis. *African Saints, African Stories: 40 Holy Men and Women*. Cincinnati: Franciscan Media, 2008.*

Richardson, Walter H. *How Great Art Thou: A Black Boy's Depression-Era Success Story*. Bloomington, IN: AuthorHouse, 2008.*

Vendryes, Margaret Rose. *Barthé: A Life in Sculpture*. Jackson: University Press of Mississippi, 2008.*

McGrath, Michael O'Neill (Mickey), OSFS. *This Little Light: Lessons in Living from Sister Thea Bowman*. Maryknoll, NY: Orbis Books, 2008.

Copeland, M. Shawn, Albert Jordy Raboteau, and LaReine-Marie Mosely, SNDdeN, eds. *Uncommon Faithfulness: The Black Catholic Experience*. Maryknoll, NY: Orbis Books, 2009.*

Copeland, M. Shawn. *The Subversive Power of Love: The Vision of Henriette Delille*. Mahwah, NJ: Paulist Press, 2009.*

Smith, Charlene, FSPA, and John Bookser Feister. *Thea's Song: The Life of Thea Bowman*. Maryknoll, NY: Orbis Books, 2009.

Bowman, Thea, FSPA, and Maurice J. Nutt, CSsR, eds. *Thea Bowman: In My Own Words*. Liguori, MO: Liguori Publications, 2009.*

Murrell, Nathaniel Samuel. *Afro-Caribbean Religions: An Introduction to Their Historical, Cultural, and Sacred Traditions*. Philadelphia: Temple University Press, 2009.*

Dwight, Edward Joseph. *Soaring on the Wings of a Dream: The Untold Story of America's First Black Astronaut Candidate*. Chicago: Third World Press, 2009.*

Martinez, Elsie Brupbacher, and Colette H. Stelly. *Henriette Delille: Rebellious Saint*. London, UK: Pelican, 2010.

Massingale, Bryan N. *Racial Justice and the Catholic Church*. Maryknoll, NY: Orbis Books, 2010.*

Hayes, Diana L. *Standing in the Shoes My Mother Made: A Womanist Theology*. Minneapolis: Fortress Press, 2010.*

Hemesath, Caroline, OSF. *From Slave to Priest: The Inspirational Story of Father Augustine Tolton (1854–1897)*. San Francisco: Ignatius Press, 2010.

Brown, Lisa Marie. *Posing as Nuns, Passing for White: The Gouley Sisters*. New Orleans: Pel Hughes Printing, 2010.

Bryant, Howard. *The Last Hero: A Life of Henry Aaron*. Rome: Pantheon, 2010.*

Skloot, Rebecca. *The Immortal Life of Henrietta Lacks*. New York: Crown, 2010.

Emanuel, Rachel L., and Alexander P. Tureaud Jr. *A More Noble Cause: A. P. Tureaud and the Struggle for Civil Rights in Louisiana, A Personal Biography*. Baton Rouge: Louisiana State University Press, 2011.*

Nyenyembe, Jordan. *African Catholic Priests: Confronting an Identity Problem*. Oxford, UK: African Books Collective, 2011.*

Agee, Gary Bruce. *A Cry for Justice: Daniel Rudd and His Life in Black Catholicism, Journalism, and Activism, 1854–1933.* Fayetteville: University of Arkansas Press, 2011.

Mukuka, George S. *History from the Underside: The Untold Stories of Black Catholic Clergy in South Africa (1898 to 2008).* Baltimore: PublishAmerica, 2011.*

Fisher, James Terence, and Margaret M. McGuinness, eds. *The Catholic Studies Reader.* New York: Fordham University Press, 2011.

Brett, Edward Tracy. *The New Orleans Sisters of the Holy Family: African American Missionaries to the Garifuna of Belize.* Notre Dame, IN: University of Notre Dame Press, 2012.

Hayes, Diana L. *Forged in the Fiery Furnace: African American Spirituality.* Maryknoll, NY: Orbis Books, 2012.*

Gjerde, Jon. *Catholicism and the Shaping of Nineteenth-Century America.* Edited by S. Deborah Kang. New York: Cambridge University Press, 2012.

Burkey, Blaine, OFM Cap. *In Secret Service of the Sacred Heart: Remembering the Life and Virtues of Denver's Angel of Charity Julia Greeley.* Denver: Julia Greeley Guild, 2012.

Marotti, Frank. *The Cana Sanctuary: History, Diplomacy, and Black Catholic Marriage in Antebellum St. Augustine, Florida.* Tuscaloosa: University of Alabama Press, 2012.

Williams, Vanessa, and Helen Williams. *You Have No Idea: A Famous Daughter, Her No-Nonsense Mother, and How They Survived Pageants, Hollywood, Love, Loss (and Each Other).* New York: Gotham Books, 2012.*

Wasburn, Kim. *Heart of a Champion: The Dominique Dawes Story.* Grand Rapids, MI: Zondervan, 2012.

Thorn, Willy. *Brother Booker Ashe: It's Amazing What the Lord Can Do.* Milwaukee: Marquette University Press, 2012.

Perry, Joseph N. *Father Augustus Tolton: A Brief Biography of a Faithful Priest and Former Slave.* Chicago: Archdiocese of Chicago, Liturgy Training Publications, 2013.*

Pramuk, Christopher. *Hope Sings, So Beautiful: Graced Encounters Across the Color Line.* Collegeville, MN: Liturgical Press, 2013.

Lewis-Moseley, Valerie D. *Kingdom Building in the Church of the 21st Century: Is there a Place for Black Catholic Lay Women in the Evangelization Mission of the Church?* Morrisville, NC: Lulu, 2013.*

Rice, Lincoln. *Healing the Racial Divide: A Catholic Racial Justice Framework Inspired by Dr. Arthur Falls.* Eugene, OR: Pickwick Publications, 2014.

Cussen, Celia. *Black Saint of the Americas: The Life and Afterlife of Martin de Porres.* New York: Cambridge University Press, 2014.

Gautier, Mary L. *Bridging the Gap: The Opportunities and Challenges of International Priests Ministering in the United States.* Washington, DC: Center for Applied Research in the Apostolate, 2014.

Hughes, Cheryl C. D. *Katharine Drexel: The Riches-to-Rags Life Story of an American Catholic Saint.* Grand Rapids, MI: Wm. B. Eerdmans Publishing, 2014.

Bassett, Molly Harbour, and Vincent W. Lloyd, eds. *Sainthood and Race: Marked Flesh, Holy Flesh.* New York: Routledge, 2015.*

Okoye, James Chukwuma, CSSp. *Holy Bible: The African American Catholic Youth Bible (New American Bible).* Winona, MN: St. Mary's Press and the National Black Catholic Congress, 2015.*

Stevens, Annie, SL, and Joan Campbell, SL. *Loretto: An Early American Congregation in the Antebellum South.* St. Louis: Bluebird Book Press, 2015.

Galawdewos. *The Life and Struggles of Our Mother Walatta-Petros: A Seventeenth-Century African Biography of an Ethiopian Woman.* Edited and translated by Wendy Laura Belcher and Michael Kleiner. Princeton, NJ: Princeton University Press, 2015.*

Heisser, David C. R., and Stephen J. White Sr. *Patrick N. Lynch, 1817–1882: Third Catholic Bishop of Charleston.* Columbia: University of South Carolina Press, 2015.

Stark, David Martin. *Slave Families and the Hato Economy in Puerto Rico.* Gainesville: University Press of Florida, 2015.

Hayes, Diana L. *No Crystal Stair: Womanist Spirituality*. Maryknoll, NY: Orbis Books, 2016.*

Norvel, William, SSJ. *A Halleluiah Song!: Memoir of a Black Catholic Priest from the Jim Crow South*. Scotts Valley, CA: CreateSpace, 2016.*

Wexler, Celia Viggo. *Catholic Women Confront the Church: Stories of Hurt and Hope*. Lanham, MD: Rowman and Littlefield, 2016.

Donnelly, Mary Queen. *Thea's Turn*. Los Angeles: Steele Spring Stage Rights, 2016.

Lloyd, Vincent W. *Black Natural Law*. New York: Oxford University Press, 2016.*

Biles, Simone. *Courage to Soar: A Body in Motion, a Life in Balance*. Grand Rapids, MI: Zondervan, 2016.*

Cressler, Matthew J. *Authentically Black and Truly Catholic: The Rise of Black Catholicism in the Great Migration*. New York: New York University Press, 2017.

Grimes, Katie Walker. *Fugitive Saints: Catholicism and the Politics of Slavery*. Minneapolis: Fortress Press, 2017.

Grimes, Katie Walker. *Christ Divided: Antiblackness as Corporate Vice*. Minneapolis: Fortress Press, 2017.

Davis, Darren W., and Donald B. Pope-Davis. *Perseverance in the Parish? Religious Attitudes from the Black Catholic Perspective*. New York: Cambridge University Press, 2017.*

Lloyd, Vincent W., and Andrew L. Prevot, eds. *Anti-Blackness and Christian Ethics*. Maryknoll, NY: Orbis Books, 2017.*

Endres, David J., ed. *Remapping the History of Catholicism in the United States: Essays from the U.S. Catholic Historian*. Washington, DC: Catholic University of America Press, 2017.

Rey, Terry. *The Priest and the Prophetess: Abbé Ouvière, Romaine Rivière, and the Revolutionary Atlantic World*. New York: Oxford University Press, 2017.*

Agee, Gary Bruce. *Daniel Rudd: Calling a Church to Justice*. Collegeville, MN: Liturgical Press, 2017.

Romaine, James, and Phoebe Wolfskill, eds. *Beholding Christ and Christianity in African American Art*. University Park: Pennsylvania State University Press, 2017.

Burke-Sivers, Harold. *Father Augustus Tolton: The Slave Who Became the First African American Priest.* Irondale, AL: EWTN Publishing, 2018.*

Duriga, Joyce. *Augustus Tolton: The Church is the True Liberator.* Collegeville, MN: Liturgical Press, 2018.

Copeland, M. Shawn. *Knowing Christ Crucified: The Witness of African American Religious Experience.* Maryknoll, NY: Orbis Books, 2018.*

Rivera, Robert J., and Michele Saracino, eds. *Enfleshing Theology: Embodiment, Discipleship, and Politics in the Work of M. Shawn Copeland.* Minneapolis: Fortress Press, 2018.

Day, Maureen K., ed. *Young Adult American Catholics: Explaining Vocation in Their Own Words.* Mahwah, NJ: Paulist Press, 2018.

Newman, Mark. *Desegregating Dixie: The Catholic Church in the South and Desegregation, 1945–1992.* Jackson: University Press of Mississippi, 2018.

Nutt, Maurice J., CSsR. *An Hour with Thea Bowman.* Liguori, MO: Liguori Publications, 2018.*

Fessenden, Tracy. *Religion around Billie Holiday.* University Park: Pennsylvania State University Press, 2018.

Johnson, Mary, SNDdeN. *Migration for Mission: International Catholic Sisters in the United States.* New York: Oxford University Press, 2018.

Curran, Charles E. *Diverse Voices in Modern US Moral Theology.* Washington, DC: Georgetown University Press, 2018.

Nutt, Maurice J., CSsR. *Thea Bowman: Faithful and Free (People of God).* Collegeville, MN: Liturgical Press, 2019.*

Nutt, Maurice J., CSsR. *An Hour with Augustus Tolton.* Liguori, MO: Liguori Publications, 2019.*

Adler, Gary J., Jr., Tricia C. Bruce, and Brian Starks, eds. *American Parishes: Remaking Local Catholicism.* New York: Fordham University Press, 2019.

Charles, Mark, and Soon-Chan Rah. *Unsettling Truths: The Ongoing, Dehumanizing Legacy of the Doctrine of Discovery.* Westmont, IL: InterVarsity Press, 2019.

Fromont, Cécile, ed. *Afro-Catholic Festivals in the Americas: Performance, Representation, and the Making of Black Atlantic Tradition.* University Park: Pennsylvania State University Press, 2019.

Rowe, Erin Kathleen. *Black Saints in Early Modern Global Catholicism.* New York: Cambridge University Press, 2020.

Copeland, M. Shawn. *Enfleshing Freedom: Body, Race, and Being.* Minneapolis: Fortress Press, 2020.*

Summerlin, LaVerne Muldow. *Gems of Cincinnati's West End: Black Children and Catholic Missionaries, 1940–1970.* Bloomington, IN: Xlibris, 2020.*

Sklar, Peggy A. *Sister Thea Bowman: Do You Hear Me, Church?* Mahwah, NJ: Paulist Press, 2020.

Tisby, Jemar. *The Color of Compromise: The Truth about the American Church's Complicity in Racism.* Grand Rapids, MI: Zondervan Reflective, 2020.*

Index

A

abolitionism
  29, 35–36, 86, 145, 154
  See also slavery
abortion rights
  213
Accra, Ghana
  43
Adams, Elizabeth Laura
  195–96, 198
Adams, William Henry, S.V.D.
  43
Adinkra
  130
adoption
  53
Africa
  19–21, 23, 25, 27, 29, 35–36, 44, 48, 53, 56–58, 60–61, 66, 94–95, 103–4, 109–13, 117, 118, 123, 128–30, 134–35, 151–54, 158–59, 178, 195, 210, 234
Africa Faith and Justice Network
  53
African American Roman Catholic Rite
  49, 57, 58, 164, 206
African Catholic Clergy Association
  60
African Conference of Catholic Clergy and Religious
  60
African Methodist Episcopal Church
  64, 128, 149
African Women Religious Conference
  60
Afro-Brazilian
  28
Afro-Creole
  35
Akers, Doris
  142

Alabama
  37–38, 41, 44, 46, 52, 134, 143, 145–46, 170–71, 173, 216
Alexander VI (pope)
  27
Allen, Celeste
  34
Allen, Richard
  128
Allen, William Francis
  155
Alter, Karl J.
  180, 221, 225, 228, 230
American Catholic Tribune
  35, 107
Anderson, Moses Bosco, S.S.E.
  53, 149
Anglo-Americans
  151–52
  See also Europeans
antebellum
  67, 69–71, 82, 90, 91, 151, 157
anti-Catholicism
  79, 87
  See also nativism
apartheid
  54
Appalachian
  218
Arkansas
  37
asceticism
  108
Asian
  10, 21
Atlanta, Georgia
  56–57, 62
Austin, Lloyd James, III
  63
autobiography
  115, 193–214
Avilés, Pedro Menéndez de
  28

B

Bahamas
  36
Baker, Ella
  146
Bakhita, Saint Josephine Margaret
  51, 58, 61, 63
Baltimore, Maryland
  7, 28, 30–38, 43, 49, 51, 54, 55, 60, 67–88, 91, 115, 138, 142, 195, 201, 202, 205, 232
baptism
  29–30, 32, 95, 105, 114, 149, 169, 203
Baptists
  53, 121, 146, 169
Barclay, Magdalene, O.S.P.
  81
Barthé, (James) Richmond
  42
Basilica of the National Shrine of the Immaculate Conception (Washington, D.C.)
  44, 60
Baton Rouge, Louisiana
  64
Baum, William A.
  52
Bay St. Louis, Mississippi
  39, 41, 43
Beasley, Delilah Leontium
  40
Beasley, Mathilda Taylor
  36
Becroft, Anne Marie (Sister Mary Aloysius)
  64
Belgium
  31, 33, 41, 73, 178, 217
Belleville, Illinois
  59, 61
Benedict XIV (pope)
  29
Benedict XV (pope)
  39
Benedict XVI (pope)
  62

Benedict the Moor, Saint (Benedict of Palermo)
  29–30
Benedictines
  34, 36, 41–43, 59, 229
Bennett, Gordon Dunlap, S.J.
  60
Bergier, Gabriel, O.S.B.
  34
Bernardin, Joseph L.
  236–237
Bible
  12, 93–94, 98, 107–8, 110–11, 113, 121, 128–29, 151–53, 157, 160, 221, 223, 234
Biden, Joseph
  65
Billings, Cora Marie, R.S.M.
  58
Biloxi, Mississippi
  51
biography
  36, 193–214
Birmingham, Alabama
  146, 173
Black Arts movement
  143–44, 147–49, 176
Black Catholic Congresses. *See* National Black Catholic Congresses
Black Catholic Hymnal Project. *See Lead Me, Guide Me*
Black Catholic Televangelization Network
  51, 58
Black Catholic Theological Symposium
  51, 62, 159, 184
Black Power movement
  4, 111, 143
Black Unity and Spiritual Togetherness (BUST)
  206
Blessed Sacrament School (La Crosse, Wisconsin)
  171–72
Bonnemere, Edward (Eddie) Valentine
  46, 48, 141

Boston, Massachusetts
 32, 85
Bourges, Anthony
 41
Bourgoin, Scholastica, O.S.P.
 81
Bowers, Joseph Oliver, S.V.D.
 43, 49
Bowman, Mary Esther Coleman
 166–67
Bowman, Thea (Bertha), F.S.P.A.
 19–26, 43, 54, 56, 65, 117, 118, 123, 126, 128–31, 149, 163–92, 207–8
Bowman, Theon Edward
 166, 170
boycott
 143, 145, 170, 171
Brady, Leo
 226
Braxton, Edward K.
 54, 59, 61
Brazil
 35
Brooklyn, New York
 62
Brooks, Gwendolyn
 147
Brown, Grayson Warren
 51, 58, 141, 160–61
Brown, James
 148
Brown, Joseph A., S.J.
 149, 176
Brown v. Board of Education
 143–44, 209
Brunini, Joseph
 184, 187
Bryant, C.C.
 146
Buffalo, New York
 55
Bureau of Catholic Indian Missions
 52
Burgess, Joseph C., C.S.Sp.
 38
Burke, John E.
 36, 37, 38

Burkey, Blaine, O.FM. Cap.
 208
Burkhardt, Andre, O.S.F.
 179
Busemeyer, Clement J.
 179, 216–22, 230
Bush, George H. W.
 58
Butler, Charles
 114
Butler, Stanislaus Kostka (Cassandra), O.S.P.
 87

C

Caeser, Raymond Rodly, S.V.D.
 51
Cailloux, André
 33
California
 30, 52, 55, 111, 147, 195
Calvert, Charles (Lord Baltimore)
 28
Camden, New Jersey
 39, 52
Camele, David
 232
Campbell, Roy Edward
 65
Canon Law Society of America
 52
canonization
 30, 35, 37, 41, 44–46, 51, 55–58, 61–62, 64–65, 115, 163, 193, 200, 207–8
 See also sainthood
Capuchins
 28, 29, 71, 110
Caribbean
 27, 67, 94, 118
Carlow College (Pittsburgh, Pennsylvania)
 182
Carmelites
 30, 49, 69, 71, 73–76, 84, 86–87
Carmichael, Stokely
 174

Carmon, Dominic, S.V.D.
  59
Carroll, Beverly A.
  55, 63
Carroll, John
  71, 74
Carter, Martin J., S.A.
  50, 51
catechesis
  30, 32–33, 35, 37, 152, 185, 189, 192
Cathedral of the Assumption (Baltimore, Maryland)
  77, 87
Catholic African World Network (CAWN)
  58
Catholic Board for Mission Work Among the Colored People (Catholic Board of Negro Missions)
  38, 52
Catholic Interracial Councils
  41, 42, 44
Catholic Theological Society of America (CTSA)
  6, 61, 65
Catholic Union of the Sick in America
  197
Catholic University of America (Washington, D.C.)
  181, 183, 225–27
Catholic Worker movement
  196
Chappell, Patricia, S.N.D.deN.
  61, 63
Charleston, South Carolina
  33, 36, 64, 85, 114
Charlottesville, Virginia
  65
Chatard, Peter
  80
Cheri, Fernand Cheri, III, O.F.M.
  64
Chicago, Illinois
  29, 35–36, 42–44, 48, 50–55, 59–60, 62, 114, 123, 146–47, 149, 203, 228
cholera
  81–84
Cincinnati, Ohio
  33, 35–36, 41, 43, 113, 136–40, 159, 179–80, 216–223, 225, 227–28, 230–32, 235–36
civil rights
  4, 21–22, 44–46, 64–65, 143–46, 158, 172–74, 176, 209
Claver, Saint Peter
  32, 35, 40
Clement, Joe
  233
Clements, George Harold
  48, 53, 59, 60, 146
Clergy Conference on Negro Welfare (Clergy Conference on the Negro Apostolate/Interracial Apostolate)
  40–41, 45, 47
Cleveland, Ohio
  47, 52, 137, 212
Clorivière, Joseph
  74
Code Noir
  28–29
Collegeville, Minnesota
  36, 43
Colombia
  32
Colorado
  64
Colored Catholic Congresses. *See* National Black Catholic Congresses
Coltrane, John
  149
Columbus, Christopher
  27, 95
Commission for Catholic Missions Among the Colored People and Indians
  35, 52
Cone, James
  1, 9–10
Congo
  29, 37, 178, 218
  See also Kongo
Congregation of Notre Dame (Montreal, Canada)
  34–35

Congress on Racial Equality (CORE)
146, 173
Connecticut
61, 232
Cooke, Terrence J.
51
Copeland, M. Shawn
6, 14, 16, 61, 65, 141–61, 176
Costen, Melva Wilson
125, 158
Council of Catholic Negro Laymen (Council of Black Catholic Laymen)
47
Cuba
21, 25, 31
Cuernavaca, Mexico
229

D

Dallas, Texas
64
dance
22, 47–48, 113, 122, 126, 129–30, 150–52, 156–57, 160, 163, 215, 232
David, Gerald
236
Davis, Cyprian, O.S.B.
43, 58, 95, 107–16, 118, 121, 208
Davis, Joseph, S.M.
49, 141, 182, 231, 233, 234
Davis, Keith
233
Davis, Mattie
232
Day (Riley), Helen Caldwell
43, 196–97
deacons
47, 49–50, 59, 66, 127, 210–12
Delgado, Anthony J.
47
Delille, Venerable Mother Henriette Diaz, S.S.F.
31, 56, 62, 115, 131, 205, 207–8
Deluol, Louis, P.S.S.
87, 89

De Neve, Don Felipe
30
Denver, Colorado
64, 208
De Porres, Saint Martin (Juan Martín de Porres Velázquez)
31, 36–37, 41, 44, 71, 115
DeSales School of Theology (Washington, D.C.)
59
desegregation. *See* integration
Dessalines, Jean-Jacques
30
Detroit, Michigan
35, 40, 43, 47–49, 52, 53, 147, 149, 203, 210, 231–33
Diekmann, Godfrey, O.S.B.
228
discrimination
42, 44, 73, 78–80, 83, 85, 87, 90, 97, 99, 100, 104, 117, 120, 144, 156, 167, 173, 183, 203
See also racism
Doherty, Catherine de Hueck
41
Dominicans (Order of Preachers)
31, 41, 63, 109, 115, 229
Dorsey, Charles Marcellus
38
Dorsey, John Henry "Harry," S.S.J.
37
Douglas, Jean K.
210–11
drama
20, 40, 139, 147, 149, 171, 215, 221, 225–27, 235, 236
Drexel, Saint Katharine
36, 38, 55–56, 61
Du Bois, W. E. B.
3, 102, 118–19, 156
DuBourg, Louis William
30, 71
Duchemin, Anthony, O.S.P.
81

Duchemin, Maria Theresa (Almaide) Maxis
32
Dukette, Norman Andrew
40
Dulin, Joseph
231–33
Du Sable, Jean-Baptiste Pointe
29
Dwight, Edward Joseph "Ed"
44
Dwight, John
155

E

East, Ray
141
Ebo, M. Antona, F.S.M.
42, 46–47, 146, 182
Eccleston, Samuel
71
Echols, Eugenia Houser
215–16
Egbulem, Chris Nwaka, O.P.
109
Emanuel, Rachel L.
209
Emmitsburg, Maryland
69, 75, 83, 90
England, John
31
Epiphany Apostolic College (Walbrook, Maryland)
35
Epstein, Dena J.
150
Esnard, Adrian, C.I.C.M.
37
Ethiopian
20, 25
Europeans
21, 106, 134–35, 216, 229
evangelization
31, 33, 36, 43, 56–58, 68, 93, 95, 105, 119, 152, 163, 186–87, 199, 201

Evans, Mari
7, 147
excommunication
56–57, 166
Ezekiel
154, 157, 215, 220

F

Fabre, Shelton Joseph
62
Fairfield, Roy
235
Federated Colored Catholics (Catholic Interracial Federation)
40
Feister, John
208
Fisher, Carl Anthony, S.S.J.
55
Fisher, Miles Mark
150
Fisk University (Nashville, Tennessee)
155–56
Flaget, Benedict
71
Florida
28, 29, 33, 55, 60
Floyd, George
65
Flynn, Harry J.
61
Foley, Albert S., S.J.
199–201
Francis (pope)
63–65
Francis, Joseph Abel, S.V.D.
50
Franciscan Friars of the Atonement
50–51
Franciscan Handmaids of the Most Pure Heart of Mary
39, 205
Franciscan Sisters of Mill Hill (Franciscan Sisters of Baltimore)
34

Index | **271**

Franciscan Sisters of Perpetual Adoration
163, 168–72, 174, 177, 180–81
Franciscans
28, 34, 36, 39, 42–43, 50–51, 131, 146, 163, 168–72, 174, 177, 180–81, 205, 223
See also Third Order of St. Francis
Franklin, John Hope
145
Friend, Shelby M.
210–12
Friendship House
41–42
Fuller, Hoyt W.
147–48

G

Gabriel-Burrow, Marjorie
141, 233
Gaddy, Kirk P.
64
Galveston-Houston, Texas
55
Garrido, Juan
27
Garrison, Lucy McKim
155
Gaudin, Juliette
31
Gayle, Addison, Jr
147–48
Gelineau, Joseph, S.J.
222, 228
gender
1, 10, 57, 68–69, 91, 146–47
Gentemann, Mary Elaine, C.D.P.
42
Genwright, McKinley
233
Georgetown University (Washington, D.C.)
32, 34, 64–65
Georgetown Visitation Academy (Washington, D.C.)
76

See also Visitation Sisters, Georgetown
Georgia
34, 36, 38–39, 45, 56–57, 62, 149, 200, 205
Ghana
20, 43, 130
Gillard, John T., S.S.J.
196
Gillespie, Avon
141–42
Gilroy, Paul
118–19
Good Samaritan Hospital (Selma, Alabama)
41
Goode, James E., O.F.M.
50, 56, 60
Gorman, Amanda
65
Goroka, Papua New Guinea
51
Gould, Virginia Meacham
208
Gouley, Marie Emilie (Mother Marie Euphrasia)
35
Greeley, Julia
64, 131, 207–8
Greening, Bruce Edward, S.D.S.
56–57
Greenville, Mississippi
39
Gregorian chant
45, 142, 171, 177, 186
Gregory XVI (pope)
31–32
Gregory, Wilton Daniel
53–54, 59, 61–62, 64, 65–66
Grey, Martin DePorres (Patricia Muriel Grey Tyree), R.S.M.
47–48, 182
Griffin, Julian, V.S.C.
44
Guidry, Mary Gabriella, S.S.F.
204–5

Guillory, Curtis J., S.V.D.
55

H

Haazen, Guido
178
Hadden, Thomas
179
Haiti
21, 25, 30–32, 38, 53, 62, 115, 207
Haley, Patricia Ann, S.C.N.
45
Harbor, Ronald (Rawn) Dean
141–42, 237
Harding, Vincent
6–10
Harlem (New York City)
39, 40, 147, 195, 203, 213–14
Harrall, Dolores, S.N.D.
53
Hartke, Gilbert V., O.P.
226
Hartwell, Anna Frances Hartwell (Sister Joseph)
36
Hawkins, Edwin R.
233
Hawkins, Isaac
46
Hayes, Diana
93-106, 118, 120
Hayes, Helen
226
healthcare
31, 34, 41, 47, 82–84, 166
Healy, Alexander Sherwood
32
Healy, Eliza
200–2
Healy, Eliza (Sister Mary Magdalen)
34
Healy, James Augustine
32, 34, 46, 199–201
Healy, Michael
200–2

Healy, Patrick Francis, S.J.
33–34, 201
Healy-Murphy, Margaret Mary
37
Hemesath, Caroline, O.S.F.
201–3
Herbert, Mary E.
34
Hickey, John, P.S.S.
32
Higginson, Thomas Wentworth
154
Hill, Herbert
148
Hogan, Peter, S.J.J.
43
Holiday, Billie
195
Holley, Martin David
62
Holy Child Jesus Mission (Canton, Mississippi)
168–69, 172–75, 180–81, 184
Holy Ghost Church (Opelousas, Louisiana)
187
Holy Ghost (Holy Spirit) Fathers (Spiritans)
34, 38, 53, 149–50, 205–6
Houck, William
187
Houma-Thibodaux, Louisiana
62
Howze, Joseph Lawson
50–51
Hughes, Edward, O.P.
41
Huhn, Martin Francis
32
Hurston, Zora Neale
153–54, 156
hymns
44, 51, 53, 128–29, 137–39, 141–44, 158–59, 164, 170, 176–78, 186, 188–92, 217, 220–1, 227, 233

I

Illinois
  29, 33, 35–36, 42–45, 48, 50–55, 59–62, 114, 123, 137, 146–47, 149, 202–3, 228, 232
imani
  110
Imani Temple (Washington, D.C.)
  56–57, 60, 164, 206
In Supremo Apostolatus
  32
Indiana
  34, 43, 55, 63, 179, 217–19, 223, 235
Indianapolis, Indiana
  34, 55, 63, 235
Indians
  See indigenous peoples
Indies
  28, 30, 94
indigenous peoples
  12, 21, 27, 29–30, 35–36, 50, 52, 62, 103, 178
Innocent XI (pope)
  28
Institut Catholique (Paris, France)
  228–29
Institute for Black Catholic Studies, Xavier University of Louisiana (IBCS)
  52, 130, 160, 184, 188
Institute on Black Sister Formation
  49
integration
  35, 37, 39–40, 47, 59, 143, 174
Isaiah
  106
Israelites
  114, 157

J

Jackson, George A. "Gus"
  178
Jackson, Jesse
  53–54
Jaggers, Garland
  48, 50, 231

Jamaica
  60
Janssens, Francis
  37
Jaxon, Joyce
  233
jazz
  44, 46–48, 54, 149, 150, 179, 194, 219, 233
Jesuits
  28, 30, 32–33, 64, 65, 71, 73–74, 222
John XXIII (pope)
  44, 115
John Paul II (pope)
  51, 53–56, 58, 60–61, 104, 115
Johnson, James Weldon
  153
Jones, Arthur
  207
Jones, Edward P.
  62
Jones, LeRoi (Amiri Baraka)
  147
Jordan, Mark
  13
Josephites
  37–38, 43, 46–47, 49, 63, 65, 67–68, 70, 201, 207
Joubert, Jacques (James Marie), P.S.S.
  31, 67, 72–73, 78–81, 83–87, 89, 205

K

Kabuleta, Francis X. E.
  44
Kaplan, Clara
  196
Karenga, Maulana (Ronald McKinley Everett)
  111, 147
Kawaida
  111
Kearns, Robert M., S.S.J.
  46
Kennedy, John F.
  45, 147

Kennedy, Robert
  147
Kentucky
  31, 34, 38, 43, 45, 55, 59, 63, 71, 154, 232
Kenya
  54
Kernodle, Tammy L.
  194
King, Martin Luther, Jr.
  3, 4, 23, 45–46, 48, 61, 147, 173, 174, 181–82, 203
Kleinfeinz, Clarice, F.S.P.A.
  171–72
Knights of Peter Claver
  38–39, 127
Knights of St. John
  35
Knights of the Holy Name of Jesus
  38
Kongo
  27, 29, 134
  See also Congo
Krol, John
  55
Ku Klux Klan
  174
Kujenga Leadership Conference
  51
kujichagulia
  110
kuumba
  110
Kwanza
  111

L

LaBauve, John
  146
La Crosse, Wisconsin
  163, 168–72, 181, 183
LaFarge, John, S.J.
  40–41, 44, 196
Lafayette Players
  235
Lambert, Rollins E.
  43

Lancaster, Mary Elizabeth (Sister Mary Wilhelmina)
  59
Lange, Elizabeth Clarisse, O.S.P.
  31, 58, 67, 81, 87–89, 115, 131, 205, 207
Lannon, Maria M.
  207
LaRochester, Barbara Jean, O.C.D.
  49
Lead Me, Guide Me
  53, 141–61, 164, 189–90, 192, 233
Leadership Conference of Women Religious
  66
Lebeau, Pierre, S.S.J.
  37
Lee, Don L. (Haki Madhubuti)
  147
Lee, George W.
  146
Leibold, Paul F.
  221–22
Le Moyne, Jean-Baptiste (de Bienville)
  29
Leo XIII (pope)
  35, 36
Lewis, Emma
  39
liberation theology
  5, 9–10, 124–25, 182–83
Lima, Peru
  31, 115
Lissner, Ignatius, S.M.A.
  39, 205
Liturgical Conference
  42, 45, 48, 137, 227–28
liturgy
  12, 24, 42, 44–45, 48–49, 51, 54, 58, 62, 95–96, 105, 109, 113, 122, 125–29, 133–40, 141–42, 150, 158–61, 163–66, 171, 175–81, 183–92, 209, 216–17, 219–21, 223–25, 227–32, 234
Lofton, William S.
  113
Long, Cordell J.
  52

Lorde, Audre
10
Los Angeles, California
30, 52, 55, 111, 147
Louisiana
29–31, 33, 35, 37–39, 42, 46, 51, 52, 55, 58–59, 61–62, 64–65, 71, 113, 115, 130, 147, 184, 187, 202, 205, 209–10
Louisville, Kentucky
34, 55, 59
Louverture/L'Overture, Toussaint (François Dominique Toussaint)
30
Luba
178
See also Missa Luba
Lucas, Lawrence E.
203–6
Lukusa, Andre
178
Luxembourg, Raphael de
29
Luykx, Boniface, O. Praem.
136, 178–79, 217–18
Lwanga, Saint Charles
25, 46
Lyke, James Patterson, O.F.M.
52–53, 57
Lynch, Patrick N.
33

M

Macon, Georgia
34, 149
Maine
34, 200
Malcolm X
4, 20, 147
Manhattanville College (New York)
195
Mannard, Joseph
86–87
Marian College (Indianapolis, Indiana)
235
Marianist
137, 141, 182

Marino, Eugene Antonio, S.S.J.
49–50, 54, 56–57
Marist Brothers
43, 60
Markoe, William
40
Marshall, Thurgood
97, 146, 209
Martin, Eva Regina, S.S.F.
149
martyrs
25, 40, 45–46, 48, 61, 170, 255
Maryland
7, 28, 30–38, 43, 49, 51, 54–55, 60, 67–91, 115, 138, 142, 195, 201–2, 205, 232
Mason, Frederick A.
59
Massachusetts
32, 48–49, 85–86
Massingale, Bryan N.
1–17, 204
Matthews, Basil, O.S.B.
41
Mbiti, John
112
McCall, Maurice Henderson
140
McCarthy, Edward
228, 230
McDaniel, William Foster
233
McKim, James Miller
155
McKim, Lucy
155
McKissick, Floyd
174
McKnight, Albert J., C.S.Sp.
205–7
McNorton, Augustine Joseph
37
McQuade, Ray, S.M.
225
Memphis, Tennessee
38, 43, 59, 62, 174, 196–97
Mendez Arceo, Sergio
229

Mendouça, Lourenço da Silva de
28
Menéndez, Francisco
29
Menéndez, Pedro (de Avilés)
28
Menkhus, James T.
142
Meredith, James
174
Meyer, Prosper Edward, O.S.B.
42
Michigan
32, 35, 40, 43, 47–49, 52–53, 147, 149, 203, 210, 231–33, 235
Mikschl, Luke, S.T.
174
Mill Hill Fathers
35–37
See also Josephites *and* Franciscan Sisters of Mill Hill
Milwaukee, Wisconsin
38, 57, 204
Minneapolis-St. Paul, Minnesota
38, 61, 64
Minnesota
36, 38, 43, 61, 64, 190, 232
Miró, Esteban Rodriguez
30
Misner, Barbara
86–87
Missa Luba
178–80, 218–19
Mission Helpers of the Sacred Heart
36
Missionary Servants of the Most Holy Trinity
168, 174
Missionary Sisters, Servants of the Holy Spirit (Blue Sisters)
38
Mississippi
23–24, 37–39, 41, 43, 46, 50–52, 65, 130, 146, 166–67, 170, 172–75, 184
Missouri
34, 40, 42, 45, 54, 59, 64, 137, 202, 227

Mobile, Alabama
38, 52
Molina, Luis de, S.J.
28
Montgomery, Alabama
37, 143, 145–46, 170–71
Montgomery bus boycott
143, 145, 170–71
Montiano, Manuel de
29
Moore, Amzie
146
Moore, Emerson John
51, 53–54, 57
Morrison, Toni (Chloe Anthony Wofford Morrison)
56, 59, 63
Morrow, Diane Batts
67–91, 201–2
Moses, Robert
145
Moultry, Prince Joseph
50
Mount St. Mary's College (Emmitsburg, Maryland)
90
Mount St. Mary's Seminary (Norwood, Ohio)
236
Muldrow, Joe
218
Mulumba, Saint Matthias Kelemba
46
Murch, Robert
226
Murray, J-Glenn, S.J.
190
Murry, George V., S.J.
59, 62, 65
music
21–22, 25, 44–45, 47–51, 126, 128–29, 136–40, 142, 146, 149, 150, 155–56, 159, 161, 167, 171–75, 177–80, 183–92, 194–95, 212, 217–19, 221–25, 227–29, 231–34, 237

N

Natchez-Jackson, Mississippi
  50
National African American Catholic Youth Ministry Network
  55
National Association for the Advancement of Colored People (NAACP)
  53, 118, 146, 173, 209
National Association of Black Catholic Administrators (NABCA)
  50
National Association of Black Catholic Deacons (NABCD)
  59, 64
National Association of Pastoral Musicians (NPM)
  50
National Black Catholic Apostolate for Life (NBCAL)
  60
National Black Catholic Clergy Caucus (NBCCC)
  47, 48–53, 57, 60–61, 64, 138, 142, 182, 189, 203–4, 231
National Black Catholic Congresses (NBCC)
  20, 25, 36, 54–55, 58–60, 63, 107, 113–14
National Black Catholic Seminarians Association (NBCSA)
  48, 52, 64
National Black Lay Catholic Caucus (NBLCC)
  49, 231–33
National Black Sisters' Conference (NBSC)
  47–49, 52–53, 64, 182–84, 231
National Catholic Conference for Interracial Justice
  44
  See also Catholic Interracial Councils
National Conference of Catholic Bishops
  45, 54–56

See also U.S. Conference of Catholic Bishops
National Office for Black Catholics (NOBC)
  49–50, 52, 60, 138, 141, 231, 233–34
Native Americans.
  See indigenous peoples
nativism
  80, 85–87
  See also anti-Catholicism
Neal, Larry
  143, 147–48
Neale, Charles, S.J.
  73
Neale, Leonard, S.J.
  74
Nerinckx, Charles
  31
Neumann, Saint John
  62
New Jersey
  39–40, 50, 52, 163, 232
New Orleans, Louisiana
  29–31, 33, 37–39, 46, 51, 55, 58, 59, 62, 64, 115, 147, 184, 202, 205, 209–10
New York
  35, 37, 39–40, 44, 46–47, 50, 55, 58, 62, 147, 195, 203, 213–14
Newark, New Jersey
  40, 50
Newport, Rhode Island
  47
Ngoi, Joachim
  178
Nguzo Saba (Seven Black Values)
  110–11
nia
  110
Nicholas V (pope)
  27
Nigeria
  20, 54, 60, 109
Nolan, Charles
  208
Norbertines
  178, 217

North Carolina
  179, 199
Norvel, William L., S.S.J.
  60, 63, 142
Norvell, Aubrey
  174
nursing
  40, 46, 81–84
  See also healthcare
Nutt, Maurice J., C.Ss.R.
  208

O

Obama, Barack
  62–64
Oblate School for Coloured Girls (Baltimore, Maryland)
  31
Oblate Sisters of Providence
  31–32, 56, 58–59, 67–91, 115, 131, 191, 202, 205
O'Brien, (Christopher) Mary, O.S.F.
  179
O'Connor, John
  57, 58, 213
O'Dea, George F., S.S.J.
  47
Odin, John
  90
Odongo, James
  58
Ohio
  33, 35–36, 41, 43, 47, 52, 62, 113, 136–40, 159, 179–80, 212, 216–23, 225, 227–28, 230–32, 235–36
Oklahoma
  136, 159, 232
Okure, Aniedi, O.P.
  54
Oldenburg, Indiana
  179, 218–19, 223, 235
Olivier, Leonard James, S.V.D.
  56
Opelousas, Louisiana
  39, 187
Order of the Brothers of St. Martin de Porres
  56
Oregon
  42
Orlando, Florida
  55
orphanages
  31, 34, 82, 83, 115, 144
O'Toole, James M.
  201–2
Our Lady of Perpetual Help Church (Chicago, Illinois)
  50

P

Paddington, George
  31
Pan African Roman Catholic Clergy Conference
  57, 61
Panama
  46
Papale, Henry
  227
Paris, Peter
  10
parishes, for Black Catholics
  33–35, 37, 40, 48, 50, 57, 66, 114, 127, 138, 188, 230, 234
Pater, Giles Harry
  217
Patterson, Bernardine Joseph, O.S.B.
  45
Paul III (pope)
  27
Paul VI (pope)
  46–48, 104, 110
Penn, Sabrina A.
  202–3
Pennsylvania
  32, 34, 36, 41, 43, 47, 49, 59, 64, 66, 84, 86, 147, 155, 182, 232
Pensacola-Tallahassee, Florida
  60

Perry, Harold Robert, S.V.D.
  45, 46, 49
Perry, Joseph Nathaniel
  60, 62, 209
Peru
  31, 115
Phelps, Jamie, O.P.
  109, 118–19, 124
Philadelphia, Pennsylvania
  34, 36, 41, 64, 84, 86, 147, 155
Pittsburgh, Pennsylvania
  32, 34, 47, 49, 66, 182
Pius VII (pope)
  30
Pius IX (pope)
  32
Pius XI (pope)
  40
Pius XII (pope)
  41, 176–77
Plessy v. Ferguson
  144–45
Plunkett, Thomas, S.S.J.
  37
population, U.S. Black Catholics
  33, 40, 42–44, 47, 50–51, 55, 66, 75, 193
Port-au-Prince, Haiti
  31
Portland, Maine
  34, 200
Portland, Oregon
  42
Port Royal Relief Committee
  155
Portugal
  27, 134
Posey, Thaddeus, O.F.M.
  51
prayer
  24, 32, 45, 56, 60, 63, 99, 108, 113, 122–23, 126–27, 138–40, 141, 153–54, 160, 167, 169, 185–86, 188–92, 197, 212, 220, 224
  See also spirituality
preaching
  94, 126–28, 139–40, 150, 165, 184, 223

Prensky, Marcus
  237
Priestly Fraternity of St. Peter
  59
Prieto, Juan
  27
Protestants
  5, 70, 79, 91, 103, 108, 113, 138, 158, 177, 188
Purcell, John Baptist
  33
Purcell High School (Cincinnati, Ohio)
  222, 225, 227–28
Putz, Lina, F.S.P.A.
  170

Q

Quigley Academy Seminary (Chicago, Illinois)
  48

R

racism
  1, 3, 10–11, 14–15, 47–48, 52, 61, 63, 65, 68, 70–71, 80, 86, 96–99, 120, 138, 143–45, 147, 167, 169, 176, 180, 182, 184, 198, 203–6, 210–11, 219, 230
Raleigh, North Carolina
  179
Rangel, Charles B.
  213–14
Rape, Jeanne Etienne
  236
Reagan, Ronald
  53
Reagon, Bernice Johnson
  145
Rehling, Charles
  218
Repp, Ray
  137
Rhode Island
  47
Ricard, John Huston, S.S.J.
  54–55, 60, 65

Richardson, Willis
  40
Richmond, Virginia
  56, 58
Rivers, Clarence Joseph
  43, 45, 47–50, 125–26, 133–40, 141–42, 149, 159–60, 179–80, 186, 215–37
Roberts, Allan John
  52
Roberts, Leon
  141, 192
Robinson, Jerome R., O.P.
  50
Rochester, New York
  50
Roudanez, Louis Charles
  33
Rousseve, Maurice
  41
Rowe, Cyprian Lamar (Donald), F.M.S.
  43, 60, 149
Rudd, Daniel A.
  35–36, 107, 108, 116

S

Sacred Heart College (Greenville, Mississippi)
  39
Sacrosanctum Concilium
  176, 180, 185, 189
St. Ann Church (Cincinnati, Ohio)
  33
St. Augustine, Florida
  28–29, 33
St. Augustine Church (Louisville, Kentucky)
  34
St. Augustine Church (Washington, D.C.)
  33, 178, 192
St. Augustine Seminary (Bay St. Louis, Mississippi)
  39, 41, 43, 46
St. Benedict the Moor Church (New York)
  35
St. Benedict the Moor Church (Pittsburgh, Pennsylvania)
  66
St. Benedict the Moor Interracial Charity Apostolate
  42, 44
St. Benedict's Home for Destitute Colored Children (Rye, New York)
  37
St. Charles Borromeo Church (New York)
  46, 195
St. Charles College (Maryland)
  76
St. Clare Hospital (Baraboo, Wisconsin)
  47
Saint-Domingue
  30–31, 45, 80–81
St. Dominic Church (New Orleans, Louisiana)
  37
St. Dorothy Church (Chicago, Illinois)
  48
St. Elizabeth Church (North Richmond, Virginia)
  58
St. Elizabeth Church (St. Louis, Missouri)
  34
St. Elizabeth Church (Selma, Alabama)
  41
St. Frances Academy (Baltimore, Maryland)
  31
St. Francis Xavier Church (Baltimore, Maryland)
  33
St. Francis Xavier Church (New York)
  44
sainthood
  57–58, 115, 131, 163, 207
  See also canonization
St. Joachim School (Carthage, Mississippi)
  174

Index | **281**

St. Joan of Arc Church (New Orleans, Louisiana)
37
St. John's Abbey (Collegeville, Minnesota)
36, 43, 228
St. John's University (New York)
214
St. Joseph College for Negro Catechists (St. Joseph's Catechetical College) (Montgomery, Alabama)
37
St. Joseph Seminary (Baltimore, Maryland)
35, 37
St. Joseph's Church (Cincinnati, Ohio)
136, 179–80, 216–23, 228, 230
St. Julien, Michael Mtumishi
231, 234
St. Katherine Church (New Orleans, Louisiana)
37
St. Louis, Missouri
34, 40, 42, 45, 54, 59, 137, 227
St. Louis University (St. Louis, Missouri)
42
St. Martin Church (Baltimore, Maryland)
142
St. Mary Seminary (Baltimore, Maryland)
30, 74, 87–89
St. Maur Interracial Priory (South Union, Kentucky)
43
St. Meinrad Archabbey (Indiana)
43
St. Monica Church (Atlantic City, New Jersey)
39
St. Monica Church (Chicago, Illinois)
35
St. Nicholas of Tolentine Church (Atlantic City, New Jersey)
39
St. Patrick Cathedral (New York)
47, 58

St. Peter Church (Charleston, South Carolina)
33
St. Peter Claver Church (Baltimore, Maryland)
36, 138
St. Vincent Archabbey Seminary (Latrobe, Pennsylvania)
43
Salvatorians
57
Sankofa
130–31
Sansaricq, Guy A.
62
Santo Domingo
27
Savannah, Georgia
34, 36, 38, 39, 205
Schoch, Phil
218
Schuyler, Philippa Duke
195
Scott, Leonard G., Jr.
52
Scott, Llewellyn J.
41
Scripture
See Bible
Seabrooks, Bernie
233
Second Plenary Council of Baltimore (1866)
32–33
Second Vatican Council (Vatican II)
44, 137, 143–44, 176, 180, 220, 223
segregation
15, 42, 78–79, 82–83, 87, 97, 104, 113, 118, 144–46, 149, 166–69, 173, 188
Selma, Alabama
41, 46, 134, 146, 216
seminaries
30, 32–33, 35–37, 39, 41, 43, 46, 48, 72, 74, 87–89, 174, 190, 230, 236, 237
Sendry, Joseph
183

Seton, Saint Elizabeth Ann
  61, 74
Sheehan, Arthur
  207
Sheehan, Elizabeth Odell
  207
Sisters, Home Visitors of Mary
  43
Sisters, Servants of the Immaculate Heart of Mary
  32
Sisters of Charity of Nazareth (Kentucky)
  38, 45, 63
Sisters of Charity of New York
  36
Sisters of Charity of St. Joseph (Maryland)
  69, 71, 74–75, 81–84, 90
Sisters of Loretto
  61, 63
Sisters of Notre Dame
  53, 61–62
Sisters of Our Lady of Lourdes of New Orleans (Louisiana)
  35
Sisters of St. Francis of Oldenburg (Indiana)
  179, 218–20, 223, 235
Sisters of St. Francis of Philadelphia (Glen Riddle, Pennsylvania)
  36
Sisters of St. Joseph of Carondelet
  46
Sisters of St. Joseph of LePuy
  33
Sisters of St. Mary of the Third Order of St. Francis
  40, 42
Sisters of the Blessed Sacrament for Indians and Colored People
  36, 38, 218
Sisters of the Good Shepherd
  195
Sisters of the Holy Family
  31, 56, 115, 202, 204–5
Sisters of the Presentation of the Blessed Virgin Mary
  31
Sisters of the Third Order of St. Francis
  36
Sisters Servants of the Holy Ghost (Holy Spirit) and Mary Immaculate
  37
Sklar, Peggy
  208
slavery
  12, 14–15, 20, 22, 27–33, 35–36, 38, 46, 51, 61, 63–65, 68, 70–71, 73, 79, 82, 86, 88, 97–98, 100, 103–4, 115–16, 118, 128, 149–57, 160, 165, 175, 186, 188, 202, 208
Smith, Charlene, F.S.P.A.
  208
Smith, Jack
  146
Smith, Mary Ann
  231–32
Smith, Vincent
  41
Society for the Propagation of the Faith
  90
Society of African Missions
  39, 45, 53
Society of Missionaries of Africa (White Fathers)
  38
Society of St. Edmund
  41
Society of the Divine Word
  37, 39, 41, 46, 47, 51, 53, 59, 200–1
Society of the Holy Family
  32
Society of the Immaculate Heart of Mary
  37
Somerville, Stephen
  229
songs
  24, 99, 116, 128, 142, 149–51, 153–58, 167, 175, 178, 180, 183, 185, 187, 191–92, 217, 219, 221, 225

Sousa, Matthias de
  28
South Africa
  25, 54
South Carolina
  29, 31, 33, 36, 64, 85, 114, 154–55
Southern Christian Leadership Council (SCLC)
  146
Southern Cooperative Development Fund (SCDF)
  206
Spain
  21, 27, 28, 134, 229
Spalding, Martin J.
  33
Spanish
  27, 29, 30, 32, 229
Spellman, Francis
  200
Spencer, James
  114
Spencer, Jon
  158
Spiritans.
  See Holy Ghost Fathers
spirituality
  20, 24, 90, 94–95, 107–13, 116, 117–25, 128–31, 141, 160, 164, 168, 173, 184, 186–87, 206
spirituals
  42, 45, 121, 129, 136–37, 142, 144, 149–61, 164, 167, 170–75, 178–80, 183, 188–89, 192, 217–19, 233
Stallings, George Augustus, Jr
  56, 164, 166, 206
Steib, James Terry, S.V.D.
  54, 59
Steptoe, E.W.
  146
Stimuli, Inc.
  48, 233, 236
Stirling, Archibald
  81–82
Stono Rebellion
  29

Student Nonviolent Coordinating Committee (SNCC)
  146
Sublimis Deus
  27
Sudan
  51, 61
Sulpicians
  30–32, 67, 71–73, 75–76, 78–81, 83–87, 89, 205
Supreme Court
  58, 143–45, 209

T

Talalay, Kathryn
  195
Tardy, Jo Anne
  209–10
Tarry, Ellen
  42, 197–98, 207
Taylor, Clarence
  2–4
Tennessee
  38, 43, 59, 62, 174, 196–97, 211–12
Texas
  32, 37, 55, 64
Theobald, Stephen Louis
  38
theology
  1–2, 5–6, 9, 11–15, 17, 28, 96, 99–100, 103–4, 140, 184, 188, 213, 239
  See also liberation theology
Third Order of St. Francis
  41, 44–45, 64
Third Plenary Council of Baltimore (1884)
  35
Thomas, Clarence
  58
Thomas, Elliot Griffin
  59
Thompson, Francesca, O.S.F.
  149, 179, 235–36
Tolton, Venerable Augustus
  35, 55, 62, 65, 202–3, 207, 209

Toussaint, Venerable Pierre
30, 51, 57, 58, 60, 115, 131, 207
Tranchepain, Marie (Sister Saint Augustine)
29
Tullock, Carlos Ambrosio Lewis, S.V.D.
46
Tupelo, Mississippi
52
Tureaud, A.P.
209
Tureaud, Alexander P., Jr.
209
Turner, Thomas Wyatt
39, 40

U

Uganda
25, 40, 44–46, 48, 104, 222
Ugandan martyrs
40, 45–46, 48
ujamaa
110
ujima
110
umoja
110
Umoja Temple (Washington, D.C.)
57
Uncles, Charles Randolph, S.S.J.
36
Union Graduate School (Union Institute) (Yellow Springs, Ohio)
235–37
Universa Laus
229
University of Detroit
231–33
University of Notre Dame (Indiana)
217
University of St. Mary of the Lake (Mundelein Seminary) (Chicago, Illinois)
43
Ursuline Academy (New Orleans, Louisiana)
29
Ursulines
29, 85
U.S. Conference of Catholic Bishops (USCCB)
61, 62, 64–65, 187

V

Valle, Lincoln Charles
38
Vatican II. *See* Second Vatican Council
Vaughn, Sarah
54
Vermont
34–35
Vernell, Rose M.
56
Vicksburg, Mississippi
37–38
Vincentian Sisters of Charity
44
Vincentians
44, 71
Virgin Islands
21, 49, 59
Virginia
56, 58, 65, 218
virtues
80, 90, 108, 112–14, 116, 202, 203, 208–9
Visitation Sisters, Georgetown (Washington, D.C.)
69, 71, 74–75
Viterbo College, La Crosse, Wisconsin
171, 173, 181, 183

W

Wade, Francis G.
41
Ward, Justine B.
42
Ware, Charles Pickard
155
Washington, D.C.
19, 32–34, 36–37, 40–42, 44–46, 48–50, 52, 55–57, 59, 60, 62–66, 69, 71, 74–75, 84, 113, 137, 146–47, 164, 178, 181, 192, 199, 206, 226–27

Waters, Donald
226
Watts, Isaac
142
Weakland, Rembert, O.S.B.
229
Webb, Vincent (Louis), S.V.D.
41
Weind, Teresita, S.N.D.deN.
62
Wendell, James, S.V.D.
39
West, Cornel
10–11, 149
West, Nadja Yudith
64
Westendorf, Omer
227
Westermeyer, Paul
190–91
White, George L.
155
Whitfield, James
72–75, 79
Wightman, Mary Rosina, S.C.
36
Williams, Anita Rose
40
Williams, Clarence, C.PP.S.
48, 51, 58
Williams, Mary Lou
44, 47, 194–95
Williams, M. Theodore (Elizabeth Barbara)
39, 205
Williams, Ralph Vaughn
237
Williams, Vanessa
53
Williams, William Augustine
32
Williamson, Adolphus
76
Wilson, Reginald
160

Wisconsin
38, 42, 47, 57, 163, 168–72, 177, 181, 183, 204
Wise, Joe
137
Wissel, Raphael
34
Woodward, C. Vann
144
worship
30, 33, 48–49, 54, 102, 106, 113, 122–23, 125–29, 133–40, 141, 153, 157, 159–61, 164–65, 175–77, 179, 185–86, 189–92, 194, 212, 215–21, 223–25, 228–31, 233–36
See also liturgy
Wright, Flonzie Brown
168–69, 177, 180
Wright, W. D.
3–4

X

Xavier High School (New Orleans)
38–39
Xavier University of Louisiana (New Orleans)
38–39, 52, 125, 130, 184, 188

Y

Youngstown, Ohio
62
youth, ministry to
51, 55, 110

Z

Zaire
20
Zimbabwe
20
Zubik, David
66